PRAISE FOR *UNSETTLING AC*

"Poetry, portraiture, life writing, and interviews edged in critical discourse intersect across race, gender, culture, and body in this beautifully constructed anthology. *Unsettling Activisms* does exactly what the title suggests, shaking our concepts of both aging and activism through the exploration of sexuality, community, family, and culture. With the 'politics of connection' and the inclusion of Indigeneity, this text can be used across academic disciplines and fields. Its accessibility and structure, however, allow the book to move outside academia into living rooms, community libraries, and reading groups, giving insight into the power of the aging voice in the process."

—Tasha Beeds, Minweyweywigaan Midewiwin Lodge Member, Assistant Professor in Indigenous Literatures, Department of English, University of Saskatchewan

"This volume is a welcome addition to aging studies, feminist studies, and social movement studies in the Canadian context. The diversity of analytical viewpoints explored is complemented by the rich variety of activist voices presented. At once both conceptually sophisticated and highly accessible to scholars, students, activists, and their allies alike, this volume will appeal to a wide variety of readers."

—Dana Sawchuk, Department of Sociology, Wilfrid Laurier University

UNSETTLING
ACTIVISMS

UNSETTLING
ACTIVISMS

CRITICAL INTERVENTIONS ON AGING, GENDER, AND SOCIAL CHANGE

Edited by **May Chazan, Melissa Baldwin,** and **Patricia Evans**

WOMEN'S PRESS

Toronto | Vancouver

Unsettling Activisms: Critical Interventions on Aging, Gender, and Social Change
Edited by May Chazan, Melissa Baldwin, and Patricia Evans

First published in 2018 by
Women's Press, an imprint of CSP Books Inc.
425 Adelaide Street West, Suite 200
Toronto, Ontario
M5V 3C1

www.womenspress.ca

Library and Archives Canada Cataloguing in Publication

Unsettling activisms : critical interventions on aging, gender, and social change / edited by May Chazan, Melissa Baldwin, and Patricia Evans.

Includes bibliographical references and index.
Issued in print and electronic formats.
ISBN 978-0-88961-603-5 (softcover).--ISBN 978-0-88961-604-2 (PDF).
--ISBN 978-0-88961-605-9 (EPUB)

1. Women political activists. 2. Aging--Social aspects. 3. Social change. I. Evans, Patricia M. (Patricia Marie), 1944-, editor II. Chazan, May, 1974-, editor III. Baldwin, Melissa, 1991-, editor

HQ1236.U57 2018   305.42   C2018-903178-6
                                                                             C2018-903179-4

Text design by Elisabeth Springate
Typesetting by Brad Horning
Cover design by Jennifer Stimson
Cover image by Jenn Cole

18   19   20   21   22   5 4 3 2 1

Printed and bound in Canada by Webcom

MIX
Paper from
responsible sources
FSC® C004071
www.fsc.org

COVER ARTIST'S STATEMENT

Wrapping trees (and city lampposts!) in red hemp was something I did for a few months in 2006/7. When I moved from Kiji Sibi Algonquin territory to Nogojiwanong, I had a very hard time leaving the land of my home territory. It took time to relate to the lands and waters of this beautiful Michi Saagiig territory. I spent a lot of time trying to get to know the cedar nation, especially in Peterborough's Little Lake Cemetery where there were old trees, which made me feel close to home. I wrapped a few cedars in that cemetery with red twine (and camped there) as a way of entering into relationship with them. To wind twine around a tree, you have to embrace it, feel its bark against your skin, say hello with your breath. I still have relationships with trees I have wrapped.

The *These Trees* wrapping work was part of a year-long exploration I was able to do under the mentorship of Maralynn Cherry (non-status, Wikwemikong First Nation) in contact with the lands of the Michi Saagiig, thinking through my relationship with the woods here and back home, and with my Nan, who got cancer that year. Red was part of being Indigenous, connected to my Nan's blood, and it expressed the life pulse of the forest. Drawings of rivers also carried touches of red. That red—it's an interconnected line of colour across places, people, and stories that were part of my small migration.

—Jenn Cole (mixed ancestry Algonquin, Kiji Sibi Watershed)

Contents

PART III   EMBODYING   121

appreciates the friendship, solidarity, mentorship, and teaching she has received over the course of this project, particularly from Elder Shirley Williams Pheasant, Jean Koning, Sally Chivers, Nadine Changfoot, Barbara Marshall, Dana Capell, Emma Langley, Maddy Macnab, Jesse Whattam, Jenn Cole, Ziy von B, and of course Melissa and Pat! Melissa heartily echoes every one of May's thanks, and would especially like to add thanks to Ben for all of his quiet everyday work and for listening through every step of this process, and to Zoe and Alex for the important teaching that loving fiercely can be a force for change. Melissa is also grateful to Joy and Cory Baldwin for their stalwart support, and Emma, Maddy, Jesse, Jenn, Shannon Culkeen, and Abi Myerscough for their friendship, sense of humour, critical perspectives, and listening ears. Melissa cannot find the words to thank May and Pat, but holds them both closely as exceptional teachers of ordinary-extraordinary activist ways of being, and as dear, dear friends. Pat adds her thanks to May and Melissa for the creativity, humour, and patience they brought to their work and for the deepening friendship that flowed from it. Special thanks also to Jesse Whattam and Sharon Swanson—collaborators extraordinaire, and Pat joins May and Melissa in expressing our appreciation to all our remarkable contributors.

Finally, we extend our thanks to Women's Press/Canadian Scholars and to the eight anonymous peer reviewers, whose comments and feedback have helped us tremendously. This book has benefitted from the funding and support of the Canada Research Chairs Program, the Social Sciences and Humanities Research Council of Canada, and Trent University.

Acknowledgements

As editors, we extend our deep gratitude to all of the contributors to this volume, for their excellent analyses, reflections, poetry, and photography, for the daily work they do toward making our world a fairer and more compassionate place, and for their generosity of spirit. They offered us critical conversations and meaningful relationships—these are reverberating well beyond this book. We also sincerely thank the entire Aging Activisms collective—all of the collaborators, research participants, research assistants, students, and supporters who have been part of this larger project since 2013. This book springs from generative spaces of thoughtful dialogue and intergenerational meeting; we acknowledge the contributions of all who have entered and shaped these spaces with us. We acknowledge, too, the territory upon which our collective is based—its lands, waters, and peoples—which has informed our intellectual and creative processes in a number of ways. The Aging Activisms collective hails from Trent University, in Nogojiwanong (Peterborough, Ontario, Canada), which is on the territory of the Michi Saagiig Anishinaabeg.

So many groups, networks, organizations, and movements have shaped how this book engages with the expansive and dynamic topic of activist aging that we could not name them all here. We do wish, however, to extend special thanks to the Grandmothers Advocacy Network, the Raging Grannies, Respecting Elders Communities Against Abuse, the Peterborough and Kawarthas Water Walkers and the Sacred Water Circle (to whom we extend the royalties from this book), the Peterborough Poetry Collective, Older Women Live, the organizers of Nogojiwanong's Solidarity Weekend 2017, the Trent Centre for Aging and Society, Ageing Communication Technologies, Critical MediArtStudio, and the North American and European Networks on Aging Studies.

We would also like to acknowledge all of the labour that has gone into this collection. A number of individuals have taken the time to read and comment on drafts of this manuscript—in full or in part—and their feedback has been invaluable: Tessa Nasca, Anisah Madden, Ziy von B, Jenn Cole, Joan McGilvray, Barbara Marshall, Sally Chivers, and Marlene Goldman. We are especially grateful to Tessa Nasca for hours of cheerful formatting assistance; to waaseyaa'sin christine sy and Ziy von B for challenging us in the most creative, productive, and important ways; and to Jenn Cole for gracing us with the art on the book's cover.

So many people have supported each of us personally through this writing and editing journey. May extends big, heartfelt thanks to Ben Hodson, who makes her work possible, and to Zoe and Alex Hodson, who infuse it with meaning. She is deeply grateful to Beverly Kraft and Elyse Chazan for sowing the seeds. She also

INTRODUCTION

Amplifying Activisms

May Chazan

In her well-known address "How Does Change Happen?" Angela Davis, professor and long-time activist, draws on the 1955 Montgomery Bus Boycott to illustrate her wider argument: that every major social movement in history has depended on the daily, often-forgotten work of groups of women (Davis 2007). Her address provides one salient example—one of many—in which "ordinary" women have trudged through the least glamorous work, unrecognized, unthanked, and omitted from historical narratives. "Often those who contribute most powerfully to movements for radical social change," she explains, "are erased in the histories that are transmitted from generation to generation." Davis eloquently captures the spirit of this book, and so I have chosen to open with her words:

> I'd like to use the civil rights movement as an example, because everybody in this country knows who Reverend Martin Luther King is ... but we don't know about Jo Ann Robinson—how she and the members of her organization were trying to start a boycott. They had tried on several occasions and then, finally, when Rosa Parks got arrested ... they stayed up all night long mimeographing. They stayed up all night long making those leaflets, and that's how the bus boycott got started.... That was really unglamorous work.... If they hadn't worked that mimeograph machine, if they hadn't gotten people to go out and distribute all of those leaflets at six o'clock in the morning when people—particularly when people who were domestic servants—were getting on the bus ... it wouldn't have happened in the way that it did. And that's a very different story ... a story about the erasure of women's contributions.

Davis's words are a poignant call to action—a plea for a critical look at whose actions are most recognized within activist movements and how the history of social change is constructed and remembered. This book takes up her call. Drawing on varied perspectives across four generations, it investigates those "quieter" or less glamorous contributions that typically fall outside the purview of historical memory. It works to amplify the diverse activisms of women and those beyond the gender binary,[1] specifically exploring how gender, class, skin colour, ability, sexuality, Indigeneity, and age combine to inform their different and uneven experiences of activist aging.

Why activist aging? And how does this connect to the story of the bus boycott?

I open with Davis's lecture because I believe that her words—and more generally the monumental moment she describes—offer insights not only into the erasure of women's contributions but also into dynamics of age and aging. According to some, Parks's infamous act of defiance might not have happened at all had it not been for the actions of little-known Claudette Colvin nine months previously (Hoose 2009). Like Parks, Colvin refused to give up her seat and move to the back of the bus; she too was arrested and later became one of four women plaintiffs in the Supreme Court case that successfully overturned bus segregation laws in Alabama. Yet, while Parks (like King) has attained heroic status, Colvin's name (like Robinson's) has been nearly erased from the Montgomery story. Why? As Colvin explained in an interview in 2009, Parks was a respected, professional woman in her 40s, while Colvin was 15 years of age at the time, darker-skinned, and of lower social status (Adler 2009). Colvin then became pregnant and, as a young, unwed mother, her credibility was further diminished. As Hoose (2009) said, "Then she became pregnant ... and that was that." Colvin was not considered to be an appropriate face or body around which to mobilize protest.

The stories of Robinson, Colvin, and Parks thus serve as a critical reminder that, while women's "quieter" roles within social movements are very often erased and forgotten, women's similar contributions to social change can be differently valued, unequally recognized, and disparately remembered, even within the same movement.[2] They also raise a series of questions particularly pertinent to this book: Among other factors, how did Colvin's age affect the perceived validity of her resistance? Had Parks been older at the time of the boycott—in her 60s or beyond—would she have commanded the same legitimacy?

Collectively, these women's stories illustrate the two central themes that interweave this volume: (1) the importance of understanding, recognizing, and valuing diverse activisms, particularly those most frequently omitted from the historical record; and (2) the need for analyses that explicitly engage with dynamics of age and aging, while simultaneously considering people's differing power, privilege, and prominence within social movements. Both Robinson and Colvin are among the frequently elided social changers whose actions have propelled transformation, while Colvin's experience also reveals how gender, class, education, skin tone, marital status, and age intersect to influence who ultimately gains heroic status and who is forgotten.

Situated in the contemporary North American context, on the land known to many First Peoples as Turtle Island, this book begins an exploration of how people of different backgrounds, ages, and abilities are engaging in a variety of activisms across different movements. Through research, conversation, poetry, personal reflection, and photography, this volume delves into the largely unexplored theme of activist aging, asking why and how different social changers engage in acts of resistance, resilience, and resurgence at different times in their lives, and what it means for them to age as activists. In some small but profound way, this collection aims to unsettle existing assumptions about activisms—about what is typically considered "activism" and who is assumed to be an "activist"—and to decentre colonial, Eurocentric, heteronormative,[3] and ableist conceptions of activist aging.

BUILDING (FROM) RELATIONSHIPS

This book has its roots in my own long-standing journey as a researcher and activist, some of which I present in various chapters throughout. While this is the outcome of a project that has both grown out of relationships and worked to build new ones, this book has most directly emerged from my program of research, and so it feels important—and accountable—for me to begin from my own journey and position within this. Over the past dozen years, I have had the privilege of working with and alongside many extraordinary individuals—people who spend their time mobilizing in a variety of ways and contexts. So many of these indomitable and brilliant people have profoundly informed my journey: hundreds of organizers who have been part of my research (most of them older women, but also many activists of all genders and ages), an even wider group of mobilizers with whom I have connected in my own activisms, and dozens of critical thinkers—students, activists, and fellow professors—whom I have learned with and sometimes mentored. This book draws together some of these varied and influential perspectives to capture a complexity of activisms and knowledges in a way that would simply not be possible in a single-authored monograph.

This volume brings together 28 contributors who have all lived and worked in a number of different territories across Turtle Island: While our life geographies vary significantly, at the time of writing we all reside in Canada. Born and raised as a settler[4] on the territory of the Kanien'keha:ka (Mohawk) Peoples, in the city now named

Montreal, my own ancestral roots lie in Jewish communities in Eastern Europe. At the time of writing/editing, I live and work in Nogojiwanong, on the territory of the Michi Saagiig Anishinaabeg (Mississauga Anishinaabe), upon which the mid-sized city of Peterborough has been built.[5] Over the course of conceiving of this book, working with contributors, and carrying the volume through to publication, I have come to understand ever more intimately how this territory—its lands, histories, and peoples—has influenced the intellectual and political directions of the project.

Nogojiwanong, known for millennia as a gathering place to First Peoples across the region, became a meeting place for many of us as contributors: a place where every one of us has, at some point, lived, visited, or spent time; a place where many of us have gathered together, across enormous difference and across four generations, to learn from each other and to build relationships. It is here, as a professor at Trent University, that I launched Aging Activisms[6] as an activist-research collective, aiming to create thoughtful spaces and relationships in which we, as academics, activists, and artists from different communities, might critically and productively challenge ourselves and each other. This volume springs from these spaces and our connections.

For me, Nogojiwanong is also the place where I have come to struggle differently, in a more daily and embodied way, with what it means to be a white settler-academic-activist-parent. It is here, in Michi Saagiig territory, that I have been blessed with opportunities to listen to and learn from Anishinaabe Elders; to participate in sun-rise and water ceremonies; and to most intimately witness the radical vision, poetic brilliance, and mobilizing know-how of students, peers, colleagues, friends, activists, and artists from Indigenous communities across Turtle Island—people who are working tirelessly toward decolonization and cultural resurgence.[7] These experiences and connections require me to continuously ask myself: What does it mean for me to research and write about aging and activism, and to do this as part of my work for social change, as an occupier of and on stolen land? What does it mean for me to hold a certain critical/feminist/decolonial politics and vision for a world I would like to leave to my children, while simultaneously building an academic career in the field of aging studies—a field that has frequently been critiqued as overlooking Indigenous knowledges and critical race perspectives?

In Nogojiwanong, I have also begun to re-engage in and with certain activist spaces—actively attending and organizing protests and rallies after a decade of near-hiatus from this kind of work. Before moving here in 2013, my focus was certainly on "quieter" approaches to social change: educating myself and others, exploring research as a tool for change, and, most immediately, gestating and nurturing the two young people in my life. As I have been stepping back into these more outward activist roles—roles that were very much part of my younger adult experiences—I have become more aware of my own changing embodiment. I re-enter older, with grey hair, with a body that has given birth twice, and often with young children in tow. In these spaces I have fielded comments about how my hair and children (and implicitly light skin tone) mark me as safe, non-threatening, and respectable. I sit uneasily with this, perhaps because comments such as these serve as a reminder of the unearned privilege I derive from my body. I am a cisgender,[8] (currently) able-bodied, light-skinned woman, now in my 40s, and I am a university professor, too: My body-mind allows me entry into spaces of protest with relative ease and minimal fear. I am not hindered by uneven ground or loud noises, nor am I likely to be targeted by police with excessive force, racial profiling, or transphobic assaults. I move through the world and through these activist spaces easily—more easily than many dear friends and colleagues, more easily than many of the brilliant contributors to this book. I understand that these inequities necessarily inform our relationships.

I try not to shy away from these tensions in this book, but nor do I expect I can resolve them. Instead, these tensions propel my continuous quest to learn—in meaningful, sensitive, and just ways—from the creative and courageous approaches that people with varying experiences of privilege bring to practicing resistance, making change, and demanding justice.

This volume draws on the perspectives of four generations, at times blurring our various roles as academics, students, and "research subjects," working to illuminate the multiplicity of ways people know and articulate activist aging. I conceived of and co-edited this volume in close collaboration with Melissa Baldwin and Pat Evans. Melissa has co-chaired Aging Activisms with me from its inception and was a Trent University graduate student when we first undertook this project. Pat is the former co-chair of the Grandmothers Advocacy Network and my long-time community research partner. With me in my 40s, Melissa in her 20s, and Pat in her 70s, our editorial trio reflects the kind of dynamic intergenerationality and academic-community collaboration—as well as deep care and friendship—that I believe are vital to the sustainability and strength of all radical movements.

We invited contributions from a collection of academics, students, activists, and artists, building from relationships that were in place or were forming in connection with Aging Activisms; some contributors then chose to work in similar intergenerational, academic-activist-student collaborations. These contributions highlight the importance of giving space and legitimacy to the many ways, individually and collectively, that we care for each other, for our communities, for past and future generations, and for the land. Our process of working together as editors, writers, and contributors has developed from and has worked to develop connections among us—connections that are critical, supportive, and radical in ways that we could not have fully anticipated at the start of the project (Pratt 2010).[9] This theme of connection reverberates throughout the book.

CONTEXT: CRITICAL PERSPECTIVES ON AGING AND ACTIVISMS

Throughout the book, all of us as contributors offer reflections on and/or analyses of activist aging. It is important, then, to understand the salience of these contributions within a wider context. Over the next 35 years, the global population over the age of 60 is expected to triple, so that by 2050, for the first time in history, there will be more people over 60 than under 15. Life expectancy is higher for women than it is for men, with populations over 60 estimated to include two to five times as many women as men (United Nations 2013). The emerging global trend is of population aging that is unprecedented, pervasive, and feminized. Meanwhile, evidence suggests that women remain politically engaged longer than previously recognized—many are actively working for social change well past the age of 65 (Chovanec, Cooley, and Diaz 2010).

While many feminist scholars have investigated how gender, class, race, sexuality, and geography combine to influence people's mobilizations, fewer have considered how age and aging intersect with these systems of power (Rich and Macdonald 2001; Twigg 2004). In response to this, some scholars—many of us part of this book—have more recently sought to document and analyze older women's activisms (e.g., Chazan 2015; K. Sawchuk 2009; Roy 2004). However, much of the work in this area remains focused on a few well-known movements of "grandmother activists," certain overt (often highly visible) forms of activism, and the contributions of relatively privileged groups of older women. Scholarship with and of older Indigenous, racialized, and LGBTQIA2S+ activists, the work of those living with disabilities, and the dynamics of aging and intergenerationality across their movements, remain especially limited (Byrnes 2016; Meadows, Thurston, and Lagendyk 2009).

This volume aims to address these profound gaps. I hope it will begin to challenge the too-frequent omission of age, aging, and intergenerationality within social movement literature. I also hope—perhaps most especially—that it might insert critical analyses of activisms into aging studies, drawing on critical feminist, decolonial, race, queer, and crip theories and approaches.

What do I mean by "critical" analyses, theories, and approaches? I draw on this language to refer to certain epistemological, methodological, and political commitments, which underpin this project and have informed our editorial processes (Brown and Strega 2014): commitments to continuously "unsettle" or "shake up" understandings of activism, pushing toward a pluralized conception of "activisms" that might resonate ever more widely among diverse social changers and with their diverse social change practices; commitments to call into question what and whose knowledges have so far been included in activist-aging scholarship and to redress, albeit in small and imperfect ways, some of the many existing omissions; commitments to intervene in unfounded scholarly and societal assumptions about aging; and commitments to continuously ask how power operates through the unquestioned deployment of certain concepts and categories, including those related to aging, gender, and social change. I enter this project with an intersectional feminist perspective, seeking to understand how multiple systems of power overlap and intersect to create conditions of privilege for some but not for others, including the privilege of knowing in ways that fit easily into textbooks. I also ground this collection in the premise that there can be no justice on stolen land (Walia 2013)—that settler colonialism, as an ongoing process on Turtle Island, needs to be actively resisted. In the case of this book, settler colonialism needs to be contested as it continues to influence the legitimacy given to different ways of knowing and doing aging, gender, and social change.

Through the editorial process, I have come to think about these commitments as a project to broaden and expand the scope of existing scholarship on aging and activisms in three interrelated ways.

(1) By Expanding the "What"

The volume's focus on unsettling activisms is about expanding and intervening in popular depictions of activism, in part by challenging widespread youth-centric assumptions. As Naomi Richards explains, "in the public imagination activism is often associated with youth," who are frequently caricatured as brash and confrontational (2012, 8). Other scholars suggest that the failure to view older people, and especially older women, as activists emerges from one-dimensional understandings of what activism is or can be (McHugh 2012). Social change work that is "quieter"—the work of educating, organizing, advocating, creating, mentoring, and record-keeping, which older women so often do—tends not to be considered "activism" to the same extent as the more outward forms of protest and rally. From this perspective, the erasure of older women's roles within social movements is likely tied to these wider misconceptions and thus, by opening up the "what" of activisms, the volume can more easily challenge dominant perceptions that activists are necessarily (or even usually) young.

But expanding the "what" in this way is not only about extending the age range of whose knowledges and experiences are considered meaningful in analyzing activisms. It is also about asking: What do dominant conceptions of activism reveal and obscure, for whom do these resonate, and for whom are these possible and safe? In this way, expanding the "what" is about valuing the activisms of people who do not necessarily have the mobilities or abilities required to attend large protests, or who are made disproportionately vulnerable at such protests, particularly in the presence of police. This expansion also responds to the many Indigenous scholars and activists of Turtle Island who have written about not readily seeing themselves in discourses of "activism," particularly discourses that position their efforts as "working against" systems of colonial and capitalist power as opposed to being in ceremony, doing what they are called upon to do, surviving, or "working to" Indigenize, heal, care for the land and water, and build a just future (Simpson 2011; Stone 2015).

This volume therefore extends "activisms" to include protest and rally *as well as* arts-based intervention, land-based practice, performance, cultural resurgence, creativity, survivance, refusal, ceremony, advocacy, and more (Meadows, Thurston, and Lagendyk 2009; Kauanui 2016; Hodgson and Brooks 2007; Pain 2014). Throughout the volume, we draw on "activisms"—in the plural form—to mean this diversity of ways of acting, resisting, intervening, animating, dismantling, creating, and building. This is, however, just the beginning, and I hope readers will continue to critically ask: What counts as activism? Who decides?

(2) By Expanding the "Who"

We (Melissa, Pat, and I) initially thought this book would focus on older women's activisms, responding to Davis's call to amplify women's activisms, and adding to this the analytic of age. We then asked: Among "older women," who remains least recognized, whose knowledges are missing from scholarly conversations, whose work is least valued, who is least likely to be remembered? These critical questions expose the overarching whiteness and heteronormativity of existing scholarship in this area. They also underpin our efforts to ensure that contributions to this book engage in meaningful ways with varied perspectives on activist aging, including the perspectives of social changers and scholars who are racialized, Indigenous, LGBTQIA2S+, and/or living with disabilities.

Furthermore, over the course of this project, contributors called on us to shift our focus from "women's activisms" to the "activisms of women and non-binary individuals." This led us to also ask: Who might the category of "woman" inadvertently erase, and how might this language re-inscribe gender binaries? While all of the contributors have, at some points, aligned themselves with women's activisms, it became evident that a rigid focus on "women" could not capture their more fluid, complex, and diverse identities. Shifting to a more nuanced perspective of gender and activisms became important to holding this volume's goal of amplifying what is frequently suppressed.

This shift is, however, also only a beginning. The volume remains composed primarily of the contributions of cisgender scholars and activists. Clearly, there is still much work to do, particularly in bringing the perspectives of trans and two-spirit activists into existing scholarship on aging and social movements. Indeed, I hope readers will continue to ask such critical questions as: Whose knowledge remains absent from these conversations? Who else is missing?

(3) By Expanding the "How"

Finally, this book seeks to push the boundaries of the "how"—to open up the question of how knowledge about aging and activisms tends to be produced and represented within scholarly texts, and to begin to make the inclusion of different knowledges and expressions of knowledge possible.

We initially thought this volume would include a series of research chapters written by academics and reflections written by activists. This structure quickly became too limiting. Some contributors asked to share their knowledge orally and/or through storytelling. These brilliant contributions and the spaces they created for intersubjectivity then became central to the book. This led us to invite the beautiful contributions of several poets, whose work opens each of the volume's sections. These, together with the recorded conversations in Chapter 3 and Reflection 3, significantly expand what this volume could offer in terms of decolonial, queer, and embodied perspectives on aging, gender, and social change.

But these, too, are only small interventions. I continue to ask, and I hope readers will as well: How else can many knowledges about aging and activisms be incorporated into such a collection?

DOMINANT NARRATIVES OF AGE/ING: CRITICAL INTERVENTIONS

As I noted, I come to this work as a "middle aged" academic-activist-parent. So, it is perhaps unsurprising that I approach this project keen to challenge youth-centric images of activism—to abandon the idea that activism is the domain of those under 30. Every section of the book indeed contests societal perceptions that "activists" are necessarily young, advancing an expanded version of who counts as an activist, what counts as activism, and how different knowledges are valued in these conversations. But there is also more to the age/ing critique offered throughout this volume; this collection also aims to make three critical interventions into dominant age/ing narratives.

First, and most obviously, the very focus of this book on activist aging contests assumptions that aging is synonymous with decline, challenging widespread portrayals of older women[10] as frail, burdensome, and apolitical (Gullette 1997; D. Sawchuk 2009; Krekula 2007). As Dafna Lemish and Varda Muhlbauer (2012) explain, ageist and sexist norms tie women's societal value to reproduction and equate their beauty and femininity with youthfulness. As a result, post-menopausal women are often considered worthless, irrelevant, and "past their prime." It is undeniable that older women can experience significant economic strain, discrimination, impaired mobility, abuse, and health challenges (Grenier 2006; Wilińska 2010), but these marginalizing, single-story narratives of decline also deny older women's agency and essentialize their experiences (Sandberg 2013; Matlok-Ziemann 2014). By contrast, every contribution to this book depicts women and non-binary activists—at every stage of the lifecourse and with varied abilities and backgrounds—asserting themselves in a variety of ways, building communities, forging alliances, being creative, laughing, learning, making connections, and often working tirelessly for social change. Each of the book's four sections highlights, in different ways, activists of "middle age" or older who are deliberately inserting themselves into political spaces; their activisms subvert ageist-sexist-ableist stereotypes and depict a heterogeneity of aging experiences.

Second, by using the language of "activist aging," the volume interrupts dominant health policy and anti-aging industry discourse of "active aging" (WHO 2002). In response to disempowering decline narratives, policy-makers have spent the last 30 years developing plans, policies, and frameworks that promote "active" and "successful" aging. These discourses have been taken up widely by the booming, multi-billion-dollar "anti-aging industry" and used to sell a certain vision of aging (Ellison 2014). However, these seemingly empowering narratives retain youth as inherently positive and desirable and aging as inherently negative and scary. "Successful" aging means remaining youthful (and thus able-bodied) longer, while "active" aging implies ramping up leisure, consumer, and physical activities (Kriebernegg, Maierhofer, and Ratzenböck 2014; Katz and Marshall 2003). These discourses thus effectively re-inscribe the very messages they were originally intended to challenge (Calasanti, Slevin, and King 2006). They also reflect and reinforce neoliberal values, tying success to consumerism and leisure (not to political engagement or societal contribution), and positioning individuals as responsible for how actively they age, with no attention to the structural drivers that shape their experiences. As Lemish and Muhlbauer suggest, "Placing the responsibility for resisting aging and maintaining good health and a stylish appearance in the hands of older adults reflects neoliberal values of individualism and personal choice and responds to market forces that deepen class divisions" (2012, 167). This volume's focus on activist aging challenges such neoliberal, ageist, ableist, and individualistic messaging; it explicitly recognizes aging as informed by systems of structural power and as imbued with possibilities for collective action and positive societal contribution.

Third, the volume considers "aging" as a process that begins at birth and ends at death, not as a condition of "later life." Throughout the volume, contributors centre the changing dynamics of activisms over people's lives, and attend to the intergenerational dimensions of different forms of resistance. In this way, their contributions shift the volume beyond its initial focus on older activists to a critical lifecourse approach. In this case, the approach is critical of predominant understandings of the lifecourse that assume a series of life stages, linear temporality, or some chronological progression of social, cognitive, or biological development, and that reinscribe heteronormative, heteropatriarchal, and colonial markers of life passage (Rifkin 2014; Fisher, Phillips, and Katri 2017). Intervening from these perspectives in narratives that equate aging with "old age," this volume examines the non-linear, ever-ongoing processes of change, learning, returning, thinking, and acting that happen from birth to death. It investigates the complex ways that people, as they age, become prominent or invisibilized, powerful or stigmatized, recognizing the socially, historically, and culturally contingent expectations attached to different perceived stages or chronological ages. The volume also explores how people's level of control over their own lives might shift at different times, and how in this way age/ing might shape their different options for practicing activisms.[11]

In response to popular conceptions of aging, then, this volume makes several critical interventions. It interrupts stereotypes of brash, confrontational, activist youth and fragile, passive "little old ladies." It contests the idea that value in "later life" is necessarily demonstrated through accelerated economic and physical activity and insists instead that, for some people, "success" at every age can be derived from a sense of new and renewed contribution to working for a fairer, more compassionate, and more sustainable world. It also challenges assumptions that aging takes place only in "old age," moving to critical and contingent understandings of activist aging over the lifecourse.

THIS BOOK: CORE THEMES AND STRUCTURE

Following Davis's powerful call to action, this book aims to illuminate the intricate, lesser-known ways women and non-binary activists work for social change across different movements and throughout their lives. It raises the questions of who and what have been most erased in discourses about social change, beginning a process of redressing such erasures. Intricately connected to this, this collection also aims to pluralize, expand, and unsettle what is typically meant by "activism." It also explicitly offers analyses of age, aging, and intergenerationality, bringing critical attention to how age intersects with multiple interlocking systems of power. In these significant ways, this book contributes to and intervenes in existing scholarship on aging, gender, and social change.

The volume is organized into four parts, each of which extends under-explored concepts within existing scholarship on aging and activisms. Each part opens with a poignant piece of poetry or prose, giving space to the many ways of sharing stories, ideas, and knowledges about resistance. Each is then introduced by a guest author who sets out key questions, considerations, and readings within their subfield. The volume includes eight analytic chapters, many co-authored by academics in collaboration with community activists, students, and other research partners, as well as eight shorter personal reflections in which contributors discuss their lived experiences of activist aging. These personal stories and perspectives, alongside the brilliant poetics, bear on, contribute to, and make more vivid the scholarly themes and discussions throughout.

Part I, "Pluralizing," sets the volume's conceptual context, shifting beyond one-dimensional understandings of activism to consider a multiplicity and diversity of activists and activisms. In her introductory remarks, Carole Roy discusses how an analysis of aging can open up who is recognized as an activist, bringing more legitimacy and prominence to older women's work for social change. At the same time, she acknowledges that, while older women's activisms have begun to garner scholarly attention, much of the work in this area privileges the activisms of groups that already occupy positions of relative privilege in society. The contributions to Part I collectively depict the plurality of older people's activisms, while also bringing a preliminary discussion of whiteness into activist aging research.

In Part II, "Persisting," waaseyaa'sin christine sy, Anishinaabekwe academic, writer, and poet, reminds readers of the multiple meanings and practices associated with activist aging, drawing attention to the importance of different forms of knowledge-sharing in these conversations. This section brings an explicitly decolonial gaze, insisting that readers understand that the activisms depicted through the book have taken place on unceded lands, where First Peoples have been activating and resisting in the face of ongoing settler colonialism for centuries. In this context, persisting and surviving over generations are as much "activisms" as blockading against land destruction, moving in ceremony for the water, or teaching children to speak their own languages. The conversations, poetry, chapters, and reflections in this section also push readers to think about activist aging as a politics of connection—indeed, as motivated by connections to land, water, place, and across generations. Without shying away from the discomforts, contributors to this section further explore how aging activists from Indigenous and non-Indigenous communities might activate together.

In Part III, "Embodying," Sally Chivers introduces concepts of embodiment and performance as they pertain to activist aging. Taking a critical-disability lens, she asks readers to consider when being "visible"—being prominent as an activist—means being valued and when it does not. She also asks: What can studies of critical disability offer to scholarship on activist aging? What does it mean to intercept not only ageist but also ableist discourses in this field? The contributors to this section refuse devaluation as they contend with what activist aging means to them—from the perspectives of aging bodies and from bodies that are aging into and/or with disabilities. In doing so, they begin to crip, queer, and un/sex studies of aging and social change, offering readers insights into their onstage, offstage, and backstage activisms.

Finally, Part IV, "Remembering," is introduced by Laura Madokoro, who highlights the political and radical importance of record keeping, archiving, and intergenerational knowledge exchange. These contributions reveal the diverse ways that activists are doing memory work, asking how recording and documenting their own activisms can transform people's subjectivities as political agents. They also explore the many creative ways in which activists of different ages are working to resist erasure and insert themselves into historical memory through archiving, art, performance, mapping, and intergenerational relationship-building. These contributors refuse a unidirectional version of knowledge transmission and instead frame intergenerational memory work as multi-directional—with younger, middler, and older nurturing each other anew as activists, as archivists, and as co-creators of their movements' stories.

The volume closes with a series of activist "theirstories"—in their own words, six activists discuss their own journeys. The stories are told by activists of different ages, by those whose activisms took shape on Turtle Island and by those whose roots lie elsewhere. They are recounted by activists whose social change work reflects "quieter" approaches, by those who have adopted "louder" ways of making a difference, and by those who embrace both. Through these stories, a powerful portrait emerges of the range of meanings, experiences, and practices that we attach to our activisms, eloquently weaving together the volume's core themes and insights.

The book's structure has emerged from a series of conversations and research events connected to Aging Activisms, taking place between 2014 and 2017. The decision to bring these particular sections together to extend scholarship on aging and activisms in these ways reflects dialogue among academics across disciplines and activists across movements. This was the product of listening and sharing, of building core relationships, of taking certain risks. Overall, the volume seeks to unsettle activisms; to expand the "what, who, and how" of activist aging research; and to illuminate new questions and perspectives. It works toward a critical approach, seeking to push the limits of what and whose knowledges count, and how this can be meaningfully included within an academic book. While this approach remains aspirational, I hope it will raise critical questions even as it sits with the tensions of an unfinished (perhaps just barely started) project.

The people who are represented throughout the book—some whose resistance work spans decades—are engaged in a variety of activisms. They work for gender equality, LGBTQAI2S+ rights, reproductive justice, environmental sustainability, equitable trade agreements, global access to medicines, peace, decolonization, just conditions for refugees, and the eradication of racism, among other causes. These are not the individuals who will go down as "the motors of history," as Davis would call them. They are not Martin Luther King, or Rosa Parks, or even Angela Davis for that matter. Instead, like Robinson and her students, and Colvin and the other young women on the bus, these social changers are the extraordinary "ordinary" ones who slog, and have slogged, foregoing many nights' sleep and taking many personal risks in their efforts to create change.

NOTES

1. The project started with an explicit focus on women's activisms (in line with Davis's call) but, over the course of the project, shifted to include women and people who are non-binary, in order to reflect the fluid and diverse gender identities of many contributors.

2. In the Canadian context, dominant historical narratives even further invisibilize the many and varied contributions of activists from racialized communities, including the lives and contributions of civil rights activists as well as Indigenous, South Asian, Japanese, and Chinese social changers.

3. By heteronormativity, I am referring to the ways in which heterosexuality, with its rigid and binary conceptions of gender, is taken as common sense in Western (colonial) society and normalized through our institutions.

4. By using the language of "settler," I mean that I am non-Indigenous to this land and that my ancestors migrated to and stayed on this land as *part of a system of settler colonialism.* Regardless of whether my ancestors were part of the earliest settlement/colonization of this land, or even whether they came from the original colonizing nations of Britain or France

(which they did not), I use the language of "settler" to indicate the structural, unearned privilege bestowed on me as a non-Indigenous person within a settler colonial context. To be clear, while both colonialism and settler colonialism are based on the domination of Indigenous peoples by colonizers, *settler colonialism is distinct in its goal of replacing the original population* of the colonized territory with a new society of settlers (some from the colonial metropole, some from elsewhere). Settler colonialism depends on access to land or territory, achieved through the creation of treaties or by conquest/taking possession. The ever-growing field of settler colonial studies (e.g., Veracini 2011; Bateman and Pilkington 2011), then, recognizes that colonialism in these contexts—Canada, the United States, Australia, and so on—must be analyzed as ongoing (not in the past), as these states continue to maintain colonial relationships with Indigenous peoples, and as settlers continue to benefit from and be complicit in their ongoing dispossession. By also drawing on the language of "white settler," I wish to further acknowledge the interconnections between settler colonialism and white supremacy, and the ongoing power and privilege held in settler colonial contexts by people who immigrated from (or whose ancestors came from) the colonial metropoles/European context broadly—people who have lighter skin tones, myself included. This volume recognizes that colonialism and settler colonialism were and are driven, at least in part, by underpinning logics of racism and white supremacy (together with capitalism and patriarchy). We specify "white settler" throughout because it cannot be assumed that all settlers are white, but skin tone (and racialization) does implicate forms and degrees of privilege and oppression. In other words, people of colour, too, can be settlers in settler colonial contexts (with the associated unearned privileges this grants), but they likely will simultaneously experience racialization and racism (see Walia 2013). These categories are contested, and not all "settlers" have ended up in this land for the same reasons or via the same pathways; nevertheless, I find value in this language for understanding social locations within structural systems of power.

5. To my understanding, based on the knowledges that have been shared with me, and recognizing the complexities of land acknowledgement in settler colonial contexts, Nogojiwanong is Anishinaabemowin for "the place at the foot of the river" or "the place at the end of the rapids." It is the territory and a gathering place of the Michi Saagiig Anishinaabeg, and was long a gathering place for Haudenosaunee and other First Peoples across the region. Home to Curve Lake, Alderville, Hiawatha, and Scugog First Nations, this land was colonized by European settlers in the 1800s. While treaties have not been respected by the Canadian government, this land "is governed by several treaties that include not only political agreements made with the Crown but also agreements that were made between Indigenous nations prior to European contact" (Migizi (Williams) and Kapyrka 2015, 129). It was treatied under Treaty 20, set out between the Michi Saagiig Anishinaabeg and the British Crown in 1818, and the Williams Treaties, set out by Canada in 1923 (ibid.). See Migizi (Williams) and

Kapyrka 2015, Blair 2008, sy 2015, and Taylor and Dokis 2015 for more information.

6. See www.agingactivisms.org for more information on this activist-research collective.

7. Here I would like to acknowledge the work of Anishinaabekwe Leanne Betasamosake
    Simpson, whose intellectual and creative contributions on resurgence have greatly influenced
    my own thinking, including *Dancing on Our Turtle's Back* and *Lighting the Eighth Fire*. I would
    point readers as well to the important collection, *The Winter We Danced*, by the Kino-nda-niimi
    Collective. I also extend particularly deep gratitude to Anishinaabekwe poet and scholar
    waaseyaa'sin christine sy, whose work is throughout this volume (see pages 22, 74, 186; see
    also sy 2014; sy 2016), Elder Shirley Ida Williams Pheasant (Chapter 3), the Peterborough and
    Kawarthas Sacred Water Circle and Water Walkers (Nibi Emosaawdamajig), Trent University's
    First People's House of Learning, the annual Trent University Elders and Traditional Peoples
    Gathering, and the many brilliant Indigenous thinkers and activists who have participated in
    Aging Activisms work, including but not limited to: Elder Audrey Kuwaquom Caskanette, Elder
    Alice Olsen Williams, Tasha Beeds, Jenn Cole, Lynn Gehl, Keara Lightning, Monique Mojica, Liz
    Stone, and Smokii Sumac.

8. By cisgender, I mean that my own gender identity (as a woman) matches the one I was
    assigned at birth ("It's a girl!").

9. On the topic of the relationships that have come to underpin this book, it is worth noting that
    there is some variation across the volume in how contributors refer to each other and to the
    participants in their research (in the case of research-oriented chapters). In the introductions
    to each part, we follow academic conventions: guest authors refer to the contributions in
    their sections by referencing authors' first and last names upon initial mention and last
    names only after that. However, in the remainder of the book, we have left it up to authors
    to determine how they refer to one another and to the others named in their pieces; in many
    cases (e.g., Chapters 1 and 2, and the book's conclusion), authors choose to use first and last
    names for initial reference and only first names thereafter, more in line with contemporary
    colloquial norms around naming people with whom closer relationships exist. Recognizing the
    import of relationships, affect, caring, and the intersubjectivity of the knowledge presented
    throughout, we have chosen not to require a standardized formal tone (using last names only)
    across the book, but instead to allow contributors to use language in a way that reveals such
    connections.

10. It is important to point out that in many of these discussions of societal narratives and
    existing scholarship, I revert to referencing "women" in large part because there is very
    limited work to date on trans and non-binary older adults.

11. Elsewhere, scholars are also calling for a rethinking of the lifecourse from critical race
    perspectives (e.g., Hulko 2009; Ferrer et al. 2017) and queered perspectives (e.g., Riach,
    Rumens, and Tyler 2014; Jones 2011)—these are clearly salient analyses in terms of the overall
    goals of this book.

REFERENCES

Adler, Margot. 2009. "Before Rosa Parks There Was Claudette Colvin" [transcript]. *NPR*. www.npr.org/templates/story/story.php?Storyid=101719889

Bateman, Fiona, and Lionel Pilkington. Eds. 2011. *Studies in Settler Colonialism: Politics, Identity, and Culture*. New York: Palgrave Macmillan.

Blair, Peggy. 2008. *Lament for a First Nation: The Williams Treaties of Southern Ontario*. Vancouver, BC: UBC Press.

Brown, Leslie, and Susan Strega. Eds. 2014. *Research as Resistance: Critical, Indigenous, & Anti-oppressive Approaches, second edition*. Toronto, ON: Canadian Scholars' Press/ Women's Press.

Byrnes, Mary E. 2016. "Grow Old with Me! Future Directions of Race, Age, and Place Scholarship." *Sociology Compass* 10(10): 906–917.

Calasanti, Toni, Kathleen F. Slevin, and Neal King. 2006. "Ageism and Feminism: From 'Et Cetera' to Centre." *NWSA Journal* 18(1): 13–30.

Chazan, May. 2015. *The Grandmothers' Movement: Solidarity and Survival in the Time of AIDS*. Montreal, QC: McGill-Queen's University Press.

Chovanec, Donna M., Miriam Cooley, and Ruby S. Diaz. 2010. "A Legacy of Women's Activism: Intergenerational Learning in the Chilean Student Movement." In *Connected Understandings: Women, Gender and Education (Proceedings of the 2010 Canadian Association for the Study of Women and Education Concordia University)*, edited by Darlene E. Clover and Vivian Smith, 11–116.

Davis, Angela. 2007. How Does Change Happen? [video]. www.youtube.com/watch?V =Pc6RHtEbiOA

Ellison, Kirsten L. 2014. "Age Transcended: A Semiotic and Rhetorical Analysis of the Discourse of Agelessness in North American Anti-aging Skin Care Advertisements." *Journal of Aging Studies* 29: 20–31.

Ferrer, Ilyan, Amanda Grenier, Shari Brotman, and Sharon Koehn. 2017. "Understanding the Experiences of Racialized Older People through an Intersectional Life Course Perspective." *Journal of Aging Studies* 41: 10–17.

Fisher, Simon D. Elin, Rasheedah Phillips, and Ido H. Katri. 2017. "Introduction: Trans Temporalities." *Somatechnics* 7(1): 1–15.

Grenier, Amanda. 2006. "The Distinction between Being and Feeling Frail: Exploring Emotional Experiences in Health and Social Care." *Journal of Social Work Practice: Psychotherapeutic Approaches in Health, Welfare and the Community* 20(3): 299–313.

Gullette, Margaret Morganroth. 1997. *Declining to Decline: Cultural Combat and the Politics of the Midlife*. Charlottesville, VA: University of Virginia Press.

Hodgson, Dorothy L., and Ethel Brooks. Eds. 2007. "Activisms" [Special Issue]. *Women's Studies Quarterly* 35(3/4).

Hoose, Phillip. 2009. *Claudette Colvin: Twice towards Justice.* New York: Macmillan.

Hulko, Wendy. 2009. "The Time- and Context-Contingent Nature of Intersectionality and Interlocking Oppressions." *Affilia* 24(1): 44–55.

Jones, Rebecca L. 2011. "Imagining Bisexual Futures: Positive, Non-Normative Later Life." *Journal of Bisexuality* 11(2/3): 245–270.

Katz, Stephen, and Barbara L. Marshall. 2003. "New Sex for Old: Lifestyle, Consumerism, and the Ethics of Aging Well." *Journal of Aging Studies* 17(1): 3–16.

Kauanui, J. Kēhaulani. 2016. "'A Structure, Not an Event': Settler Colonialism and Enduring Indigeneity." *Lateral: Journal of the Cultural Studies Association* 5(1). www.csalateral.org/issue/5-1/forum-alt-humanities-settler-colonialism-enduring -indigeneity-kauanui/

Krekula, Clary. 2007. "The Intersection of Age and Gender: Reworking Gender Theory and Social Gerontology." *Current Sociology* 55(2): 155–171.

Kriebernegg, Ulla, Roberta Maierhofer, and Barbara Ratzenböck. 2014. "Re-thinking Material Realities and Cultural Representations of Age and Aging." In *Alive and Kicking at All Ages: Cultural Constructions of Health and Life Course Identity*, edited by authors, 9–17. Bielefeld, Germany: Transcript-Verlag.

Lemish, Dafna, and Varda Muhlbauer. 2012. "'Can't Have It All': Representations of Older Women in Popular Culture." *Women & Therapy* 35: 165–180.

Matlok-Ziemann, Ellen. 2014. "'Old Women that Will Not Be Kept Away': Undermining Ageist Discourse with Invisibility and Performance." In *Alive and Kicking at All Ages: Cultural Constructions of Health and Life Course Identity*, edited by Barbara Ratzenböck, Roberta Maierhofer, and Ulla Kriebernegg, 259–274. Bielefeld, Germany: Transcript-Verlag.

McHugh, Maureen. 2012. "Aging, Agency, and Activism: Older Women as Social Change Agents." *Women & Therapy* 35(3): 279–295.

Meadows, Lynn M., Wilfreda E. Thurston, and Laura E. Lagendyk. 2009. "Aboriginal Women at Midlife: Grandmothers as Agents of Change." In *First Voices: An Aboriginal Women's Reader*, edited by Patricia A. Monture and Patricia D. McGuire, 188–199. Toronto, ON: INANNA Publications and Education Inc.

Migizi, Gitiga (Doug Williams), and Julie Kapyrka. 2015. "Before, During, and After: Mississauga Presence in the Kawarthas." In *Peterborough Archaeology*, edited by Dirk Verhulst, 127–136. Peterborough, ON: Peterborough Chapter of the Ontario Archaeological Society.

Pain, Rachel. 2014. "Seismologies of Emotion: Fear and Activism During Domestic Violence." *Social & Cultural Geography* 15(2): 127–150.

Pratt, Geraldine. 2010. "Collaboration as a Feminist Strategy." *Gender, Place and Culture* 17(1): 43–48.

Riach, Kathleen, Nicholas Rumens, and Melissa Tyler. 2014. "Un/doing Chromonormativity: Negotiating Ageing, Gender and Sexuality in Organizational Life." *Organization Studies* 35(11): 1677–1698.

Rich, Cynthia, and Barbara Macdonald. 2001. *Look Me in the Eye: Old Women, Aging and Ageism.* Tallahassee, FL: Spinster's Ink.

Richards, Naomi. 2012. "The Fight to Die: Older People and Death Activism." *International Journal of Ageing and Later Life* 7(1): 7–32.

Rifkin, Mark. 2014. "Queering Indigenous Pasts, or Temporalities of Tradition and Settlement." In *The Oxford Handbook of Indigenous American Literature*, edited by James H. Coz and Daniel Heath Justice, 137–151. Oxford, UK: Oxford University Press.

Roy, Carole. 2004. *The Raging Grannies: Wild Hats, Cheeky Songs, and Witty Actions for a Better World.* Montreal, QC: Black Rose Books.

Sandberg, Linn. 2013. "Affirmative Old Age—The Ageing Body and Feminist Theories on Difference." *International Journal of Ageing and Later Life* 8(1): 11–40.

Sawchuk, Dana. 2009. "The Raging Grannies: Defying Stereotypes and Embracing Aging through Activism." *Journal of Women & Aging*, 21(3): 171–185.

Sawchuk, Kim. 2009. "Feminism in Waves: Re-imagining a Watery Metaphor." In *Open Boundaries: A Canadian Women's Studies Reader*, edited by Barbara Crow and Lise Gotell, 58–64. Toronto, ON: Pearson.

Simpson, Leanne. 2011. *Dancing on Our Turtle's Back: Stories of Nishnaabeg Re-creation, Resurgence, and a New Emergence.* Winnipeg, MB: Arbeiter Ring Publishing.

Stone, Liz. 2015. "Episode 10: Liz Stone." Interview by Melissa Baldwin and Maddy Macnab. *Aging Radically*, Trent Radio, December 2, 2015. Audio, 29:30. www.aging activisms.org/#!agingradically/ohfvr

sy, waaseyaa'sin christine. 2016. "At the Boiling Place: Reading Sap for Future Anishinaabeg Sugar Bush (Re)Matriation." *GUTS Magazine* (May 2016). www.gutsmagazine.ca/boiling-place/

sy, waaseyaa'sin christine. 2015. "Dance the Curves." In *This Place a Stranger*, edited by Vici Johnstone, 102–111. Halfmoon Bay, BC: Caitlin Press.

sy, waaseyaa'sin christine. 2014. "Through Iskigamizigan (The Sugar Bush): A Poetics of Decolonization." In *Indigenous Poetics*, edited by Neal McLeod, 185–204. Waterloo, ON: Wilfred Laurier Press.

Taylor, Anne, and Melissa Dokis. 2015. *Oshkigmong: A Place Where I Belong, the Story of the Michi Saagiig (Mississauga) of Curve Lake First Nation* [film]. Curve Lake First Nation.

Twigg, Julia. 2004. "The Body, Gender, and Age: Feminist Insights in Social Gerontology." *Journal of Aging Studies* 18: 59–73.

United Nations. 2013. *World Population Ageing 2013*. Department of Economic and Social Affairs Population Division. www.un.org/en/development/desa/population/publications/pdf/ageing/worldpopulationageing2013.pdf

Veracini, Lorenzo. 2011. *Settler Colonialism: A Theoretical Overview*. New York: Palgrave Macmillan.

Walia, Harsha. 2013. *Undoing Border Imperialism*. Edinburgh, UK: AK Press.

WHO (World Health Organization). 2002. *Active Ageing: A Policy Framework*. Geneva, Switzerland: WHO. www.whqlibdoc.who.int/hq/2002/WHO_NMH_NPH_02.8.pdf

Wilińska, Monika. 2010. "Because Women Will Always Be Women and Men Are Just Getting Older: Intersecting Discourses of Ageing and Gender." *Current Sociology* 58(6): 879–896.

PART I

PLURALIZING

POEM I

Grandmother

waaseyaa'sin christine sy

waaseyaa'sin christine sy is Anishinaabe of mixed ancestry from Lac Seul First Nation and Sault Ste. Marie, Ontario. A poet, scholar, mother, activist, granddaughter,
and Anishinaabe language learner, she was 43 years old when she wrote this poem.
sy is actively engaged in learning about sustenance land-based practices in her
Anishinaabe homelands. She currently lives in Coast Salish Territory, where she is
an assistant professor in gender studies at the University of Victoria.

… and all these things too, but you know also, look, tonight—the crescent moon. nokomis. grandmother. she reminds me of shape-shifting. a shape-shifter.
imagine sliding on a brand-new pair of moleskin-textured mucklucks made out of
brain-tanned deer hide that she petitioned her nephew to prepare just so she could make
you something for your feet because she wants you to always try to walk the good walk,
dance the good dance, skip, get up tall when you trip. imagine having someone who
loves you so much they want you to walk a good walk.
or, a hefty bandolier bag made to hold your sacred items, made for you with her special
velvets and threads. imagine all those shining, shiny beads orchestrated into meanings
and designs created by her, specifically for you, so you could do all the work you have to
work and carry all the weight you have to carry, in softness and beauty. or, however you
like. she, tonight, a beading needle. long, thin, bendy. barely there, still there.
a tool for tattooing intricately stylized ceremonial symbols into our bodies&being in
blue. or, drawing out grief, pain or little balls of coagulated messes that distract us, get
in the way of who we are and what we're supposed to be doing. a tool for etching in,

siphoning out. imagine she is there using herself to divine you back forward to yourself. a curvy knife.

an elongated, curvy knife shaped through years of butchering autumn kills or filleting freshly fished ogaa or shagan. for cutting into a tender roasted goose got that day and let to set in its heat for just the right amount of time—until the juices to stop bubbling and the aromas to fill the air. for cutting into a fresh loaf of bread that she made you run to the grocery store to get at the last minute because what good is roasted goose if you can't sop up its juice. paanjike. wipe your folded piece of bread slowly and carefully along the curve of the plate. nokomis is the curve of a plate glistening with goose juice waiting to be sopped up.

she is an awl. an awl for making a basket or preparing sheets of wiigwaas—birchbark— to be sewn together to make protection, to make cover, to make walls, to make round; to make a softly shaped, breathing home.

she is the bone for making an awl.

the penile bone of a bear.

she is the penile bone of a bear used for making an awl.

she is a bear, a softly shaped home. a tool for making a softly shaped bear home. she is a tool for making a softly shaped breathing…

she is the shape of the first copper i fumbled with and hammered my fingertips into with a rock, copper just scoopy enough to hold a thin layer of nibi that could be clarified into, "okay, it's clean enough now for all of us to take a slurp from."

the way nokomis holds the earth shine tonight, too, on her darker side. the way the light shows her dark, her dark more expansive than her light, right at the moment. it reminds me that while she glows, she is not all glowy.

still, she is worthy of respect and honour. she is worthy of poetic pining. she is still so worthy a poem.

INTRODUCTION TO PART I

Pluralizing

Carole Roy

A decade ago, in response to calls from such feminist writers as Baba Copper and Ruth E. Ray to pay more attention to older women, I wrote about a network of older women activists—the Raging Grannies. I also participated in making documentaries about these women with filmmaker Magnus Isacsson. The Raging Grannies cut a dashing, outspoken, and daring presence. In a society that equated activism with youth (and still does to a large extent), theirs was a refreshing, radical voice that articulated their views through engaging satirical songs and flamboyant actions. As a feminist interested in social movements, it was a privilege to document their activisms; to witness the expression of anger and outrage in sassy and outlandish ways. The idea was not to reify their particular brand of activism, but to dispel the notion that "little old ladies" are meek, feeble, and of no consequence.

Revealing invisibility is always a demanding task, and the Grannies allowed older women and older women's activisms to be recognized. Now the task is to pluralize the notion of activisms and illuminate the many diverse activisms of women, non-binary, and gender fluid activists of varying ages, including activisms that are not always overt in their delivery, but are no less effective in their impact. Paths of expression and action are often contingent on social locations, affected by intersections of age, race, Indigeneity, citizenship/immigration status, social class, sexual orientation, gender expression, and ability. Broadening activisms to include the labour necessary to sustain decades-long work in community health promotion or women's organizations, for example, reveals the many contributions that otherwise go unrecognized. Allowing activisms to include "listening" challenges the current societal value placed on "action," bringing attention to the critical work of reflection that is so necessary for resistance efforts to create change. Listening includes receiving individual activists and allowing them to express their feelings, views, and experiences; it also involves the ongoing emotional labour done to sustain individuals, groups, and organizations. This work is often done quietly and away from public view, yet it is work that contributes enormously to individual and community development and to a more just and democratic society.

This part of the book explores the different ways activists organize, resist, and survive, including reflections on how the lifecourse influences their activisms. For some, activism is lifelong, while for others it is a response to becoming a grand-mother; for some their lifelong work may not fit under the typical rubric of activism (i.e., formal protest) at all. The activisms of the older women depicted in this sec-tion include a wide range of approaches from the outlandish to the very subtle. The personal is still political, but the political is also personal. While older age may bring concerns related to health, for some it also brings into focus issues of power and politics, wanting to express support for family, friends, and communities to ensure that democratic societies endure and to safeguard the Earth so it can sustain life into the future. These "aging activisms" are far from homogenous—activists of various backgrounds, ages, and abilities are portrayed engaging in many forms of activisms for many different purposes. Using the lens of aging allows an analysis that can connect what happens in the early years to later life. What is remarkable is that many activists engage in activisms all along their lives, although the forms of their resistances might change significantly as they get older.

In the first chapter, May Chazan, Melissa Baldwin, and Jesse Whattam critically examine the dominant assumption that motherhood and grandmotherhood are times of retreat from working for social change, based on oral histories with members of the Raging Grannies and the Grandmothers Advocacy Network. They further broaden conceptions of activisms to include everyday, often invisible forms of resistance—some-times even survival—that can take place in the domestic sphere. For many of their participants, their child-rearing years might have appeared apolitical from the outside; yet, as they fought personal battles around domestic abuse, divorce, and custody of children, most often through the 1970s, they became part of the wider struggle to improve lives for women and children. The authors also suggest that, while political involvement can take different forms along the lifecourse, for many, aging seems to amplify older women's resistance. These authors make explicit that their participants were predominantly white, settlers, and working-/middle-class, and in doing so raise important questions about how experiences and meanings of (grand)motherhood are contingent. The chapter is followed by a reflection by Peggy Edwards who connects her concrete experience as a grandmother and health consultant to her renewed activism in solidarity with grandmothers responding to the HIV/AIDS crisis in southern Africa. She suggests that, in her experience, older women demonstrate persistence, bring stra-tegic thinking, and activate their extensive networks to express solidarity.

Kim Sawchuk and Constance Lafontaine focus their work on Respecting Elders: Communities Against Abuse (RECAA), a network of predominantly older women from a number of "ethnocultural communities" (as RECAA calls them—predominantly immigrant communities who are racialized in the Canadian context) in Montreal. They explore the creative activist tactics deployed by this group, including the use of silent skits and media pieces, to work across differences in language and culture to raise awareness about elder abuse. The authors contribute to understanding older age as a time of creativity and connection, and they explicitly document the very little-known organizing brilliance of older, racialized women. The following reflection by Sadeqa Siddiqui, who immigrated twice, first from India to Pakistan and then from Pakistan to Canada, represents an example of how her activisms found different expressions at different times, yet migration issues and women's rights remain a focus of her engagement.

This section broadens our understanding of aging, drawing on a critical and non-linear lifecourse perspective, and depicts a wide range of activisms—from outward and overt to more quiet approaches that are no less effective. What forms do activisms take for different activists, each with a unique lifetime of experiences? What sustains their engagement—or re-engagement—with issues of social justice and social change? Power and privilege are always relative terms: How is activist aging experienced differently as a result of race, social class, culture, immigrant experience, sexual orientation, gender identity, and Indigeneity? This section explores activists' personal reflections and scholars' analyses of what it means to resist, activate, survive, create, and work for change.

RECOMMENDED READINGS

Byrnes, Mary E. 2016. "Grow Old with Me! Future Directions of Race, Age, and Place Scholarship." *Sociology Compass* 10: 906–917.

Calasanti, Toni M., and Katherine F. Slevin. Eds. 2006. *Age Matters: Realigning Feminist Thinking.* New York: Routledge.

Chazan, May. 2015. *The Grandmothers' Movement: Solidarity and Survival in the Time of AIDS.* Montreal, QC: McGill-Queen's Press.

Ferrer, Ilyan, Amanda Grenier, Shari Brotman, and Sharon Koehn. 2017. "Understanding the Experiences of Racialized Older People through an Intersectional Life Course Perspective." *Journal of Aging Studies* 41: 10–17.

Hulko, Wendy. 2009. "The Time- and Context-Contingent Nature of Intersectionality and Interlocking Oppressions." *Affilia* 24 (1): 44–55.

Ray, Ruth E. 1999. "Researching to Transgress: The Need for Critical Feminism in Gerontology." In *Fundamentals of Feminist Gerontology,* edited by D. J. Garner, 171–185. New York: The Haworth Press.

Roy, Carole. 2004. *The Raging Grannies: Wild Hats, Cheeky Songs, and Witty Actions for a Better World*. Montreal, QC: Black Rose Books.

Roy, Carole. 2017. "Older Women, Humor, and Social Activism." In *Gender: Laughter*, edited by Bettina Papenburg, 199–214. Farmington Hills, MI: Macmillan Reference.

Sawchuk, Kim. 2013. "Tactical Mediatization and Activist Ageing: Pressures, Pushbacks, and the Story of RECAA." In *MedieKultur* special issue on mediatization, edited by Stig Hjarvard and Line Nybro Peterson.

SUGGESTED MULTIMEDIA AND FILMS

Edwards, Peggy. Writer/Producer. 2010. *Voices of Advocacy: Older Women Speak Out* [Documentary short]. Ottawa: Rooney Productions. www.grannyvoices.com

Isacsson, Magnus, and Jocelyne Clarke. Directors. Carole Roy. Researcher. 2014. *Granny Power!* [Documentary film]. Montreal, QC: Pleiades Productions.

Ophelian, Annalise. Producer/director. StormMiguel Florez. Co-producer/editor. 2016. *Major!* [Documentary film]. What Do We Want Films with Floating Ophelia Productions. www.missmajorfilm.com

Ressources Ethnoculturelles Contre l'Abus Envers les Aîné(e)s / Respecting Elders: Communities Against Abuse (RECAA). 2015. *In Their Own Words: Volunteer Voices from Montreal's Cultural Communities* [short video project]. www.recaa.ca/projects/in-their-own-words-volunteer-voices-from-montreals-cultural-communities/

SUGGESTED WEBSITES

Ageing + Communication + Technologies (ACT Network): www.actproject.ca

Aging Activisms (activist-research collective): www.agingactivisms.org

Grandmothers Advocacy Network (GRAN): www.grandmothersadvocacy.org

Raging Grannies: www.raginggrannies.org

Respecting Elders: Communities Against Abuse (RECAA): www.recaa.ca

CHAPTER 1

Rethinking the Politics of (Grand)Mothering: Activisms and the Lifecourse

May Chazan, Melissa Baldwin, and Jesse Whattam

This chapter draws on research with older women (in their 60s through 80s) who shared their stories with us—stories of why and how they have acted for change over the course of their lives. It is based on oral histories with 32 older activists from across Turtle Island (Canada and the United States). By delving into important, intricate, and sometimes painful details of their activisms over time, the chapter challenges certain simplistic assumptions about (grand)motherhood[1] as synonymous with disengagement. It contests, in other words, "the myth that bearing and raising children alters a woman's consciousness in some fundamentally conservative way, silencing her voice and disarming her rebellion" (Jetter, Orleck, and Taylor 1997, back cover), and it intervenes in assumptions that grandmotherhood is a period of political decline and that "grandmothers" (or those who might appear to be grandmothers) are necessarily harmless, apolitical, and passive. This chapter instead reveals the continuities, contingencies, and changes in particular women's activisms over decades—activisms that (re)surge in their later lives. We open with Ingrid's story, in which she narrates a common theme from this research: the creativity, persistence, and resilience it takes to resist and to act over time.

Ingrid[2] was born in 1940 into what she described as a "patriarchal Roman Catholic family" in Acadian New Brunswick, Canada. Like her 18 siblings, much of her childhood was shaped by experiences of poverty, trauma, and abuse. She spoke candidly, connecting her early experiences to the lifelong values that shaped her activisms in later life:

> In the first 10 years of my life, I was twice in an orphanage because both my parents were in the hospital.... [My father] was very old school, right wing, women [were] property. When I was little—eight, nine, ten, eleven, twelve—he

was an alcoholic. He would invite his drinking buddies over and line us [me and my sisters] up, for them to choose one of us. Mother was in the bedroom crying, totally, totally victimized, helpless.... But they were old, they were drunk, we could outrun them....

School was horrible! ... Every day I would get the strap and have to stand behind the piano in the classroom.... At 15, I thought, "Whatever is out on that street cannot be as bad as what I am experiencing in this house. I'll take my chances." It was probably these early experiences that made me always for the underdog.

Ingrid left her home at 15 and hitchedhiked across Quebec. She soon became pregnant, got married, and then followed her husband to Elliot Lake, Ontario, where he had been offered a job in a mine. She said:

I would have been about 17, maybe 18.... I was four months pregnant when I got married, and then I had six children in eight years.... After the sixth, I knew I was going to have a nervous breakdown if I had another one, so that was it.... The next many years were like zombie-land, just trying to survive! ... The attitude [of my husband] was very familiar. You know you kind of pick a man that's like your father.

Ingrid focused on caring for her children and navigating a difficult relationship in the years when her children were young. Later, when they were all school-aged, she took a job as a bus driver to support them. Although her husband made a decent wage, he was, in her words, "financially abusive" and never provided adequately for them. She felt that, in those years, it would have been impossible for her to engage in activism: She did not have the time and her husband would not have allowed it.

Ingrid's turning point came in her mid-40s, when her children were mostly grown up: After 29 years of marriage, she began a very long process of divorce. Within two weeks of her husband leaving, she had enrolled in a degree program in feminist counselling at the University of Ottawa, paying her way by bus driving. She became passionately involved in feminist struggles: "When I went to university, I was exposed to a whole lot of different ideas and views ... I remember having the *big feminist meltdown*." After six years of legal battles, she received a sizeable settlement from her divorce. She gave some of it to each of her children and the remainder freed her up to begin working at a feminist sexual assault centre.

While working at the centre, she and some of her colleagues started a women's organization, which she represented at the 1995 United Nations World Conference on Women, in Beijing. Later, she taught English in various places across Asia. She lived in China for a number of years, where her activism involved smuggling political books, films, and other censored materials across the border from Hong Kong. After retiring from teaching abroad at age 60, she moved to Vancouver. At the time of our research, she was working daily for the causes she cared most deeply about: women's rights, the environment, and peace.

Ingrid's story is one of resistance and resilience. She *twice* cultivated the courage to escape abusive conditions. She raised six children, putting each of them and herself through university. She then worked in feminist counselling with survivors of sexual abuse and assault. Her story—one of the many activist stories that Angela Davis (2007) and others might consider as among the erased, omitted, and forgotten—illustrates many of the themes revealed throughout our research.

Two aspects of her narrative are particularly salient for thinking about activist aging, or about people's activisms at different times in their lives. First, Ingrid did not see herself as an activist during her child-rearing years: She did not then have the time or opportunity to work outwardly for social change. Yet she managed to resist her husband's control by supporting herself and her children, and she extricated herself from her marriage at a time when divorce was still stigmatized and divorce laws did not support women.[3] Far from being apolitical during her child rearing years—a frequent assumption (O'Reilly 2012)—her politicization was very much tied to her own struggles: to the challenges of freeing herself psychologically, financially, and physically from her husband and from enduring further trauma. Second, unlike the well-known narratives of aging as decline (discussed in the book's introduction, see also Gullette 1997), Ingrid described herself as coming to more overt forms of activism in her 40s. It was then that her feminist organizing took off; it was then that she could take the risks she did. Her post-retirement years were the most politically active of her life.

This chapter analyzes research on aging and activism carried out between 2013 and 2015. Why and how were older women from different movements engaging in activisms? What drew them in? How did their activisms change over their lives? How were they engaged in later life? What sustained them in this work?[4] In our analysis, we adopt a critical lifecourse perspective, which considers how the passage of time changes one's positions and circumstances—and thus activisms—although not in any straightforward or linear way (Hulko 2009; Jones 2011).[5] We also draw on a broad definition of "activisms," as discussed in this volume's introduction, to encompass a range of ways of acting, including outward forms of protest and everyday acts of resistance (Hodgson and Brooks 2007). Our research did not set out to investigate experiences of motherhood or grandmotherhood specifically, but rather considered women's activist life histories broadly. However, in this chapter we explore the theme of (grand)motherhood because, in telling their own stories, these activists returned frequently to their own experiences as (grand)mothers, the narrow patriarchal expectations they faced in these roles, and, in one case, the decision to not become a mother (a decision that still evoked discourses of the social expectations around reproduction faced by women in the 1970s). In our analysis, we consider whether and how motherhood and grandmotherhood might be sites that prompt activisms, and how (grand)motherhood (as discourses, institutions, identities, and positions) can be mobilized toward political ends.

Our study took as its entry point women who were involved in at least one of two "granny activist" networks: the Grandmothers Advocacy Network (GRAN, see www.grandmothersadvocacy.org, as well as Chapter 8), which is a network of older Canadian women who advocate for Canadian policies and practices to support the struggles of women and children affected by HIV/AIDS in southern Africa, and the Raging Grannies (see www.raginggrannies.org, as well as Chapters 4 and 6), which is a North American movement of older women environmental, peace, and social justice activists who act primarily by parodying "little old ladies" and performing satirical songs to get their political messages across. We selected these networks because, while different in their goals, activities, structures, and governance, both are composed predominantly of women over the age of 60. Many of the women in these networks are (and have been) active in varied political struggles that extend well beyond their "granny activism," so the project also delved into a broad range of resistance stories.

Largely reflective of the broader GRAN and Raging Grannies communities, participants in our study were born between 1922 and 1954, with roughly two-thirds born in the 1940s.[6] Given that most were part of the same age cohort—in their 60s and 70s during the time of our interviews—the North American feminist, peace, and civil rights movements of the 1960s and 1970s were common reference points in many of their activist histories. In addition, all of our participants were cisgender, white settler women.[7] Among diverse migration stories, some described how their families were given unceded Indigenous land as part of Canada's nation-building project, while others described their families arriving in North America as refugees from Europe. Further, participants were predominantly post-secondary educated and working-/middle-class, with some diversity in where they were raised (urban/rural, across North America), their parents' political leanings, and their families' class backgrounds. Given this relatively homogeneous age, gender, and racial/ethnic demographic, we acknowledge the partiality and contingency of the analysis we offer. Different stories and different conclusions would likely emerge in interviews with activists of colour, Indigenous Elders, or older trans activists, among others. Participants' social locations have undoubtedly informed their activisms, as well as their experiences and conceptions of motherhood and grandmotherhood.

CONCEPTS: ACTIVISMS, THE LIFECOURSE, AND THE POLITICS OF (GRAND)MOTHERHOOD

We focus in this chapter on two "life stages" that are often assumed to be apolitical: motherhood and grandmotherhood. In so doing, we draw together a number of themes and concepts at the intersection of critical motherhood and critical aging studies. Some of these concepts reverberate throughout the volume, and thus it is worthwhile outlining these briefly here.

First, we engage with critical scholarship that considers the varied ways in which "motherhood" can be politicized, performed, and politically mobilized.[8] Like the works of Adrienne Rich (1995), Andrea O'Reilly (2012), and others, the stories we draw upon intervene in dominant narratives about "motherhood" as a period of disengagement—a time when many are deemed to be isolated with their children, happily self-sacrificing, and far removed from politics and social struggle. Our work resonates with the insights of Annelise Orleck (1997), Jewelles Smith (2012), and others, who depict motherhood not as a time when women's activisms end but rather as an impetus for shifting methods and forms. Our research also supports O'Reilly's (2012) observation that maternal activisms can blur the boundaries between the private and the public. Indeed, in exploring these blurry public/private boundaries, we build on Rachel Pain's (2014) work to suggest that "quiet" acts of resistance in the domestic sphere may be as much part of women's activisms as brazen protest.

Second, we investigate women's activisms into their later lives, challenging lingering notions that older women's resistances are undertaken "despite" their age. While numerous feminist scholars look at the intersection of *motherhood* and activisms, fewer have extended this to include an analysis of *grandmotherhood* and activisms (Chazan and Kittmer 2016; Chazan and Baldwin 2017). We build on the work of aging scholars who critique the ageist and sexist narratives surrounding grandmotherhood (Sawchuk 2009) and consider the ways in which some older women activists mobilize "grandmotherhood" to gain entry into political spaces (Chazan and Kittmer 2016).

Third, we recognize the possibility that there are times in people's lives when their actions become limited—due to health issues, disability, restrictive relationships, economic situations, and/or extreme calls on their time—but that such restriction is not necessarily synonymous with disengagement. Here again we see small, daily acts of resistance as having the potential to create broader change, holding open the possibility that women's activisms do not necessarily stop during periods of restriction. For some of our participants, we find Pain's (2014) work extremely useful. Pain explores the small, quiet, "messy and non-linear" acts of resistance that many people experiencing domestic violence engage in daily. Although women often practice these daily acts of resistance in the private and isolated spaces of their homes, she argues that "quiet politics … still contribute to a wider process that ultimately may lead to change" (143). Like Pain and others, we consider the politics of survival (surviving control, devaluing, isolation, financial manipulation, domestic violence, and all other forms of abuse) to be processes of resistance and of norm-changing.[9]

Finally, in considering our conceptual framing, we offer one important caveat. The scholarship that resonates most with our research is based on fairly Eurocentric (North-centric, white) understandings of motherhood and grandmotherhood. However, scholars working in different contexts and with different groups have also done important work, which we wish to acknowledge. For instance, working with communities in the Global South, some have sought to analyze the ways in which (grand)motherhood is contingent on social history and political economy (Scheper-Hughes 2003; Chazan 2015; Chilisa and Ntseane 2010; Stevenson 2011). Others remind us of the particularities of (grand)motherhood and of the diverse ways of knowing (grand)mothering from the perspectives of communities indigenous to Turtle Island (Huago 2016; Lavell-Harvard and Lavell 2006; Simpson 2011) and migrant/immigrant/refugee communities (Tungohan 2013; Baldassar, Baldock, and Wilding 2007). In this chapter we hope to dispel assumptions about (grand)mothers fading into apolitical domesticity, while also acknowledging the socio-historical specificity of our analysis.

MOTHERHOODS AND ACTIVISMS

Many participants in our research, though certainly not all, discussed their involvement in formal protest—peace, civil rights, and feminist rallies—in their late teens and early 20s, often while they were in university or college. Yet many who described themselves as "active activists" in these earlier years went on to describe their 20s through 40s as years when they were less engaged or even "apolitical." These women explained that, in the years when their children were young, they were taken up with the demands of family life and work, sometimes living in quite restrictive emotional, social, and economic conditions. This finding led us to examine participants' 20s through 40s—the child-rearing/motherhood years for many—in more detail, questioning whether, for these women, motherhood was indeed apolitical or, in line with Orleck (1997) and others, this time was *differently political* but still a potential site for change. What we found in the stories was much diversity and some patterns; collectively, these stories strongly challenge assumptions of disengagement.

Most participants described their middle adulthood as a spectacular "juggling act." Many worked outside their homes; they described careers as teachers, journalists, politicians, paramedics, designers, financiers, executive directors, psychologists, mediators, marketers, nurses, professors, probation officers, ministers—and this includes only a fraction of their compensated activities. Most also got married and raised children. Here, however, we note one important and divergent narrative. One participant in our study, Jo, neither birthed nor raised children, and her distinctive story punctuates some of our findings. Jo was also the only participant who was "out" as a lesbian in the 1970s–1980s. She explicitly discussed her decision not to have children as a personal and politicized choice that facilitated her activisms through the 1970s, when she was in her 20s and 30s. She associated her decision not to have children with her capacity to work extensively with the iconic Status of Women Canada campaign through that decade. We hold her story as part of this collective.

Among the 31 participants who raised children, almost all described themselves as their children's primary caregivers: 22 out of the 31 who raised children did so with very minimal support. All 31 women also, at some point in our interviews, discussed the very regressive laws and policies in Canada and the United States in the years they were entering and negotiating motherhood: the struggles for access to birth control, for parental leaves, for child care, for no-fault divorce, and so on. When it came to describing their activisms during these years, however, there was much variety in what was shared. Some, like Sam, Anna, and Betty, depicted supportive relationships but nonetheless felt that these were years of less overt engagement as a result of the hours required to care for children. We noted that these women turned their non-child-care hours to advocacy-related work of various sorts, both paid and volunteer. They felt less able to attend rallies or protests with babies and children in tow, but they continued their work in pursuit of social and environmental justice. By contrast, other participants, such as Maeve and Flo, spoke of continuing the activisms "full force" through the motherhood years; their children were brought right into the work with them. For these women, motherhood definitely remained a time of overt activism, advocacy, and engagement.

In contrast, a large group of participants, including Ingrid, Amelia, Paige, and others, shared deeply personal recollections of living in restrictive or abusive marriages, seeking divorces at a time when divorce remained stigmatized, and being forced to fight long, protracted custody battles. More than two-thirds of participants were no longer living with their first spouses at the time of our interview, and about one-third explicitly labelled previous marriages as abusive. More than half disclosed that they had been in very unhappy or unduly controlling marriages, while nine participants discussed the enormous challenges associated with ending their marriages, obtaining a divorce, and keeping custody of their children. It was this group that most explicitly depicted their child-rearing years as apolitical. They described "fighting the battles at home"—"surviving"—and noted how the battles were particularly intensified in the years when their children were young. However, when we shift to consider everyday acts of resistance and the politics of surviving as interventions into a patriarchal, capitalist society, we begin to think differently about this supposed disengagement (Pain 2014). Instead, we recognize that the "battles" fought by many were not merely individualized but also part of the larger struggle to change norms for women and families across North America.

Here, Violet's story, like Ingrid's, is illustrative. Violet was born in 1942 into a highly politicized New York family. In her late teens and early 20s she pursued a degree in education, and at 22 she married a man who was studying to be a doctor:

> I didn't think I had that much in common with him, but he was a ticket into mainstream America: He was going to be the doctor and I could get married and have a house with a picket fence and a dog and a station wagon.... I was 22 at the time—we had been dating for a while, and I think you tend to marry the guy you're dating at the time you think it's time to get married.

The years that followed were tumultuous. She had two sons, while moving cities frequently, teaching part-time, and doing advocacy work, including starting programs for disadvantaged preschoolers and working in voter registration in Black communities. Throughout all of this, her marriage was extremely difficult.

Reflecting on her eventual divorce, she said that for a long time she "didn't have the courage or the resources to leave the marriage and [she] was afraid of losing the kids." Connecting her situation to the structural oppression of so many other women at that time, she went on: "I had [the legal system] working against me. He was not only the man, but he was also a well-established pediatrician.... So the next decade really had me embroiled in a whole new world of what women face. I was devastated and scared." She fought for divorce and for custody of her children in New York State, a state that did not adopt no-fault divorce laws until 2010. She explained that her husband frequently used his power and position against her. When she did extricate herself and her children, she was left with no financial support. In her words: "I didn't have the benefit of standardized child support laws or alimony. There were no formulas in place at that time, so I was totally at the mercy of my husband's attorneys.... As long as I could have my boys I didn't care about the rest." After her divorce, she worked at a community college for 12 years in order to support herself and her sons.

Violet identified her intense personal struggles as highly politicized, and, like Ingrid, her struggles led her to later work for justice for others facing similar conditions. After attending a support program for people going through separations, she launched her second career: "As I was sitting there hearing over and over again these stories of how the legal system was chewing people up and spitting them out, I realized there had to be a better way. So I got my training as a divorce mediator." In 1989, she started a private practice in divorce mediation, from which she retired in 2004.

For Violet and so many others, activism was not necessarily absent from the mid-adult years, but instead was deeply personal: Their struggles as mothers often blurred the personal and the political. Their "battles" around divorce, custody, maternity leaves, child care, reproductive rights, and so on were part of a larger societal transformation. Collectively, these daily individual struggles worked to propel broader changes for women and families in North America in the 1960s and through the 1990s. Most participants referred to the personal impacts of changing laws, policies, and norms around divorce and domestic abuse, reproductive rights and sexual health, women's rights to financial autonomy, and support for working mothers; many also explicitly described their own struggles as part of a wider women's movement. For them, motherhood was politicized and a site for social change, connected intricately to these struggles.

Our analysis of these diverse stories thus suggests that motherhood was not a time of inactivity, but a time when the nature of resistance shifted for many, although not all, of our participants. At the same time, it became evident that participants' personal circumstances both *shaped* opportunities for social and political engagement and were *part of* the broader social and political change underway, and that understanding these nuances requires a broad conceptualization of activisms. These conversations unveiled the many ways motherhood, as institution, experience, and discourse, was political and politicized. Further, it is noteworthy that all participants described themselves as holding true to their personal politics and feminist values even if these could not be acted on in ways that they identified as overt activism. Some saw returning to overt activisms in later life as a continuation of these values but informed by the growth, difficulty, richness, and restriction of their experiences of marriage and motherhood.

GRANDMOTHERHOODS AND ACTIVISMS

Discussing their mid- to later-life activisms, participants most frequently portrayed this time as one of activist resurgence: With calls on their time decreasing, they could engage in social change work around the issues that matter most to them. At the time of our interviews, five of 32 participants were still working in some form of paid employment and 25 described themselves as "retired." Of our 32 participants, 26 described having grandchildren (including step-grandchildren); some described themselves as "grandmothers in waiting" or "grandmothers to be." While not every participant described later-life activisms as a *continuation* of their earlier activisms, all identified as activists and saw older age and/or grandmotherhood as a time of *intensified* resistance. Some spoke of coming to activism post-retirement, being freed up to act on their lifelong values in more explicit ways. Similar to our discussion of the child-rearing years, these stories challenged notions of older women and grandmothers as apolitical, or of aging as a process of political decline. Five central findings emerged in relation to later-life activisms.

First, for many participants, later life has been accompanied by an increasing awareness of their own privilege, an acknowledgement of the complexities and tensions inherent in their activisms, and a self-consciousness around their roles and social locations as activists. Many discussed at length what it means for them to be allies or to work in solidarity with Indigenous movements or transnational feminist movements, remarking that these kinds of considerations and conversations have become more evident as they have aged (Chapter 4 in this book takes up some of these ideas). Participants reflected on the struggles they faced through their lives, but also on the privilege afforded to them because of their white skin (McIntosh 1988). Some also reflected on their privilege among older activists— they positioned themselves as among those older people who are able-bodied and financially comfortable enough to be able to keep up this work. As we heard these statements of privilege, we were also aware of the potentially contradictory realities that many were living solely on their old-age pensions and/or in subsidized housing, and many were living with various disabilities or going through treatment for serious health conditions.

Second, in considering what it was about later life that led to their new or renewed engagement with activism, many said they had more "time and space" as they aged—time and space that enabled them to act on long-held (but not always overtly expressed) feminist politics. With kids grown and demands of paid work abated, they described a less encumbered life—while this was particularly true for those who were in tenable financial situations, all participants expressed these kinds of sentiments. Some participants framed later life as a time of fewer social risks; their jobs and their children were not in jeopardy. Some discussed the responsibility that comes with being older, precisely because the social risks they face are fewer. Others also remarked that law enforcement officers tend to be more lenient in their dealings with older women activists, recognizing that they were conferred certain protections as older, working-/middle-class, white women. They thus felt they should be the ones to put their bodies on the line when needed: "I think as Grannies … we get listened to, and we can do things that other people can't.… The police have been nice to us … the young people can't get away with that. So we try—when there's a gathering of the homeless, the Grannies will go with their hats on, their boas, just to be a protection. So I think we have a duty there." This certainly stands in sharp contrast to ideas that older women's worlds necessarily constrict as they age; it also challenges narratives of older women engaging in activisms "despite" their age. Rather, in the stories shared with us, older age and grandmotherhood were depicted as sites of social change, offering an expansion for some in time, space, and political opportunity.

Third, in considering what sustains their activism, many participants talked about the perspective that comes with the passage of time and how this perspective strengthens their convictions. Some talked about the growing urgency they feel to leave the world a better place; as one woman said, "As I get older, I hold to my views more strongly. I am more convinced that things have to change and that I have to try to change them." For others the realities of inhabiting aging bodies seemed to be propelling their advocacy in various ways. For instance, some discussed the emotions associated with coming to terms with health issues and with their own eventual mortality; with these issues more present than ever before, they felt strongly that "now is the time" to make a contribution. Some further connected their age to their ability to reflect on what has changed and, importantly, on what has not. They saw unfinished business, especially around stopping pipelines, scaling back the power of mega-corporations, dealing with global wealth disparities, and putting an end to violence against all women and girls, with particular attention to the disproportionate violence experienced by Indigenous women and girls in North America and women and girls in the Global South.

Fourth, the theme of "grandmotherhood" was raised explicitly in a number of ways in conversations about later-life activism. Some discussed entry into grandmotherhood as shaping their engagement with GRAN and/or the Raging

Grannies, and, more broadly, as a turning point in their lives. Among these, several noted that this did not necessarily mean becoming a grandmother in a biological sense but rather was about a life passage that involves returning to having young children in their lives whom they care deeply about, while having the space that comes with not needing to be the primary caregiver. Others found their activism was sustained by their care for the future generations more broadly. Sam's words are illustrative and draw a connection for her (a "coming back to") between motherhood and grandmotherhood as sites of advocacy:

> Being a grandmother, and I don't necessarily mean a biological grandmother … I think what happens is we come back to little children, and when we come back to little children, we think about what we want to do on behalf of little children—usually, but not always, our grandchildren.… [For a period of time before becoming a grandmother], you are away from small children, and then grandchildren bring back to you the wonder of life and the vulnerability. For our children and grandchildren, it's lucky that the wonderment is perhaps larger than the vulnerability, but not so for others.

For some, then, the shift in consciousness that many tie to entering grandmotherhood does not pacify them but rather amplifies their resistance. For others, their later-life activisms were not associated with "grandmotherhood" as a passage; they connected to these networks of "granny" activists more strategically. They mobilized grandmotherhood as a discourse in strategic ways that conferred protection and provided them entry into political spaces (resonating with Chazan and Kittmer 2016; Chazan 2015; Sawchuk 2009; Roy 2004). As with maternal activisms, which are often not recognized as activism "or is dismissed as not 'real' activism" (O'Reilly 2012, 3), "granny activism" is often disregarded as "cute" or "fluff." Yet "granny activists" strategically mobilize the unexpectedness of their activism as grandmothers, along with performances of their moral authority, to achieve political ends. In this way, their positions as grandmothers offer particular opportunities to enhance their political struggles (as also noted in Chapter 6).

Finally, many participants discussed the ageism they experience in their lives as part of the impetus for their later-life activism. Most described a growing sense of obscurity as aging women (a theme that is reflected in other chapters and reflections, and particularly in Reflection 6); this was compounding their desire to be acknowledged (or, as some said, to be "seen and heard") as activists. For them, advocacy is, in some part, a resistance to this invisibility and to the stereotypes of older women as marginalized, frail, and passive (Kutz-Flamenbaum 2007;

Matlok-Ziemann 2014). In fact, many of the women we interviewed talked about the double purpose of their current activism: to lead to change in the myriad of issues in which they are involved *and* to resist sexist-ageist narratives and experiences of ageism and isolation. As Amelia aptly described: "It's the image of people surging to the forefront at a time in their lives when the public perception would have them fade into the background.... I'm not willing to be insignificant, and I've got the time and energy right now to make sure I won't be. I've always felt strongly about leaving the world a better place and making what difference you can."

CONCLUSIONS: RETHINKING ASSUMPTIONS OF DISENGAGEMENT

This chapter explores activisms across the lifecourse, focusing on the diverse activist histories of 32 older, cisgender, white settler women across North America. While their experiences vary significantly, their stories collectively challenge certain assumptions about motherhood and grandmotherhood as apolitical periods in women's lives. This chapter's explicit focus on the lifecourse and its broadening conception of activisms resonates through many of the contributions to this book.

Why and how people become activists, and what sustains them over time in their activisms, depends on both personal circumstances and the broader social, political, and ideological contexts in which they live and work. Our research provides particular insight into how socio-political and personal contexts shaped the ways certain women constructed (grand)motherhood and practiced resistance. As stated at the start of this chapter, far from "the myth that bearing and raising children alters a woman's consciousness in some fundamentally conservative way, silencing her voice and disarming her rebellion" (Jetter, Orleck, and Taylor 1997, back cover), these women described how their activisms became intertwined with their personal circumstances as mothers. They likewise portrayed grandmotherhood not as a period of decline but as a time of new and renewed engagement—a time when they were able to become politically active in overt ways and when the well-being of future generations became a clear priority. Unlike their earlier activisms, their later-life engagement was less interwoven with their domestic struggles and more connected to the ageism and sense of invisibility they were experiencing.

Bringing together critical motherhood and aging studies, we have explored certain less-recognized activisms of personal struggle (Pain 2014; O'Reilly 2012), raising these in the context of activisms throughout participants' lives. We have begun to draw on writings on invisiblized resistance and to connect these to questions of invisibility and aging. We have considered activisms not as "despite" but rather as intricately intertwined with (grand)motherhood, analyzing (grand)motherhood as a potential site for social change and as a discourse, institution, identity, and position that can be mobilized toward political ends. We have posited that the private and public struggles of (grand)mothers may well be blurred or intertwined. In doing this, we ultimately call for rethinking the politics of (grand)mothering.

This discussion moves this book toward an ever-broadening conceptualization of what is typically deemed activism and who is most often deemed an activist, as discussed in the book's introductory chapter. By unveiling "invisibilities" within certain women's activisms—the "quiet politics" of resisting domestic violence and the illegibility of older women as political agents—it exposes interconnected narratives of silent struggle and brazen protest.

NOTES

1. In this chapter, we use *(grand)motherhood* and *(grand)mothering* as a short form to refer to the related discourses, roles, performances, identities, institutions, expectations, and experiences of motherhood and grandmotherhood. We also use this combined word to allude to the complex shifts and continuity of these experiences, and to indicate that motherhood and grandmotherhood are not simply bounded periods of time in one's life.

2. Throughout this chapter, we use pseudonyms for research participants.

3. In Canada, the Divorce Act was amended in 1986, enabling people to obtain a divorce without having to prove "fault" in a court of law. Though divorces were still a site of struggle for many women, this major legislative change made the process safer and more accessible for many women. In the United States, similar laws were passed, though at different times and in different ways for each state legislature. Ingrid's legal battles began in 1985, shortly before this change, and continued through to 1991, exposing how this significant change in Canadian law did not necessarily have an immediate positive impact for many women.

4. In keeping with an epistemological underpinning that emphasizes the lesser-told stories of social change and social changers, this research was open to participants who identified as women as well as those who identified as transgender or gender non-binary. Largely reflective of the networks in this work, all of our participants identified as women. The activist histories in this study were generated by asking participants to reflect on their lives, politics, and activisms decade by decade. Following Pamela Sugiman (2011) and others, we recognize the importance of remaining critical of how these stories are retold and reconstructed in different contexts. In particular in research on aging and with older people, we urge examination of the role of intergenerationality in such research, including the implications of cross-generational research relationships in the shaping of how such stories are told, heard, analyzed, and written about.

5.   By "lifecourse perspective," we do not refer to the predominant understanding of the lifecourse as a series of life stages, or a chronological progression of social/cognitive/biological development. Nor do we understand the lifecourse to fit within a rubric of heteronormative markers of life passage. Instead we draw on what we call a critical lifecourse perspective to enrich the broad definition of aging taken up throughout this book, considering the non-linear, ever-ongoing process of changing, learning, returning, thinking, and acting that happens from birth to death. In so doing, we also recognize the different socially, historically, and culturally contingent expectations attached to different perceived stages or chronological ages. We engage with the different and complex ways people become visible or invisible, powerful or stigmatized, as they age; we consider how people's level of control over their own lives can shift at different times, and how age/ing might shape the different options for activisms available to them. Further, we heed the works of scholars who have called for a rethinking of the lifecourse from critical race perspectives (e.g., Hulko 2009; Ferrer et al. 2017) and queered perspectives (e.g., Riach, Rumens, and Tyler 2014; Jones 2011).

6.   In this chapter, we do not compare GRAN participants with Raging Granny participants, though it is worth noting that the Raging Granny participants were, on average, 10 years older that the GRAN participants.

7.   As noted in the book's introduction, we use "cisgender" to mean that participants identify with the gender they were assigned at birth, though this is not language that participants used. We use "white settler" to mean that participants were non-indigenous to Turtle Island, that their ancestors migrated to and stayed in this land as part of a system of settler colonialism, and that they have light skin and trace their ancestral lines back to European contexts—some participants used this language. We feel it is important to state these social locations explicitly in a move to consider the contingency of our analysis—that is, to begin to understand how people's positions vis-à-vis systems of structural power influence how they experience, understand, and practice activist aging, and indeed the options available to them. We also make this explicit in our move toward a critical race perspective; we refuse to further invisibilize whiteness or not to account for the systemic power of race as this pertains to those who are not racialized or who occupy dominant positions.

8.   We recognize that using the language and concepts of "(grand)motherhood" centres the experiences of cisgender women who are raising or have raised biological or adopted children. We use this language because it was regularly deployed by participants in our research, and because our work speaks to a body of feminist literature engaging directly with these concepts. In line with our effort to challenge binary conceptions of gender and to make visible the experiences of people who identify as non-binary or gender fluid, we do however feel that a move toward a language of "(grand)parenthood" could be warranted. We also recognize that many of the points raised through the chapter could equally pertain to people in primary caregiving roles who do not necessarily identify as "mothers."

9.   See the introduction to Part II for waaseyaa'sin christine sy's thoughtful discussion of Indigenous survivance and "persisting life" as resistance. For other considerations of convergences of survival and political struggle, see Hande and Kelly 2015; Haddad 2004; and Bailey and Shabazz 2014.

REFERENCES

Bailey, Marlon M., and Rashad Shabazz. 2014. "Gender and Sexual Geographies of Blackness: New Black Cartographies of Resistance and Survival (Part 2)." *Gender, Place & Culture* 21(4): 449–452.

Baldassar, Loretta, Cora Baldock, and Raelene Wilding. 2007. *Families Caring across Borders: Migration, Aging and Transnational Care-giving.* London: Palgrave Macmillan.

Chazan, May. 2015. *The Grandmothers' Movement: Solidarity and Survival in the Time of AIDS.* Montreal, QC: McGill-Queens University Press.

Chazan, May, and Melissa Baldwin. 2017. "Understanding the Complexities of Contemporary Feminist Activism: How the Lives of Older Women Activists Contest the Waves Narrative." *Feminist Formations* 28(3): 70–94.

Chazan, May, and Stephanie Kittmer. 2016. "Defying, Producing, and Overlooking Stereotypes? The Complexities of Mobilizing 'Grandmotherhood' as Political Strategy." *Journal of Women and Aging* 29(1): 297–308.

Chilisa, Bagele, and Gabo Ntseane. 2010. "Resisting Dominant Discourses: Implications of Indigenous African Feminist Theory and Methods for Gender and Education Research." *Gender and Education* 22(6): 617–632.

Davis, Angela. 2007. *How Does Change Happen?* [video]. www.youtube.com/watch?v =Pc6RHtEbiOA

Ferrer, Ilyan, Amanda Grenier, Shari Brotman, and Sharon Koehn. 2017. "Understanding the Experiences of Racialized Older People through an Intersectional Life Course Perspective." *Journal of Aging Studies* 41: 10–17.

Gullette, Margaret Morganroth. 1997. *Declining to Decline: Cultural Combat and the Politics of the Midlife.* Charlottesville, VA: University of Virginia Press.

Haddad, Beverly. 2004. "The Manyano Movement in South Africa: Site of Struggle, Survival, and Resistance." *Agenda: Empowering Women for Gender Equity* 61: 4–13.

Hande, Mary Jean, and Christine Kelly. 2015. "Organizing Survival and Resistance in Austere Times: Shifting Disability Activism and Care Politics in Ontario, Canada." *Disability & Society* 30(7): 961–975.

Hodgson, Dorothy L., and Ethel Brooks. Eds. 2007. "Activisms" [Special Issue]. *Women's Studies Quarterly* 35(3/4).

Huago, Ann. 2016. "Decolonizing Motherhood: Images of Mothering in First Nations Theatre." *Theatre History Studies* 35(1): 269–284.

Hulko, Wendy. 2009. "The Time- and Context-Contingent Nature of Intersectionality and Interlocking Oppressions." *Affilia* 24(1): 44–55.

Jetter, Alexis, Annelise Orleck, and Diana Taylor. Eds. 1997. *The Politics of Motherhood: Activist Voices from Left to Right*. Hanover, NH: The University Press of New England.

Jones, Rebecca L. 2011. "Imagining Bisexual Futures: Positive, Non-Normative Later Life." *Journal of Bisexuality* 11(2/3): 245–270.

Kutz-Flamenbaum, Rachel. 2007. "Code Pink, Raging Grannies, and the Missile Dick Chicks: Feminist Performance Activism in the Contemporary Anti-War Movement." *NWSA Journal* 19(1): 89–105.

Lavell-Harvard, Dawn Memee, and Jeannette Corbiere Lavell. 2006. *"Until Our Hearts Are On the Ground": Aboriginal Mothering, Oppression, Resistance and Rebirth*. Bradford, ON: Demeter Press.

Matlok-Ziemann, Ellen. 2014. "'Old Women that Will Not Be Kept Away': Undermining Ageist Discourse with Invisibility and Performance." In *Alive and Kicking at All Ages: Cultural Constructions of Health and Life Course Identity*, edited by Barbara Ratzenböck, Roberta Maierhofer, and Ulla Kriebernegg, 259–73. Bielefeld, Germany: Transcript-Verlag.

McIntosh, Peggy. 1988. "White Privilege: Unpacking the Invisible Knapsack." *Race, Class, and Gender in the United States: An Integrated Study* 4: 165–169.

O'Reilly, Andrea. 2012. "Outlaw(ing) Motherhood: A Theory and Politic of Maternal Empowerment for the 21st Century." In *What Do Mothers Need? Motherhood Activists and Scholars Speak Out on Maternal Empowerment for the 21st Century*, edited by Andrea O'Reilly, 63–80. Bradford, ON: Demeter Press.

Orleck, Annelise. 1997. "Tradition Unbound: Radical Mothers in International Perspective." In *The Politics of Motherhood: Activist Voices from Left to Right*, edited by Alexis Jetter, Annelise Orleck, and Diana Taylor, 3–22. Hanover, NH: The University Press of New England.

Pain, Rachel. 2014. "Seismologies of Emotion: Fear and Activism during Domestic Violence." *Social & Cultural Geography* 15(2): 127–150.

Riach, Kathleen, Nicholas Rumens, and Melissa Tyler. 2014. "Un/doing Chromo-normativity: Negotiating Ageing, Gender and Sexuality in Organizational Life." *Organization Studies* 35(11): 1677–1698.

Rich, Adrienne. 1995. *Of Woman Born: Motherhood as Experience and Institution*. New York: WW Norton & Company.

Roy, Carole. 2004. *The Raging Grannies: Wild Hats, Cheeky Songs, and Witty Actions for a Better World*. Montreal, QC: Black Rose Books.

Sawchuk, Dana. 2009. "The Raging Grannies: Defying Stereotypes and Embracing Aging through Activism." *Journal of Women & Aging*, 21(3): 171–185.

Scheper-Hughes, Nancy. 2003. *Death without Weeping: The Violence of Everyday Life.* Berkeley: University of California Press.

Simpson, Leanne. 2011. *Dancing on Our Turtle's Back: Stories of Nishnaabeg Re-Creation, Resurgence, and a New Emergence.* Winnipeg, MB: Arbeiter Ring Publishing.

Smith, Jewelles. 2012. "DisAbled Mothers in the 21st Century: Finding Empowerment through Activism." In *The 21st Century Motherhood Movement. Mothers Speak Out on Why We Need to Change the World and How To Do It,* edited by Andrea O'Reilly, 156–164. Bradford, ON: Demeter Press.

Stevenson, Judith. 2011. "'The Mamas Were Ripe': Ideologies of Motherhood and Public Resistance in a South African Township." *Feminist Formations* 23(2): 132–163.

Sugiman, Pamela. 2011. "Passing Time, Moving Memories: Interpreting Wartime Narratives of Japanese-Canadian Women." In *Rethinking Canada: The Promise of Women's History, 6th edition,* edited by Mona Gleeson, Tamara Myers, and Adele Perry, 264–282. Don Mills, ON: Oxford University Press.

Tungohan, Ethel. 2013. "Reconceptualizing Motherhood, Reconceptualizing Resistance: Migrant Domestic Workers, Transnational Hyper-Maternalism and Activism." *International Feminist Journal of Politics* 15(1): 39–57.

REFLECTION 1

"Climbing into My Granny Pants": Reflections from a Grandmother Activist

Peggy Edwards

Peggy Edwards is a writer and retired health promotion consultant based in Ottawa, Canada. She has worked with Health Canada, the Canadian Public Health Association, and the World Health Organization, and is the co-author of three bestselling books on healthy aging and grandparenting. She is an activist and leader in the Grandmothers Advocacy Network (GRAN) and the Grandmothers to Grandmothers Campaign, which support African grandmothers who are raising their children and grandchildren in the context of the HIV/AIDS crisis. In this reflection she considers what becoming a grandmother has meant for her own activisms.

I have always been an activist, raised by a feminist mother and her stories of my suffragette grandmother. I was born in 1948. As a middle-class white woman who came of age in Canada in the 1960s, I was among the first of my generation to have full access to higher education, reliable birth control, and the opportunity to work outside the home while raising a family. I grew up with the peace movement and the women's movement—fighting for social justice and equality.

I was only 40 when my first grandchild was born. I was anxious and exhilarated … and pissed off at how my daughter was treated. Things had improved since I gave birth to her in 1971, when mothers were routinely shaved, cleansed with enemas, drugged and cut, and were cloistered with strict hospital rules—no husbands or attendants allowed at the delivery, and babies remained locked in the nursery except for feeding times. In 1990, some 20 years later, birthing was still highly medicalized. Although she had a healthy pregnancy, my daughter was considered "high risk" because she was just 19. I was allowed to be with her, but she had so many monitoring wires hooked up to her she could not get out of bed. Efficient nurses hurried in and out to check the monitors and probe her vagina, giving her little information on how things were going. It was an uncomfortable, long wait in a sterile hospital cubicle until she was told it was time and wheeled off to the delivery room. My old concerns about women's right to control their sexual and reproductive health and to enjoy giving birth in a loving environment came flooding back.

After mom and baby were cleaned up and settled, I held Ben in my arms. In spite of my frustrations with the birthing process, nothing can describe the absolute joy and love I felt for this newborn miracle of life. That sense of wonder and bliss has not diminished with the births of many more grandchildren and five great-grandchildren, and the arrival into my family of several new step-grandchildren.

In 2006, as a grandmother of 11, I wrote a book on grandparenting called *Intentional Grandparenting: A Boomers' Guide* with my friend and co-author Mary Jane Sterne. We knew that grandparenting had tremendous potential to enrich our lives and those of our adult children and grandchildren. For me, grandmothering also provided an opportunity to think about and act on the local and global concerns I had about aging, grandparenting, and the generations coming up. Years of experience raising children and watching our parents' grandparenting told us that we must be purposeful in constructing this exciting new role in our lives.

I believe you do not have to be a biological grandparent to take on the grandmothering role. There is a community of older women—aunts, friends, stepparents, and others—who become surrogate grandmothers. So, while every child is unique and every woman's experience of grandmothering is distinct, "grandmothers" share a common bond—a love for the next generation and a desire to make the world a good place in which to grow up.

In the same year we published our book, I attended a gathering in Toronto organized by the Stephen Lewis Foundation that brought 100 African grandmothers to meet with 200 Canadian grandmothers on the eve of the World AIDS Conference. We heard their stories—of burying their adult children and raising their grandchildren and other vulnerable young people orphaned by AIDS. We witnessed their resilience and strength in the face of crisis and inadequate support. We laughed and danced and cried together.

As a grandmother, I felt a connection with the courageous women I met from sub-Saharan Africa, despite my understanding of our tremendous differences. I was sad and outraged at their situation. When I left, I knew that doing nothing was *not* an option.

After returning to Ottawa, Mary Jane and I started a voluntary group called the One World Grannies. Our group, like hundreds of others across Canada in the

Grandmothers to Grandmothers Campaign, is dedicated to supporting and working in solidarity with the African grannies.[1] Being part of a grandmother group has widened my network of dear friends and provided me with the social support I so need and appreciate at this stage of my life. It has also sharpened my appreciation for the power of grassroots community action.

At the same time as we were busy forming grandmother groups, I knew that systemic, political change required a strong cross-country advocacy arm. We formed the National Advocacy Committee, which subsequently became a separate organization called the Grandmothers Advocacy Network (GRAN).[2] Being part of GRAN has confirmed for me (and others) that older women have the experience, skills, strategic thinking, and persistence to be really good at advocacy. GRAN has become a force to be reckoned with on Parliament Hill and a trusted partner for other organizations working in social justice. We challenge stereotypes that paint older women as passive, invisible, and without influence.

How have grandmothering and growing older changed my activism?

First, I have more time than I did as a busy working mother to share what I know and what I value, to listen, and to advocate for causes I believe in. I am far less concerned about what other people may think of me. I can say what I want … and I do.

Second, it has deepened my commitment to an intergenerational focus and the importance of justice and equity for both the young and old. It has sharpened my concerns about the need for policies and programs that foster the well-being of vulnerable families of all types.

Third, it has made me better understand how many women experience the double jeopardy of both ageism and sexism, and to reflect on how this jeopardy multiplies when racism, ableism, poverty, and homophobia interact with these systems of discrimination. It has deepened my commitment to fight against this and to work to support and protect the human rights of all older people.

Finally, my grandchildren have provided me with moments of great humour and inspiration.

One of them watched in disbelief as I climbed into my granny pants and asked, "Grandma, why do you have such big underwear?" I laughed, realizing that he had only seen his mother's thongs. While growing older has freed me of my socially driven obsession with being slim, I was reminded that body acceptance and women's rights to body integrity are still issues today.

Another grandchild marched with me to Parliament Hill in a rally insisting that Canada pay its fair share to international development and affordable medicines. He said to some of the other marchers: "I can't imagine what it would be like to watch my parents die. Or to not be able to go to school or have enough to eat.

It's just not right." I thought about how important it is to include young people in our activism and to respect and treasure their contributions.

Grandmothering and growing older allows me to explore new ways of being. It has helped me see how my values, passions, strengths, and weaknesses interconnect and sometimes collide. But perhaps most importantly, it enables me to share my passion with other aging activists, and with a younger generation—my grandchildren.

NOTES

1. For information on the Grandmothers to Grandmothers Campaign, see www.grandmotherscampaign.org.
2. For more information on GRAN, see www.grandmothersadvocacy.org.

CHAPTER 2

Activist Aging: The Tactical Theatrics of RECAA

Kim Sawchuk and Constance Lafontaine

This chapter introduces the concept of "tactical theatrics" as a way to reflect on the variety of activist interventions practiced by a community of culturally diverse elders, RECAA (Respecting Elders: Communities Against Abuse). RECAA's mandate centres around advocating for communication, reciprocity, and respect in ways that challenge how service provision for older adults in Quebec tends to ignore dilemmas faced by "ethnocultural communities"[1] due to cultural-linguistic differences. Through activism, RECAA members challenge narrow representations of aging—which rarely include those operating at the intersections of race, age, and gender—to illuminate the possibilities and creativities of later life. From Forum Theatre to media arts, RECAA has developed a multiplicity of modes for communicating about elder abuse. This multiplicity allows groups to engage mindfully and meaningfully in RECAA's activities as their membership ages, respecting the variegated and changing capacities of the members of this collective.

This chapter highlights the import of RECAA's activist practices. We suggest the idea of "tactical theatrics" as a term to advance an understanding of how one might maintain and develop one's identity *as* activist throughout the lifecourse. We understand tactical theatrics to be the repertoire of plural and varied performance-based interventions that are mobilized by RECAA as part of its activist mission. We argue that the strength of tactical theatrics for RECAA lies in its recognition of what it means to age together—a recognition that posits a diversity of interventions. These tactical theatrics constitute a repertoire of activist possibility that takes into account the heterogeneity of experiences in later life.

We begin this chapter by introducing RECAA and explaining the concept of tactical theatrics. We then explore how RECAA activists address elder abuse through Forum Theatre workshops, short-term creative projects that use digital media, and timely interventions in response to specific political or social situations. This set of different practices, tactically deployed, allows members of RECAA to participate in public interventions on the street, in a mall, or in a community centre, in a manner that is flexible, open-ended, and mindful of the embodied nature of activisms; these themes resonate with the contributions in Part III. In all of their different practices, RECAA members are mindful that, whether marching on the street, holding a sign, or distributing pamphlets, these particular kinds of activism involve time, energy, and the physical ability to participate.

These reflections on tactical theatrics and what this means for the authors as we age as academic-activists are inspired by our long-term and close engagement with RECAA as community-based researchers studying aging in the context of an increasingly digital world. Since 2012, we have been collaborating with RECAA as members of Ageing, Communication, Technologies (ACT), a research team housed at Concordia University in Montreal.[2] RECAA is a core community partner of ACT and both share offices and equipment on the Concordia University campus. As a research partner and part of our governing board, RECAA is involved in developing projects with ACT and steering the intellectual trajectory of our work. Throughout this chapter, our firsthand experience with RECAA, gleaned from years of collaboration, is supplemented by recent interviews with two of RECAA's founding members, Anne Caines (who also shares her own activist trajectories among the "theirstories" in the concluding chapter of this book) and Marguerite Kephart.

RECAA

Founded in 2003, RECAA is a group of Montreal elders, ranging from 65 to 92 years of age at the time of writing. RECAA founders initially came together as a response to the implicit racism and lack of cultural awareness on the part of municipal, provincial, and federal government agencies dealing with the challenges, including the issue of elder abuse, faced by older adults from Montreal's ethnocultural communities. While RECAA is mostly composed of women, men are also active members of the group. RECAA avoids identifying itself as a "women's group" because members advocate for all genders; however, its leadership and coordination duties are largely assumed by a strong group of women who have long histories of leadership within their communities. RECAA has grown over the past 15 years. It is now composed of a large network of about 100 supporters who regularly attend public events, such as a World Elder Abuse Awareness Day event held every June and an annual general meeting every fall. RECAA belongs to an alliance of community-based organizations in Montreal, such as the South Asian Women's Community Centre, the Council for Black Aging Community of Montreal, Chinese Family Services, the Centre d'orientation paralégale et sociale pour les immigrants (COPSI),[3] and the Notre-Dame-de-Grâce (NDG) Seniors Citizens' Council. Many of RECAA's members have participated in these organizations. Over the past few years, younger people have joined RECAA, as members, allies, and collaborators.

Now in its fifteenth year, RECAA's mission is not only to reach out to Montreal's ethnocultural communities but also to work with people of all ages to build a culture of respect for older adults and to find ways to create a society in which "our elders should be able to live in dignity, safety and free of exploitation and physical or mental abuse" (RECAA 2016). As the original founders of RECAA—including Anne, Marguerite, and Sadeqa Siddiqui (whose personal journey with activism follows in Reflection 2)—have noted, many elders living in residences, long-term care facilities, and even with family experience emotional neglect, financial exploitation, and/or physical violence; most, however, would not come forward to speak to governmental agents or authorities. The founders explain that this silence is a result of two primary factors: First, many elders from these communities have not been made aware of their rights, and, second, some recently immigrated elders are afraid of unwanted interventions by government agents.

While RECAA recognizes the important work done by many caregivers in Montreal, its goal is to reach people who may avoid contact with established government and community services and to find ways to assist older adults in identifying situations of abuse in a way that acknowledges the complexity of any given situation. It is within this confluence of motivations that RECAA members have come to use tactical theatrics, starting with Forum Theatre, to reach out to communities safely, so that elder abuse can be discussed in multiple languages and with emphasis on potential solutions.[4]

TACTICAL THEATRICS

RECAA has expanded from using Augusto Boal's (1979) techniques of Forum Theatre—a particular set of practices that involve engaging audiences with and in non-verbal skits to present and collectively address a social challenge or conundrum—as its primary mode of communicating its message.[5] It has developed multiple modes for communicating with diverse communities, across differences in language, religion, culture, and ethnicity. In addition to Forum Theatre, RECAA uses embodied short performances, dance, food events, and storytelling, as well as face-to-face exchanges and social media, to create a "repertory of tactics" (Jasper 2008). Its expanding repertory draws on experimentation and uses RECAA members' cultural know-how, creativity, and lived experiences (including their knowledge of recipes, dance, and film traditions) to bring attention to the issue of elder abuse. We refer to RECAA's repertory of practices as *tactical theatrics*: These are a set of performance-based activist interventions that enable older RECAA members to advocate in a way that accounts for heterogeneity in later life. Tactics emphasize that people move through the lifecourse in different ways, with different interests and availabilities, and with different and shifting physical and emotional capacities. From a flash mob in a mall, to demonstrations in the Montreal metro system, RECAA members have used their talents to occupy spaces that both assert the presence of seniors and enable differing levels and modes of participation.

Our approach to considering RECAA's tactics is based on French scholar and author Michel de Certeau's chapter "Making Do: Uses and Tactics" from *The Practices of Everyday Life* (1988). In that chapter, de Certeau considers the matter of resisting a system. Tactics are the ways in which those who are subordinated within these systems—those who do not immediately and readily benefit, who are left out or are marginalized—can act in order to make a system work for them. According to de Certeau, tactics represent some of the everyday ways in which people who are not in a position of power deal with and resist a system. Notably, tactical manoeuvres do not deal with systems of power from the outside. Instead, tactical manoeuvres originate from within. Organizations such as RECAA are adept at "making do" (ibid., 35), and their approach to this "making" allows for a meaningful, considered, and experimental engagement to push for social change, paying attention to what bodies can do, together.

Organizations that resort to tactics depend on the current systems within which they work, yet are unable to gather or easily find resources. Community-based organizations that are engaged in a constant struggle to survive must make vigilant and inventive use of the cracks that exist in a system, and they must use these cracks to their advantage (ibid., 37). In the case of RECAA, tactical theatrics involve devising different ways of intervening that draw on long-standing performative techniques and new skills in digital media production. This attention to the embodied nature of performance, its timeliness, and its audience have led RECAA members to develop a suite of low-cost and highly portable skits that require only a few props, as well as small-scale media projects that can flexibly be adapted to the circumstances at hand.

RECAA's tactical theatrics have been built over time and have evolved. They are the product of a diverse membership that has spent many years developing friendships through disagreements and discussions, working through shared problems and imaginatively overcoming obstacles. As James Jasper points out in his study of social movements, "tactics represent important routines, emotionally and morally salient in these people's lives" (2008, 237). RECAA's weekly meetings include a communal lunch, which is important to its consolidation as a group. RECAA's weekly get-togethers are more than a means towards activist efficacy; these rituals—of eating together and practicing routines to be ready for the next event—structure the everyday activities of the group. These practices create its social fabric and contribute towards building community as much as they serve outward political goals.

A sense of play, creativity, and informality are central to RECAA's planning activities, including holding lively potluck-style planning sessions, developing skits or choreographies, having prop-making sessions, and so forth. The preparatory activities work towards building community internally through a set of shared processes. These working meetings generate new expertise, knowledge, and materials that sustain the future public performances of the group. All of this extensive "behind-the-scenes" work—the kind of work referred to in Chapter 5 as the "backstage" activism—comprises the tactics that sustain RECAA in ways that allow it to carry out *activist* work. These meetings provide opportunities for friendships to develop and for aging activists to enjoy spending time with, and caring for, one another. As RECAA co-founder Anne explains, "We love to have a good time.… We try to get people to come and if you say, 'We're dealing in elder mistreatment,' would I want to come to your group? Well probably not!" Putting creative play and fun at the centre of RECAA's theatrics is a tool for engagement, while also being a tool that generates the levity needed to work within and cope with a difficult cause (Shepard 2014).

RECAA's internal community building and unique notion of "community development" is a part of its activist project. Operating in this way has led to the creation of a fluid support network that is both flexible and always being renewed, or as Anne explains, "We have a structure but we're also structureless, in a way." In the following pages, we consider RECAA's three modes of tactical intervention in temporal terms: RECAA's long-term tactical commitment to Forum Theatre; RECAA's use of short-term tactics, such as engaging in digital media interventions for activist purposes; and finally, RECAA's timely activist interventions to issues of immediate concern that demand action.

LONG-TERM COMMITMENT: FORUM THEATRE

RECAA's central activist practice is a variant of Forum Theatre in which members perform short skits that are presented without words, fictionalizing everyday life stories of elder abuse—subtle disrespect, willful neglect, physical intimidation, or financial exploitation. RECAA has chosen to present these skits non-verbally in order to reach as many communities as possible, and in particular to reach seniors from communities who might not be reached by other groups, including health and government services. Audience members are then encouraged to become "spect-actors" by coming up on stage, replacing the character who is being oppressed, and devising and trying out solutions to the situation. In this way, through active intervention followed by discussion, the audience can examine how to rewrite the scene to find solutions to complicated, emotionally charged situations. By working with the audience to test out scenarios, the socio-political efficacy, as Baz Kerkshaw (1992) terms it, lies in Forum Theatre's ability to demonstrate the malleability of outcomes. In demonstrating a malleability of outcomes, Forum Theatre provides the spect-actors with an understanding that their reality can be changed, and also gives them some of the tools to intervene in their own everyday lives and to effect a degree of political and social change.

For example, a skit titled "Aunt Enid" involves a bottle of beer, a table and chair, a crutch or walking stick, a ball cap for the actor playing the nephew, a housedress for the person playing the care worker, and a wallet to depict the action of Enid's nephew taking her money when she is not looking. This scene makes visible the problem of elder abuse in an intimate, non-threatening way. As an audience member replaces Enid, they are asked to improvise an outcome that addresses the problem, thus "rehearsing for social change," as Mady Schutzman and Jan Cohen-Cruz put it (1994, 2). Asking the spect-actors to participate in the scene, and effectively change it, gives them the tools to understand how these difficult situations of elder abuse can be addressed, and indeed shows them that they are not without power in these situations.

When the skit is over, the spect-actors are invited to come up with other potential solutions. While the skits are non-verbal, relying instead on movement and gesture, the discussion is typically hosted by one of the RECAA members. If the gathering is in a seniors' centre or cultural centre where there is one predominant language, then a host from the centre will act as a translator for the discussion. The performances are highly interpretive and abstract and, at the same time, direct and embodied. Movements, facial expressions, and a few key props are used to build a communicative bridge between the RECAA members and their audience (see Williams 1977, 1983; Drotner 2008, 70). For RECAA, the import of Forum Theatre for activism is apparent in its ability to reach those who otherwise might be excluded, and to acknowledge their agency and abilities, as they are called upon to develop solutions that might be used to address their shared problems. RECAA does not intervene in situations of abuse: this is beyond its mandate. Instead the idea is to educate and inform so that individuals and communities know how to access help. In this long-term cultivation of Forum Theatre as a method of tactical theatrics, what matters is the "subtle, but significant, shifts in participants' critical faculties and socio-political outlooks," shifts that are needed for enduring social change (Schutzman 1994, 137).

At the beginning of the intervention, the spect-actors are encouraged to partake in ice-breaking activities that challenge the actor-spectator divide and hierarchy, and to elicit participation from audience members that recognizes their expertise, knowledge, and solution-finding abilities. These activities demand that RECAA members be attuned to the audience's context. These preliminary ice-breaking exchanges are often centred on gesturing and non-linguistic sound-making, and often prompt laughter. RECAA sets an informal tone for its theatre activities in order to create space to safely discuss difficult issues, conflicting feelings, and systemic contradictions. In potentially difficult settings, laughter, informality, and play become crucial; these have been a pillar of RECAA's work over the years. Indeed, as noted earlier with reference to RECAA's planning activities, this sense of play has been key to developing a loyal and tight-knit membership that remains committed to the activist mission and actions through later life.

RECAA's mission of fighting elder abuse does not just extend outwardly to a mission of awareness-building: RECAA is also at work in creating a space of inclusion and collaboration where a group of diverse seniors are engaged and valued. For RECAA, building a Forum Theatre practice includes not only interventions with communities, but also planning, script-writing, and overall preparation.

SHORT-TERM TACTICS: FROM FORUM THEATRE TO DIGITAL ENGAGEMENT

Another way in which RECAA intervenes as an activist organization is through the development of short-term projects that are based in digital engagement. These short-term activist interventions represent a way of "making do" within a system in which core funding for community groups is scarce and attributed competitively through programs such as the Canadian government's New Horizons for Seniors (NHS). Over the past five years, most of the funds that have allowed RECAA to exist have been granted by NHS, which funds short-term projects that "help seniors make a difference in the lives of others and in their communities" (Employment and Social Development Canada 2016). Organizations like RECAA run on very small, tight budgets. While there is usually one part-time contract worker who provides expertise in theatre facilitation and coordination, the bulk of the work of

RECAA is ensured through the volunteering efforts of its membership, most of whom are 65 and over. In the absence of stable funding, RECAA has had to, in de Certeau's parlance, "vigilantly make use of the cracks" in the system.

Non-renewable and short-term government funding opportunities allow RECAA to conduct activities that look "for new ways to make our message fresh," as Marguerite puts it, and to carry out its core activist work: Forum Theatre. Yet, it is important that the NHS program does not fund projects unless the organization can justify that they represent a new endeavour for the organization. The prioritization of new and distinct projects within the NHS funding guidelines creates a context in which RECAA cannot be funded for its core face-to-face Forum Theatre activities; this propels the tactical need to develop related projects that are varied but allied with the RECAA mandate and its interests and commitments as a group of elders, many of them long-term activists. Further, if a funded project is successful, an organization will not have access to sufficient funding to repeat it. One must innovate. One must find new partners. It is for these reasons that some university-based researchers, including those of us in ACT, work with RECAA to navigate this set of systemic arrangements, identify how to "pervert" the strategic goals embedded in the new governmental language of neoliberalism, and collaborate with community groups to put resources into the hands of important intellectual allies from the community sector. Each year, RECAA thinks of a new project that resonates within its overall mission of promoting a cultural respect towards elders, but also adds new approaches and tools to its activist arsenal. Developing these annual projects has been a tactical workaround for RECAA to survive despite a scarcity of governmental resources available to community organizations in Quebec and Canada. This progressive adaptation to a project-by-project mode of operations has provided invaluable funding for many of their digital projects that are related to their core mandate.

Indeed, over the past five years, RECAA has undertaken a series of short-term projects that consist of carefully considered and negotiated engagements with digital technologies. These projects usually take shape through collaborations with other groups, and many of these collaborations have an important intergenerational component. Some of the recent short-term digital projects undertaken by RECAA (as collaborations with ACT) have been a one-year-long food blog called *Food Talks*, a documentary film titled *Madhu's Saris*, and a media capsule series entitled *In Their Own Words*, among many others.[6]

The *Food Talks* food blog, for example, is a year-long project in which seniors affiliated with RECAA appropriate the youth-dominated medium of online food blogging to reflect upon the importance of food as a tool for community building, and of food as a political issue that has local and global implications. For RECAA, the focus on food is fitting because, as mentioned, food and eating together have "always been important to RECAA," as Marguerite points out. For part of the food blog project, ACT students give a workshop on blog writing, posting, and photography, and both young and old share food and stories that centre on aging, culture, respect, and food. And, though it is not impossible that *Food Talks* will continue beyond one year, the impermanence of the food blog or similar short-term activist interventions, both in design and application, matters.

Carrying out these projects has extended the reach of RECAA's activities and influence, enabling the formation of new partnerships within the larger Montreal community, and building the skills, knowledge, and expertise among its membership, supporting them to reach different audiences within an increasingly networked society. As Marguerite explains: "The food blog adventure is not directly related to our Forum Theatre workshops but has enabled us to work together in a different environment (either cooking or writing our recipes together) and to have fun as well. The food blog is hopefully enabling us to reach a wider audience to discuss issues which are dear to us like social injustice, ageism, and poverty." Some of the *newness* in the short-term projects for RECAA also brought about a turn towards the use of digital technologies and the integration of new media within RECAA's practices (see K. Sawchuk 2013).

Further, RECAA members find that working collaboratively within RECAA and with other groups, and working in both intra- and intergenerational settings, generates an environment that challenges them. Anne explains: "I'm not going to say that working intergenerationally makes us young. It challenges us. These intergenerational projects have been a way for all parties to learn and share, to discover common ground and to build a safe space where people can make mistakes." There is an assumption that younger people use media, that old people do not, and that younger people have a proficiency that far outweighs that of older people. Working together allows the space for contesting these presuppositions, and for revealing the sometimes surprising reality of what people know or do not know. A new form of digital activism that challenges ageism by setting up contexts for learning from each other through projects and through conversation is key, and is directly related to Virginia Eubanks's (2011) discussion of CARR, or Collaborative Action and Reflection Research. As Eubanks writes, CARR represents and emphasizes the "conversational nature of the research" (178). Advocates for popular technology approaches take seriously all people's everyday interactions with information technologies (IT), and use these experiences as a starting point for exploring what it means to be a critical citizen in the information age through collaborative knowledge creation (34). CARR "starts from the assumption that poor and working-class people already have vast experience with

IT and thus come to technology and social justice programs as knowledgeable and asset bearing rather than as deficient and needy" (32).

RECAA has enabled its members to learn skills (digital and otherwise), specifically building up "collaboration by selecting to work with groups that offer interesting projects or activities that enable us to enhance various skills," as a member pointed out. Members of RECAA want to keep learning and creating in their old age, and their shorter-term activist practices are ways for them to do so.

TIMELY INTERVENTIONS THROUGH PUBLIC PERFORMANCES

The third type of activist intervention undertaken by RECAA involves organizing timely public performances or live or digitally-mediated interventions. RECAA undertakes these punctual interventions in three ways. First, RECAA members stage interventions as part of societal debates, as they did when they recorded a *Rap against the Quebec Charter of Values* (Bill 60) in 2015. Second, they stage interventions that coincide with broader public demonstrations, as was the case when they took part in a march against austerity held in Montreal in 2015. Third, they make use of annual events like World Elder Abuse Awareness Day (WEAAD), which has a broad resonance, to present public performances. In 2012, they also developed a musical, called *We Are Old, We Are Wonderful*, under the direction of Theatre Agile's Lib Spry.

For WEAAD 2016, RECAA and its allies organized an event at a downtown metro station. They sang songs and rode an escalator up and down to engage Montrealers in a discussion on the rights of, and responsibility of society towards, older people. As part of this intervention, RECAA held a banner stating "Elders can make waves." This motto aptly encapsulates what these three forms of timely public performances have in common. They seek to assert the presence of seniors and advocate for the inclusion of their perspectives and interests in societal matters. These performances emphasize the pivotal roles that seniors can play in social justice activism and challenge the idea of activism as an activity reserved for the youth.

Often (but not always) the punctuated interventions take the form of lively and carefully crafted performances like their choreographed flash mob, which they performed at a local mall for WEAAD in 2014.[7] This performance incorporated elements borrowed from Forum Theatre into the choreography: To open the dance, members of RECAA did three poses representing isolation, neglect, and disrespect. As noted previously, protests like the flash mob are carefully designed to be inclusive of its membership, and they configure public protest in a way that allows older members, with varying physical abilities, to participate. For instance, the flash mob took place inside a mall precisely because RECAA determined that performing in an outdoor space would have been too difficult for those using walkers.

Part of RECAA's cultural activism associated with age and ageism is experimentation with tactical appropriation of modes of expressions or genres that are typically associated with youth, such as the flash mob. Similarly, RECAA's *Rap against the Quebec Charter of Values*[8] borrows some features of the hip-hop genre. The rap came about when the written deposition that RECAA submitted to the Quebec government was rejected because elections were called. RECAA members wanted to share their deposition in a different way and publicly express their opinions against what they considered to be a racist bill, but they thought that releasing text online would not have the reach they sought. As a member explains, "We felt it should be something different. We were exploring different things." Rap was selected as a genre that packed the "punch" with which RECAA wanted to deliver its message. In doing so, RECAA subverted the age-based (and indeed gender-based) expectations of the genre. The unexpected juxtaposition of the older women, the rap music, and the political message delivered stood out against the backdrop formed by a representational system that is dominated by a narrow representation of aging that rarely includes those operating at the intersections of race, age, and gender. As another member explains: "We are creative by using the new activities that we are learning such as performances, dance, song, et cetera, to put our message about prevention of elder abuse, and the respect of elders in general, 'out there' in a novel fashion." In doing this, RECAA purposely does not conform to the narrow societal representations of seniors, and instead creates unexpected and surprising interventions to make their political messages stand out, interventions that resonate with the parodic performances of aging sexuality detailed in Chapter 6.

However, RECAA members are also well aware that one of the potential liabilities of genre appropriation is the labelling of these activities as "cute." Thus, members continue to debate the value of using tactics and genres typically associated with youth culture. Not all are willing to participate. RECAA's flexible structure does not demand allegiance to or participation in all RECAA activities. Part of its political agenda is to allow for divergence, yet at the same time let those who are willing continue to explore new media and new genres for activist expression.

In Dana Sawchuk's (2009) analysis of the Raging Grannies, she points out that many members of this network suggest that their public image as "little old ladies" serves a "protective function" for their activist practices, keeping police repression at bay. In other circumstances, their humorous and innocuous image allows them to more easily infiltrate spaces (including media spaces), which permit them to voice their radical message in settings that could be unwelcoming to younger activists. In this sense, these older women's exclusion from the youth-centric public image of activism and prevailing societal stereotypes affords them a particular ability to harness the image of innocuousness and passivity to cut through some of the typical barriers to activist expression. Miya Narushima (2004) similarly describes this as a sort of Trojan horse–like capacity to infiltrate otherwise inauspicious spaces.

There is a similar sense among RECAA members that something about their image and their activities has widespread appeal and could be considered palatable to an audience that may otherwise be unwelcoming to their messages about elder abuse and their activist efforts as a group of those seen in such highly racialized terms as "immigrants." This includes mainstream media outlets looking to feature local "positive news" stories or social media platforms through which digital content can be shared quickly and widely. Yet, unlike the Raging Grannies, RECAA members also express a hesitation to reach out to media and a reluctance to make some of their activist work too visible or too mediatized, specifically in contexts within which the group would lose some of its control over their image and message. About five years ago, RECAA began documenting its public performances, usually through video recordings, so as to preserve a legacy of interventions and also spread their message online. The use of digital recording technologies offers a way for RECAA to mediatize their performances and include pre-recorded video or sound, to capture poignant moments and disseminate RECAA's activist actions. Learning digital recording and editing skills over the past five years has enabled the group to reach a broader audience (for instance, the video of a 2014 flash mob on Facebook has proved to be very popular).

For RECAA, developing an understanding of circulation and of the interplay between their image as older activists and a broader system of representation is an important element in their ongoing discussion of how to establish digital renderings of their tactical theatrics. This reflection upon their creative practices counters a prevalent tactic of staging "media events" in social movements (Delicath and DeLuca 2003), where elaborate performances are designed specifically to entice mediatization, media dissemination, and accelerated circulation.

An example of RECAA's reflexive and negotiated approach towards the mediatization of its punctual interventions: The group choreographed and presented a Bollywood dance during "Age3.0: The Creative Aging Fair," a public event that ACT co-organized during the summer of 2016. Eight women members of RECAA, including Madhu, donned their saris and danced to a Hindi version of the Donna Summer song "Hot Stuff," chosen by Madhu herself to represent her life and her accomplishments. The dance itself was part of a day and an exhibit devoted to thinking critically and creatively about representations of aging and celebrating community arts as "social innovation." RECAA filmed and digitized this choreography but, at the time of writing this chapter, members had decided to keep it private and not to share it beyond a small circle of individuals. When asked why, a RECAA member explained that the dance "doesn't stand on its own." RECAA is working on a write-up to provide the full context of the performance, including the motivations for the dance and the aesthetic choices made. In this way, RECAA is attempting to forestall its performance being usurped and transformed by a media system where narrow stereotypes dominate popular representation of the aging process and of older people, particularly those who are racialized by the media. For RECAA, the video on its own risks being framed within a patronizing, dismissive, and infantilizing discourse that would celebrate the "cute old women dancing" to the song "Hot Stuff," obliterating their political efforts and nuanced message. While RECAA takes calculated risks to reach audiences through mediated means, it also makes reflexive and careful use of social media. RECAA understands the potentials and limits of digital circulation, and both action and inaction on this front factor as part of their tactical theatrics.

CONCLUSION: AGING AS ACTIVISTS

What the members of RECAA share, besides their age, is a commitment to politics, human rights, and social justice. Their entire mandate is centred on advocating for communication, reciprocity, and respect. In the context of Quebec, the typical models for caring for older adults either ignore cultural communities or are unaware of the specific dilemmas they face due to linguistic and cultural differences and to persistent, systemic racism and xenophobia. RECAA members are in large part seniors from these communities, and mostly women, working for and with other seniors. RECAA does not consist of older adults who are "actively aging," the governmental mantra that has gone global (World Health Organization, 2002). The women and men of RECAA are aging as activists and providing a welcome alternative view of spirited oldness.

Employing tactical theatrics, in the case of RECAA, entails dealing with their own aging as members of an activist group, and the overall aging of the group. As Anne puts it, "Our aging is a great challenge to us, because energy can be lost. And energy is something that is very important for any organization. Physical fitness, mental fitness, and emotional fitness, and also evolving of reference points." Yet what is important is that RECAA's activities challenge aging as an individual process that must be "endured" alone as an isolated individual. She continues: "I think that transition is like … coming to terms with your own aging and then having to do it in a group." Yet while this aging together is a resource, it is also a source of worry:

> I look at us and think "wow, you know, our membership is low; are we going to disappear?" Because it's extremely difficult to find that line between somebody who has been an activist … to say I am going to continue. Because there is this moment when you don't want to do anything, and I can relate to that. You just want to sit back.… And there are other things that come in the way, like being a grandparent.

RECAA members are aging with activism as a part of their life, but one that evolves and changes and demands great attentiveness to each other. Activism is embodied. For RECAA members, continuing to live and act as activists are deliberate decisions, which entail creative workarounds to emerging challenges. By diversifying its modes of intervention and promoting an activism that both creates and is integrated into a community of support, RECAA provides opportunities for members to participate in the ways in which each is able at different moments in time. This flexibility allows members to continue, to the extent that they want to and can, and to contribute through activities that build on the individual capacities and experiences.

Being a RECAA activist and contributing to its mission does not *only* mean marching on the streets or *only* choreographing a dance or *only* acting out a skit in public or *only* having a lively debate over a shared meal. The strength of tactical theatrics is in its celebration of togetherness through a diversity and plurality of related interventions that have different temporal commitments. These tactical theatrics allow for a building of a repertory of activist possibilities that accounts for the heterogeneity of later life, and that is inclusive of the different ways its members live their old age—with an understanding that, sometimes, one might feel 31 one day and 90 the next.

NOTES

1. RECAA has used the term "ethocultural communities" in its documents to broadly refer to the plurality and diversity of communities in Montreal with minority racial, ethnic, and cultural backgrounds, and who speak languages other than French and English.

2. See www.actproject.ca.

3. COPSI can be roughly translated from the original French to "Paralegal and Social Orientation Centre for Immigrants."

4. Forum Theatre is a RECAA-grown technique that draws upon Augusto Boal's Theatre of the Oppressed, which relies on participatory theatre interventions aimed at collaborative problem solving. We will further discuss RECAA's Forum Theatre activities in section three of this chapter.

5. Forum Theatre is designed to disrupt the active-performer/passive-audience dichotomy, as it asks the audience to intervene and alter the scene. This seeks to provide participants with the tools to alter their own realities and to promote social change.

6. Food blog: www.foodtalks.recaa.ca; upcoming documentary film tentatively titled *Madhu's Saris*: www.actproject.ca/act/madhus-saris; and the media capsule series *In Their Own Words*: www.recaa.ca/projects/in-their-own-words-volunteer-voices-from-montreals-cultural-communities.

7. RECAA flash mob: www.recaa.ca/recaa-flash-mob/.

8. The Quebec Charter of Values, or provincial Bill 60, was proposed by the Parti Québécois in 2013. It would have banned public sector employees from wearing certain religious symbols. The bill was the subject of significant controversy, including outcry from many groups denouncing it as xenophobic. Bill 60 was ultimately not passed.

REFERENCES

Boal, Augusto. 1979. *Theater of the Oppressed*. London: Pluto Press.

de Certeau, Michel. 1988. *The Practice of Everyday Life*. Berkeley: University of California Press.

Delicath, John W., and Kevin M. DeLuca. 2003. "Image Events, the Public Sphere, and Argumentative Practice: The Case of Radical Environmental Groups." *Argumentation* 17(3): 315–333.

Drotner, Kirsten. 2008. "Boundaries and Bridges: Digital Storytelling in Education Studies and Media Studies." In *Digital Storytelling, Mediatized Stories: Self-Representations in New Media,* edited by Knut Lundby, 61–84. New York: Peter Lang.

Employment and Social Development Canada. 2016. *Funding: New Horizons for Seniors Program.* www.canada.ca/en/employment-social-development/services/funding/new-horizons-seniors-community-based.html

Eubanks, Virginia. 2011. *Digital Dead End: Fighting for Social Justice in the Information Age.* Cambridge, MA: The MIT Press.

Jasper, James. 2008. *The Art of Moral Protest: Culture, Biography and Creativity in Social Movements.* Chicago: The University of Chicago Press.

Kerkshaw, Baz. 1992. *The Politics of Performance: Radical Theatre as Cultural Intervention.* London: Routledge.

Narushima, Miya. 2004. "A Gaggle of Raging Grannies: The Empowerment of Older Canadian Women through Social Activism." *International Journal of Lifelong Education* 23(1): 23–42.

Respecting Elders: Communities Against Abuse (RECAA). 2016. *About Us*. www.recaa. ca/about-us/

Sawchuk, Dana. 2009. "The Raging Grannies: Defying Stereotypes and Embracing Aging through Activism." *Journal of Women & Aging* 21(3): 171–185.

Sawchuk, Kim. 2013. "Tactical Mediatization and Activist Ageing: Pressures, Push-Backs, and the Story of RECAA." *MedieKultur* 29(54): 47–64.

Schutzman, Mady. 1994. "Brechtian Shamanism: The Political Therapy of Augusto Boal." In *Playing Boal: Theatre, Therapy and Activism*, edited by Mady Schutzman and Jan Cohen-Cruz, 137–156. London: Routledge.

Schutzman, Mady, and Jan Cohen-Cruz. 1994. "Introduction." In *Playing Boal: Theatre, Therapy and Activism*, edited by Mady Schutzman and Jan Cohen-Cruz, 1–16. London: Routledge.

Shepard, Benjamin. 2014. *Community Projects as Social Activism: From Direct Action to Direct Services*. New York: Sage.

Williams, Raymond. 1977. *Marxism and Literature*. New York: Oxford University Press.

Williams, Raymond. 1983. *Towards 2000*. London: Chatto & Windus/Hogarth.

World Health Organization. 2002. *Active Aging: A Policy Framework*. www.who.int/ aging/publications/active/en/

REFLECTION 2

Continuity and Change: A Personal Reflection on Activism across Time and Space

Sadeqa Siddiqui

Born in India but raised in Pakistan, Sadeqa Siddiqui reflects on the roots of her activism and the ways it has changed, influenced by social conditions, her education, and aging. Recounting her parents' active involvement in the India/Pakistan Partition movement, her experience as a student activist in Pakistan, her move to Montreal in 1968, and her more recent work to bring attention to issues of elder abuse, Sadeqa tells a compelling story of change and continuity.

In 2011, at the age of 69, I announced my intention to retire from the South Asian Women's Community Centre (SAWCC)[1] in Montreal, where I had worked as coordinator for 30 years. The first question my fellow workers, board members, and founding members of my organization asked was, "What are you going to do once you retire?" I considered all the suggestions I received, from "travel around the world" to "write a book on your experience of 30 year's work at SAWCC and in the women's movement"; appealing ideas for sure.

I started recollecting my memories of my journey of activism in my youth, in my adulthood, and present. My mother's image was very prominent. I thought, "I will continue what I have inherited."

My involvement in social change work started with my parents. While my father and maternal uncles were engaged in the independence movement of India from British rule and the creation of Pakistan, my mother was concerned about families that were being displaced within India and their physical and emotional suffering. She decided to get training as a nurse to help women and children who were escaping violence and turmoil by coming to our relatively peaceful city of Hyderabad.

Following the partition, our family moved to Pakistan. We were fortunate that my father found a job and a suitable place for us to live. All around us there were families who had lost not just their belongings but also their family members during the move from India to Pakistan. I accompanied my mother whenever she visited families in our community or when people sought her help. Because of her community work, she was invited to be on the board of the All Pakistan Women's Association, founded by Ra'ana Liaquat Ali Khan, the wife of Pakistan's first prime minister. She encouraged girls to join Girl Guides and my sisters and I were the first to enrol. So, at a young age I was exposed to the vulnerability of the human condition and the way activism could affect people's lives.

My activism transformed with my age, education, and changes in social conditions. Our family moved from a small town to Karachi, the then-capital city of Pakistan, which is where I went to high school. On our way to school, we used to see so many children on the street who were not going to school because their parents could not afford the books or the school fees. This image stayed with me and I wondered what we could do to provide them with books. During this time, I joined an organization called the Girls' Student Congress (GSC), which had been created to encourage girls of all ages to be conscious of self-development and their education and to be active in the student movement. The GSC was also encouraging parents to send their daughters to school. There were many obstacles for them, and one of them was financial—paying for books. We discussed this in our meeting and the group decided to organize students across the city to collect old books and to have a place to bring the books. The city library agreed to give us a space and we started collecting books by going door to door. In that library, we mended the books and prepared them for distribution. In the beginning of the school year we distributed the books to those who could not afford them. During my high school years, we continued collecting and repairing books for two months every summer. It was a very rewarding experience.

The GSC gave women, young and old, a vision and courage, and developed an activism in them. It helped me to understand the socio-politics of the country. Within 15 years of the creation of Pakistan, it went under army control. Students were organizing themselves against the military dictatorship. In my first year in college, I joined the National Student Federation and was further involved in the political movement in Pakistan. My parents and maternal uncles encouraged me and my siblings to participate in the students' movement, even after I came close to being arrested by the police, twice.

My involvement continued until I graduated and got married. Family dynamics vary from family to family and sometimes we need to compromise with the changes that married life brings. So I did; I became less active and also had my first child. Soon after came another change in my life. My husband was accepted as a PhD student at McGill, so we moved to Montreal in 1968. After a year or so, we met some South Asian people who introduced us to the Indian Peoples Association of North America, which had members from the Indian subcontinent and met weekly to have discussions about the political situation in South Asia. During the 70s, when more South Asians were migrating to Canada, women in the group discussed the issues of isolation and economic dependence as they affected South Asian migrant women. The idea of an organization for South Asian Women was realized in 1981 as a service, support, and advocacy organization that evolved into what is now the SAWCC.

In 1983, I became a full-time community worker at the SAWCC. Helping newly arrived immigrant and refugee women and their families reminded me of my younger days when I worked at my mother's side. One significant experience that sustained me for 30 years at SAWCC was helping women who were victims of violence and encouraging women's economic independence.

I initiated many economic development and education projects, including an awareness-raising project on violence against women. We took the approach of "Theatre of the Oppressed," seeking social and cultural change through the empowerment of women by increasing their understanding of the impact of male violence on women and children. This took the form of a non-verbal theatre workshop on the situation of violence, designed so that women can relate to what is happening to them. These workshops were offered to different communities and institutions.

My work as the coordinator of SAWCC went beyond services to women and their families to also involve work to bring about systemic change. I was active in the Quebec Women's Movement and was a member of the coordinating committee of the 1995 World March of Women, organized to bring together women from all over the world working to end violence against women and fighting the feminization of poverty. The project of the World March of Women gave me the opportunity to travel abroad and meet and organize women's groups to become part of the march.

In 2012, I retired from my position at SAWCC, but I continue to be active in working for changes, particularly in the lives of women. Currently, I am a member of the coordinating committee of the International Migrant Alliance (IMA), a global alliance of migrants, refugees, and displaced people. The IMA aims to strengthen and put forward migrants' voices on issues affecting them and their families at the national, regional, and international levels to ensure that the countries that send migrant workers, and the countries that receive them, respect their human rights and provide them with better working conditions and proper wages.

In Canada, the IMA is demanding changes to provisions to the Temporary Foreign Workers Program and the Caregiver Program (domestic workers).

I am also active in Respecting Elders: Communities Against Abuse (RECAA),[2] a collective of seniors from diverse ethnocultural communities striving to create a culture of respect for elders. RECAA members collectively create and organize non-verbal Forum Theatre workshops that profile the issues of disrespect, mistreatment, and elder abuse (see Chapter 2).

I believe that as long as I am healthy and physically active, I will continue my activism work, which began in my childhood, thanks to my mother. While we may all be women activists, we each have our own histories, each with a unique starting point and an individual journey that have led us to where we are now.

NOTES

1.   For more information on the SAWCC, see www.sawcc-ccfsa.ca.

2.   For more information on RECAA, see www.recaa.ca.

PART II

PERSISTING

POEM II

Firekeeper

Keara Lightning

Keara Lightning is a member of Samson Cree Nation, who has had the privilege of growing up as an uninvited guest on Anishinaabe and Haudenosaunee territories. As an activist in her 20s, she has worked on fossil fuel divestment campaigns and in climate justice organizations, as well as Indigenous student and community groups. She hopes to continue writing and learning Cree language.

Kohkum doesn't want to be called kohkum
she's called "nana" but she's still kohkum,
secretly. Like when she sends extra money
because the herbal medicines and probiotics
aren't covered by band healthcare, but
she always tells nikawiy not to tell me who it's from.
Like when she's biting angry that she hasn't been forgiven,
so coldhard but I see her
protecting a spirit like an open wound.
I want to elegize all you could never be,
nikawiy, nohkum, surviving coldhard in
a world burning up with our ancestors as tinder
(we watch the plains burning harder every year,
and I wonder if in your Edmonton apartment,
you can feel the flames like on your own skin)
I wonder all you could have been,
and maybe what you are—yet,

your closest to warmth still isn't melting,
it's ice cracking, and through the cracks
I see the open wound, there, still.
You were ripped from home, gradually, and
all at once right from birth, you never got to
carry water or keep the fire like they say we should.
You had brown babies and you couldn't
keep them. You didn't bathe them
in the cool moon waters of sacred women.
We didn't wear long skirts like they say we should.
We didn't bow heads down, sacred, to the moon,
praying. Whatever length of skirt we wore,
it was ripped off and either way, violated.
I want to own my body and choose its offerings.
Whatever I choose, sacred, still sacred.
I sit in the centre of ceremony, told to be separate
for moon time, wearing the long skirt, sweating,
face burning up blistering in the summer sun.
Hold my head up defiant, thinking my legs
are not shameful, don't need to be covered,
I don't feel waters in my womb, I'm not pulled
by the moon. I feel burning up, I feel sun.
I want to elegize all you could never be,
nikawiy, nohkom, surviving in this world,
still coldhard, strong
as you have to be.
I live in my body like an elegy, I reclaim
tradition. Reclaim sacred. Reclaim body.
We always leave so much unsaid, but I hope
you watch me burning harder every year.
I hope you feel the flames like on your own skin

INTRODUCTION TO PART II

Persisting

waaseyaa'sin christine sy

> We were able to re-establish ourselves because it was our turn. It was our turn then,
> back in the 60s. Now it's your turn. Now this lady that's fasting, it's her turn. She's
> doing what any of us would do. She's doing what we have to do. You need to shout, be-
> cause it's working. It's your turn.... It's their turn. You can't be quiet. If you shut up, you
> know what's going to happen, it's going to get messy and there's going to be another
> genocide. So keep it up! Keep shouting. Keep fighting. If all you have is your body, put
> it there. Your ancestors did. They fought for every right you enjoy.... And you know
> what? Your great-great-great-grandchildren will do the same thing.... We're gonna be
> Indian and that's how we are. That's why we're here. All my relations.
>
> —*Elder Ramona Bennett, Puyallap Tribe, "Idle No More" video (Bennett 2013)*

Spoken in Seattle, Washington in 2013, to a circle of people who had gathered in
solidarity with Idle No More (INM) and Chief Theresa Spence of Attawapiskat
First Nation, Ramona Bennett's words are invoked by and towards the spirit and
practice of Indigenous persistence.[1] Within the specific context of settler colonialism in Turtle Island (Canada/United States), which includes but is not limited to
genocide, Bennett invokes her lived experience enacting Puyallap responsibilities,
offering her Nations' relational responsibilities to the salmon as an example.[2] She
provides a snapshot of the vibrant transnational, historical, and intergenerational
actions that Indigenous peoples take to maintain life in territories they call home.
She asserts the hereditary nature of this work—invoking it from the past and
inscribing it into the future. In doing so, Bennett shapes futuristic consciousness
and, reaching beyond geographical place through cyberspace, her insights extend
beyond those she addresses on the ground, to us, the viewer.

At the time of INM, my family was living in Nogojiwanong (Peterborough,
Ontario)—one significant place in the home and territory of the Michi Saagiig

Anishinaabeg (Mississauga). Colonized through British and Irish settlement vis-à-vis Canadian-negotiated treaties with the Mississauga beginning in the early 19th century, Nogojiwanong remains a place of Mississauga endurance, resistance, and persistence, and it is home or visiting place to diverse non-Mississauga Indigenous urban peoples.[3] Nogojiwanong is also home, or visiting place, to all of the contributors in this section. The work of continual Indigenous regeneration that occurs here is individual and collective, spontaneous and planned (sy 2013). In Nogojiwanong during INM and after, many collective actions were organized by women across generations of varied Indigenous Nations, some which are introduced in this section. Each was grounded in spirit vetted through ceremonial practitioners that importantly included Mississauga peoples such as Dorothy Taylor and Gitiga Migizi Doug Williams.[4] I recall many steady, sure-moving bodies entering these spaces with the assistance of helpers, walkers, or canes; the smell and sights of burning sage; the vibrations of songs and drums; and the lulling cadence of soft, articulate words spoken in both fluent and adult-learned Anishinaabemowin—evidence of survival, resistance, and continuance. Non-Indigenous peoples always participated. There was always the vital presence of teens, children, and babies.

Mni Wiconi, named after the Lacota word for "water is life," was the first baby born at Standing Rock Tribal Reservation in North Dakota in 2016 (Williams n.d.). She was named in situ at a historic gathering of Indigenous nations who collectivized to protect the Missouri River against the Dakota Access Pipeline. Sky Bird Woman (Lacota), Mni Wiconi's mother, invokes birthing and child-bearing as an act of resistance against settler colonial sterilization of Indigenous women's reproduction. In myriad ways, Mni Wiconi is testimony to a disrupted notion of aging and activism in Indigenous communities. Naming infuses spiritual power, ancestral legacy, and future-bearing relationality into our children's lives and lifeline. It simultaneously inscribes responsibility to the communities that children inhabit—reminding the older generations that maintaining responsibilities and persisting life in the face of difficulty is shared work. In this way, the future is not only greeted by our children but is reflexively mirrored back to adults and Elders. For Indigenous communities, aging and activisms in this regard are limitless, looping through time with each generation and spiralling outward through human relations, as illustrated by the contributors.

We read both ancestral echoes and contemporary patterns in the following four dynamic contributions, made by Elder Shirley Ida Williams Pheasant, actor/playwright Monique Mojica, academic May Chazan, and Elder Jean Koning. In conversation with Chazan, both Williams Pheasant (Chapter 3) and Mojica (Reflection 3) reveal how violence compels intergenerational resistance and persistence—be it strategic, intuitive, or spontaneous. We learn about the settler, racialized, and gendered violence Williams Pheasant resisted and refused to accept as a young girl and how Mojica honours the bundle bestowed on her as a young person witnessing the varied ways each of her parents negotiated the trauma of surviving genocide in Europe and the United States. Following the trajectories of their respective lives through employment, vocation, parenthood, and aunt-hood, these women each beautifully complicate meanings of activism and converge in articulating relational responsibilities and responsible relations to and with the natural world. So vitally, they also show us that activisms can look different amongst Indigenous women. For instance, Williams Pheasant teaches culture and spiritual relationalities to women, reveals particular sentiments about being bold, and works often with non-Indigenous communities. In contrast, Mojica considers herself an outlaw/outlier with (and sometimes within) activisms, unapologetically claims to be fuelled by a new kind of anger as she enters granny territory, and openly challenges contemporary white feminisms for their continued lack of support in opposing violence against Indigenous women.

Making room for orality, as these two contributions do, is crucial. These methods enunciate Indigenous actions and the philosophies and motivations that shape them. Not only are Indigenous insights important, but the ways readers engage with, and learn from, them are critical acts in the disruption of dominating forms of knowledge production (Smith 1999). In important ways, what we want to know, how we strive to know, who we want to know it from, and what we do with knowledge is connected to whether we are reproducing colonial worlds or creating decolonial, reconciliatory, new worlds. Centring the oral transmission and construction of knowledges is an indicator of responsiveness to Indigeneity and the lands in which they are being produced. This centring is a strategic, intentional effort towards decolonization.

In Chapter 4, Chazan introduces us to the Raging Grannies—a network of predominantly settler women across Turtle Island who illuminate, interrogate, and utilize humour and play strategically to chastise social injustice. In her chapter, Chazan importantly reveals and addresses a gap in the literature about this dynamic group of women. In doing so, she reveals the solidarity work that the Raging Grannies engage in with Indigenous peoples, and their efforts in exposing Canada in its dishonourable relationships with Indigenous peoples. Neither Chazan nor the Raging Grannies retreats from discomfiting questions about power dynamics that exist in Indigenous/non-Indigenous relationships. In Reflection 4, Koning, speaking from her conscientious position as a settler woman, reflects on building and being in relationships with Indigenous peoples. Her individual and relational work is purposefully, critically, and strategically oriented towards decolonial change in Canada. Drawing from her almost century-long life, Koning shares her best lived insights and wisdoms.

The echo of individual life-living in action, moving across generations and communities, resonates throughout the section. Aside from complicating normative meanings of activisms, this section creates space for considering further questions towards unsettling. In her introduction to the book, Chazan emphasizes the need to pay critical attention to the ways power, privilege, and prominence operating in social movements intersect with age and aging. Applied here, questions that emerge include: How do Indigenous peoples across age, class, gender expression and sexualities, kinship ties, geographies, nations, and differing social histories negotiate power in achieving their shared visions or in reconciling divergent ones? How does the value of reciprocity operate in decision-making, for example, between Elders and youth? And, whose work, ideas, or visions become popularized and whose get erased or diminished? Why/how is this? Further, how do power, privilege, and prominence operate within Indigenous relationships and Indigenous/non-Indigenous solidarities, to highlight and invisibilize Indigenous women and genderqueer and non-binary peoples engaged in everyday (unseen) and popularized (public) activisms? Finally, Bennett (2013) asserts a world of activism in the future. Beyond the work and the aesthetics of this work (e.g., beaded gas masks), what will aging activisms look like and be like in the future? Perhaps, as suggested in the poem in Part IV, "Lip Point for Bearded Womxn," it will all be different *and* it will all be the same—the constant being the ongoing existence of opposing or conflicting visions of what makes a good life.

RECOMMENDED READINGS

Anderson, Kim. 2011. *Life Stages and Native Women: Memory, Teachings, and Story Medicine.* Winnipeg, MB: University of Winnipeg Press.

Corntassel, Jeff. 2013. "We Belong to Each Other: Resurgent Indigenous Nations." *Voices Rising*, November 27, www.manataka.org/page2661.html

Hunt, Sarah, and Cindy Holmes. 2015. "Everyday Decolonization: Living a Decolonizing Queer Politics," *Journal of Lesbian Studies* 19(2): 154–172.

LaDuke, Winona. 2017. *The Winona LaDuke Chronicles: Stories from the Front Lines in the Battle for Environmental Justice.* Black Point, NS: Fernwood Publishing.

Lawrence, Bonita. 2003. "Approaching the Fourth Mountain: Native Women and The Ageing Process" in *Strong Women Stories: Native Vision and Community Survival*, edited by Kim Anderson and Bonita Lawrence, 121–134. Toronto, ON: Sumach Press.

Meadows, Lynn M., Wilfreda E. Thurston, and Laura E. Lagendyk. 2009. "Aboriginal Women at Midlife: Grandmothers as Agents of Change" in *First Voices: An Aboriginal Women's Reader,* edited by Patricia A. Monture and Patricia D. McGuire, 188–199. Toronto, ON: INANNA Publications and Education Inc.

The Kno-nda-niimi Collective. Eds. 2014. *The Winter We Danced: Voices from the Past, the Future, and the Idle No More Movement.* Winnipeg, MB: Arbeiter Ring Publishing.

Tuck, Eve, and K. Wayne Yang. 2012. "Decolonization is Not a Metaphor." *Decolonization: Indigeneity, Education & Society* 1(1): 1–40.

Women's Earth Alliance and Native Youth Sexual Health Network. n.d. "Violence on the Land, Violence on Our Bodies: Building an Indigenous Response to Environmental Violence," www.landbodydefense.org/uploads/files/VLVBReportToolkit2016.pdf

SUGGESTED MULTIMEDIA AND FILMS

Viceland. 2017. *Rise.* Documentary series. www.viceland.com/en_us/show/rise

Intercontinental Cry. 2016. "Everyday Acts of Resurgence: A Talk by Taiaike Alfred, Jeff Corntassel, and Lisa Strelin." www.intercontinentalcry.org/everyday-acts-of-resurgence-talk/

Obomsawin, Alanis. 2014. *Trick or Treaty?* Ottawa: National Film Board of Canada.

Roque, Sara. 2009. *Six Miles Deep.* Ottawa: National Film Board of Canada. www.youtube.com/watch?v=tuK_5syA-34

Standing Rock Sioux Nation. 2016. *Mni Wiconi—Water Is Life.* www.standwithstandingrock.net/mni-wiconi/

Welsh, Christine. 1994. *Keepers of the Fire.* Ottawa: National Film Board of Canada.

SUGGESTED WEBSITES

Chocolate Woman Collective, www.chocolatewomancollective.com/

Honour the Earth, www.honorearth.org/

Idle No More, www.idlenomore.ca/

Indigenous Nationhood Movement, nationsrising.org/

Mother Earth Water Walk, www.motherearthwaterwalk.com/

Native Youth Sexual Health Network, www.nativeyouthsexualhealth.com/

#StandingRockSyllabus, www.nycstandswithstandingrock.wordpress.com/standingrocksyllabus/

NOTES

1.   The discourse of Indigenous life, life force, and living in settler colonial contexts has been conceptualized, theorized, and set out as praxis in myriad ways including but not limited to ideas of continuance, reclaiming, revitalization, restoring, renewal, resurgence, resistance, reconciliation, survival, survivance, thriving, re-creation, flourishment, decolonization, and

endurance. A literature review of these concepts would be worthwhile in elucidating how "activism" is theorized and practiced by Indigenous peoples and communities.

2.   On settler colonialism and Indigenous endurance, see Kauanui 2016.

3.   For more on the Williams treaties, see Blair 2008. See also the 2015 film by Anne Taylor and Melissa Dokis, *Oshkigmong: A Place Where I Belong, The Story of the Michi Saagiig (Mississauga) of Curve Lake First Nation.*

4.   Taylor and Williams embody Mississauga life force through diverse spheres of Indigenous-settler communities. Their work reflects activisms through intersectional lenses of age, mobility, class, and gender.

REFERENCES

Bennett, Ramona. 2013. "Idle No More." [video]. Directed by Dave Wilson. January 2, 2013, www.youtube.com/watch?v=ksESR2BVlqY

Blair, Peggy. 2008. *Lament for a First Nation: The Williams Treaties of Southern Ontario.* Vancouver, BC: UBC Press.

Kauanui, J. Kēhaulani. 2016. "'A Structure, Not an Event': Settler Colonialism and Enduring Indigeneity," *Lateral: Journal of the Cultural Studies Association* 5, no. 1. www.csalateral.org/issue/5-1/forum-alt-humanities-settler-colonialism-enduring-indigeneity-kauanui/

Smith, Linda Tuhiwai. 1999. *Decolonizing Methodologies: Research and Indigenous Peoples.* London: Zed Books, Ltd.

sy, christine. 2013. "Idle No More Proclaim Oct. 7: So, What Does Being a Treaty Person at Trent University Mean?" *Arthur,* October 7. www.trentarthur.ca/idle-no-more-proclaim-october-7/

Williams, Valerie. n.d. "Mom Gives Birth at Standing Rock: 'Having Babies Is My Act of Resistance.'" www.scarymommy.com/native-american-mom-gives-birth-at-standing-rock/

CHAPTER 3

"That's My Bridge": Water Protector, Knowledge Holder, Language Professor

Elder Shirley Ida Williams Pheasant

This chapter features a conversation with Elder Shirley Ida Williams Pheasant from Wikwemikong First Nation, Manitoulin Island. Elder Williams Pheasant has made profound contributions to Anishinaabewin cultural resurgence, especially through her language teaching as a professor at Trent University. In 2010, Elder Williams Pheasant and her niece, Elizabeth Osawamick, started an annual "water walk" in the Peterborough/Nogojiwanong and Kawartha area, as well as a regional group called the Sacred Water Circle.[1] In this conversation with May Chazan, which took place on December 17, 2015, she discusses the roots of her social change work, her residential school experience, her role as learner and professor, and the meanings and practices of the water walks. She reflects on whether, and in what ways, water walking is an illustration of older women's activisms. For her, water walking is a form of spiritual activism and an opportunity for cross-generational cultural teaching. It also raises awareness about the need to protect our fresh water and to redress the injustice of the ongoing lack of access to clean drinking water on First Nations reserves.

HISTORY WITH ACTIVISM

MC: When did you first become involved with activism, or what do you consider the roots of your work for change?

SWP: I guess it started with myself. I was living in an abusive relationship and I wanted to get out. I think my activism started, personally, at that age, in my 30s. There were four things my father told me when they put me in the residential school, when I was getting on the bus. They would have put him in jail if he didn't let me go. I was 10 years old and the four things he told me were: "Remember who we are; don't forget your language; no matter what they do to you in there, be strong; and go and learn about the Indian Act. We don't know what this Indian Act is. Learn about it, and come back and tell us." But we were not allowed to talk about the Indian Act, and we were forbidden to speak in our language. So when the time came and I wanted to change my life, I thought about those four things he told me and I decided to go back to school.

MC: Is that when you came to Trent?

SWP: Yes! And they kept me here [laughs]. No, in between I went away for a few years. I went to teach in Toronto, and took some other courses on life skills. I was teaching about land rights, women's rights, and life skills. I guess much of my activism has come through my teaching.

I left Toronto to go teach in Niagara and I developed a program for Natives in transition. These were men and women who wanted to go back to school and work. The program was run through the provincial government but they cut it off after two years. Just at that time, someone sent me a job posting. Trent was trying to replace Professor Wheatley, who was an Elder who was teaching the language here. I had taken his course, even though I was fluent, but he told me to take it anyway. He said to me when I left Trent after being a student, "You should be teaching the language." I wasn't even thinking about teaching the language; I was looking more into hospital work and things like that. But anyway, I never thought I would be a teacher or professor. But when I saw the job posting, I thought maybe that is where I am supposed to go, and when I got that little piece of paper encouraging me to apply I thought I would never get it. I thought, "It's a university, I will never get it, and even if I did, how would I teach it? Even if I was fluent, how would I teach it for new learners?" I thought, "I don't know of the linguistic aspects of it to teach it." But I applied anyways, and I got it.

I had quit school when I was 16, at the residential school, not because I didn't like the education but because I didn't like the way we were treated. When you are 16, it is better to be dumb than to endure the kind of treatment we were getting in the schools. Not only that, but there was an incident. At 16 years old in our culture, it's a very special time. Mothers usually buy their daughters dresses.

You have to wear something nice on your sixteenth birthday because that's your passages of rites and there are ceremonies for this. Of course, we couldn't do that because practicing our culture was forbidden. But my mother said, "Because you helped contribute, I am going to buy you a brand new dress." My mother always looked forward to the future, so she thought, "She's growing, I am going to get her one size bigger." When I got the parcel at the residential school I was so happy! I opened it and it was a dress. I showed it to the nuns because of course we had to show them everything. She sent me upstairs to the teacher still there, who said, "Go try it on, see how it is."

December the 8th was coming up; it was the Immaculate Conception day and there was a feast and it was very special for the girls. We all looked forward to it, because we could wear our own dresses, only if you were 16, for this occasion. It was when you got your orange and corn flakes and real milk, so we looked forward to that. That was the time we got white cloth tables and sometimes even real toast. Anyway, because we looked forward to that, she said I could wear that dress. So I tried it on, and low and behold it was one size too big. It was not proper, I guess, because it was one size bigger and my flesh was showing. The dress was kind of saggy and hung a little low. And that was when the teacher said to me, "What is your mother trying to do to you? Make you a whore?" I didn't like the way she said it. I didn't like the word "whore." I didn't know what it meant, but I knew I didn't like it. And so I said, "My mother is a church-going woman; she would not do that." Whatever that was. I just said that. I wasn't trying to be bold or anything.

She pulled my ear and said, "We are going downstairs to the superintendent. You are very bold and I am going to tell her." We both went. She told her story first and I came second. I got the strap and had to stand on the post for three or four days. Anything we did like that we had to stand at the pole for four days with just water, no food, no nothing. The other girls would keep candy sometimes and would walk by and sneak us some of that, or half a piece of bread, so you might eat a little bit. But that time I thought, "This is enough. I can't take this anymore." So at Christmastime I asked my father if I could quit school. My father said, "Well if you quit school, you have to help your mother. You will have to find a job." He took a feather and pointed to one side and said, "We raised you with all kinds of things. This is your side of learning on this side, and then you went to the residential school and you learned academics on that side. Perhaps you have to fill the first side now and maybe in the future you will finish that one." He said, "Maybe you don't know what I'm talking about now, but you will one day." I didn't know what he was talking about, but I understand now.

Well—because of my education—I think it really helped me to help my own people, to restore all the things that have been stolen from us. I have helped and worked to restore the language to our people, and also telling the stories of what happened to those who don't understand. That's my bridge. A lot of our women don't know some of our traditional teachings because the cultural wisdom was lost. So re-teaching them, you know, this is the way it was before the English teachings came into being. It is restoring some of the education that was taken away from us. That is one of the things I said on the CBC recently, when I was interviewed and they asked me the question, "What is the greatest reconciliation that you think should be done?" I said, "Restoring language and education. Putting in programs for language and culture to restore what was taken from us." That would be the greatest reconciliation from the churches and that's because it was the churches, and the government that hired them, that took it from us.

MC: Teaching the language and the culture has been a huge part of your work for social change, your life's work. You mentioned to me once before that you had siblings but you were the only one among them to be able to hold onto some of that knowledge. Were you the oldest?

SWP: No, I am the second youngest. My father noticed that all my siblings were coming home from the residential school and didn't want to speak the language anymore or practice some of the cultural things that our parents did. They didn't believe in it or they would make fun of it. He noticed it and so what he did was he wouldn't let me go to school when they came for me, when I was seven years old. What he did was promise the priest he would teach me the catechism, but he didn't say what language he would teach me in. So he used our language to teach me things, from when I was seven until I was ten. He taught me all of the cultural things we did. Because I was the age of 10, the language had firmly grounded in my brain. He did tell my mother, "One of our daughters is going to hold on to the things we've always had. She is the one who is going to carry on these things." I remember my father telling my mother that.

MC: How has your own work changed or shifted over your life? In your community, do women's roles in working for change tend to change as they age?

SWP: For me, I guess since I've finished teaching, retired, I have been more active in the community, both the Native and non-Native communities, but maybe moreso non-Native communities. I have been active with many more organizations, talking about residential schools, education, Native values, the water walk. I have done a lot of work on water issues and on the TRC (Truth and Reconciliation Commission), the recommendations. First Nations women have always been leaders in the community for social things. The role of the Elders is to teach the young ones about life and how to live a good way of life.

THE WATER WALKS

MC: You mention that you've been very active in the water walks and water issues in more recent years. Would you like to explain what the water walks are, how they started, how you got involved?

SWP: A water walk is where women and men gather to bless the water, to sing, and to pray. They carry a copper pail for water, along with an eagle staff. The women carry the water and the men carry the eagle staff, as this is part of the role of man, to help women as partners. They usually begin with a sunrise ceremony, where they give thanksgiving for the sun energy for what it brings, including daylight and the beginning of the new day. The women are then selected to get the water that will be carried out in the pail, stopping in places of significance to the four directions to bless the water, sing, and pray.

Josephine Mandamin, an Elder woman from the Midewiwin Lodge, started the first water walk to bring awareness to water issues in the Great Lakes in Ontario in 2003. In 2010, the Kawartha First Nations women along with surrounding First Nations women started the water walks in this area. I was part of starting it, with my niece Elizabeth. It was because of the flash flood that year: The structure of the water system in Peterborough could not hold the water, so the sewage flooded over into Rice Lake. So the cottages, Alderville First Nation, and Hiawatha First Nation were told they couldn't drink the water. They were on water-boiling alert. That was the first thing.

At first we didn't do anything about it but we knew we should. She and I gathered at the tipi here at Trent [University] to pray and ask what we should do. How could we help? But we were at a standstill because we didn't know what to do, because this isn't our reserve. On our reserve we could do anything to bring political awareness to the people. But here we couldn't, because it's not Native land as it was before the settlers, and probably we would never be listened to. So we gathered and prayed. And then we started to talk about doing a water walk. Josephine was doing the water walk and of course we could always bring more awareness to the people and help in this way.

And then that same year, Tom Jackson was a Chancellor here at Trent (2009–2012) and had a conference at the Environmental Centre that April. All the scientists were coming and then Tom's committee called me and said, "We would like to hear from First Nations and we were wondering if you could be on the panel?" And I thought, "Oh god, me on the panel with all the scientists?"

I struggled with it for about a week, struggled with what I could say and do. But then I thought about our ceremonies around the water. I looked up the work of a scientist from Japan, Dr. Emoto. One of the things he did was to give his students two bottles of water. To one, the students send all their good thought, and to the other they focus all the negative thoughts they can send. Then he takes the bottles away and freezes them. The following week he brings the bottles out. The one with the good thoughts is crystal clear and sparkling, really nice. He described it as shiny, with little stars. Then he brought the second bottle out, where the students had sent all the bad thoughts, and the quality of it was dirty. It was brownish, had all kinds of marks on it. He said, "The water is alive, you can send your messages and thoughts, and the energy it goes into that."

And that is what we talk about in our ceremonies. You have to treat the water in a very kind way. When we do the teachings, the Elder women, older than I am, when they talk about it, when they pray, when we drink that water, it purifies your thoughts, your brain, so you can make a good decision. Another drink, it purifies your body, you are walking with that spirit, so you cleanse that body because the spirit doesn't want a dirty house. And the third one is your heart. When you drink that water again, it is to purify your heart, so that your heart is pure and you can send love to all human beings. Without love, we cannot live together. We strive to be kind to one another. We strive to love one another, with good thoughts and good energy so that we can go on in life. That is what sustains us. That is what they talk about in some of the prayers. We understand the significance of the water—it is alive, it is sacred, and it must be honoured and respected. We cannot continue to abuse it as this water is what sustains us as people. If we do not look after it, it will become sick and so will we.

Until now we have done a water walk in this region every year since 2010. This year, 2016, will be our seventh walk.

CULTURAL RESURGENCE, SPIRITUAL ACTIVISM, BEING IN CEREMONY?

MC: Do you consider the water walks to be a form of "activism" initiated by Elder women? Are there political objectives associated with the water walks?

SWP: It is not a political group, but we are a group of Native women who have come together to do our duty to bless the water. In the lodge, it is the women who bless the water and as women we have responsibility to sing, talk, and bless water. The water needs us now, as we see that the water is not seen as holy, but is considered [a] commodity by settlers here in Canada. They believe that there will always be water and that it will be there for forever without ever thinking that it will be gone if we do not look after it. It is becoming polluted now and we need to do something about it.

MC: Would you describe this work as a type of "activism," or a spiritual practice, or ceremony?

SWP: It is like an activism, I guess. As women Elders, we are initiating it to make a better world for everyone, including the water, and everything will benefit, including trees, plants, fish, and the organisms living in the water. There is a movement of Native women coming together to do water walks in Ontario, following Josephine Mandamin, who walked the Great Lakes and has done the four corners of the world to try to bring awareness of the water issues in Canada. The water has been very strained from pollution, from oil spills, plastics, and sewage being thrown [in] without any thinking for consequences in the future. We need to think for seven generations, for our children so that they can drink good water in their life. Doing the water walks will help to increase awareness and appreciate the water more and will also bring awareness to people to be more cautious of how we use the water in everyday living. So I guess in a way it is activism; there is a level of that. For us Elder women, we were just doing our duty to bless the water through the water ceremony. And teaching younger women this tradition too, about blessing the water, and teaching them this part of our culture, not letting this be taken from us.

Other people started joining us because they care for the water. We are trying to come together, so that together we can bring awareness to a lot of people, including in the political arena. When we first started the walk, there was nobody doing anything about the water and there were many First

Nations around here that were on alert about their water conditions. When we were doing the first walk, the Chief from Attawapiskat who was fasting was also trying to bring awareness to a lot of things—education, housing, and the water works. They are having a really hard time. And so it was coming to our awareness also, we need to be doing something to support the First Nations, those of us who know the issues. Here in Peterborough, we are urban Natives—First Nations from different reserves, but we are considered urban. I am a professor at the university here and I am a translator for the Ontario unions, so I get to hear all kinds of issues of First Nations and one of them is water.

There is the lack of clean water and the lack of access for First Nations. Non-Native communities just need to go to the tap and turn the water on, but our people have to go get the water from the lake and bring it up and boil it if they want to drink it. The First Nation reserves near here, they have been on a "boil water advisory" for the last 10 years. With a lot of boats going that way, they were told that the water is not safe for them to drink. They have to use wells, but even the wells aren't as good as they should be. They have been asking for 25 years for service for the water works. They still haven't gotten it. Curve Lake, Hiawatha, they get it from the lakes there and have to boil it. Alderville is at the tip of Rice Lake and some are still on water alert.

LOOKING FORWARD

MC: You say this is the last year for the water walks in the Nogojiwanong area. What is your feeling about the future for the water, for First Peoples, for this country?

SWP: I am very hopeful right now. I think we have a really good Prime Minister. There has never been a Prime Minister that has sat with the chiefs, the Assembly of First Nations. They get together twice a year and this is the very first time that I have seen a Prime Minister going to address all the chiefs together. And he met the TRC (Truth and Reconciliation Commission), and I think he will support the 94 recommendations, even though we might not be able to do all of them.

I see change even with the equality with women, and Native women. We have a lot of Native women who are educated, compared to the 1970s when there were only three who had a BA [Bachelor of Arts]. Our communities are strong. Our women are strong and they are getting stronger. There is a lot of work to do still to relearn our culture, our languages, and to care for the Earth and the water, to teach this society how to take care. But I have hope for the future.

NOTE

1. The inspiration for the Peterborough and Kawarthas regional water walk was the Mother Earth Water Walkers, begun in 2003 by grandmother Josephine Mandamin, former resident of Wikwemikong First Nation. She started the first water walk to bring awareness to the importance of protecting the Earth's fresh water (www.motherearthwaterwalk.com). Since then, people from Indigenous and non-Indigenous communities have come together to walk the perimeter of large bodies of fresh water—including each of the Great Lakes—to honour, heal, and protect the water. Since 2003, the Nibi Emosaawdamajig ("those who walk for the water") have walked more than 1,000 kilometres. As Elder Williams Pheasant shared in a recent article by Angela Long: "Water is a relative. Water is alive. Water is protected by Indigenous law. People have a responsibility to care for the water" (see www.trc.journalism. ryerson.ca/walking-for-water). Information about the Peterborough and Kawathas Sacred Water Circle can be found at www.sacredwater.ca.

REFLECTION 3

"And Then We Let Them Go, and We Have Their Backs"

Monique Mojica

This reflection features a conversation with actor/playwright Monique Mojica (Guna and Rappahannock Nations). Monique is passionately dedicated to a theatrical prac- tice as an act of healing, of reclaiming historical/cultural memory, and of resistance. Spun directly from the family-web of New York's Spiderwoman Theater, her theat- rical practice embraces not only her artistic lineage, by mining stories embedded in the body, but also the connection to stories coming through land and place. At the time of this conversation with May Chazan on February 21, 2017, 63-year-old Monique was "turbo-charged and full steam ahead" in creating Sideshow Freaks & Circus Injuns, with the Chocolate Woman Collective[1] and co-author LeAnne Howe. This piece, set to go to production in August 2017 in Toronto, is about the hundreds and hundreds of "mounds" that are aligned in multiple ways across Turtle Island, even in urban landscapes; these seemingly innocuous and largely invisible earthen mounds, found in downtown parks and at the centre of suburban roundabouts, are burial grounds to thousands of Indigenous people and effigies of their cosmovisions. These mounds, in the words of Chickasaw scholar Chadwick Allen, are "the first lit- erature of this land." In this conversation, Monique tenderly reflects on her life's work, her journey with time, and her role as she enters "the Grandma territory."

✿

BECOMING AN OUTLAW

MM: Nuedi, a nuga Olonadili Oloedidili, Ganosoktha. My name is Monique Mojica. I was born into Guna and Rappahannock Nations, and adopted into the Cayuga Bear Clan of the Haudenosaunee.

I'm the third generation of four generations of performers in my family.

MC: How would you describe what drew you into working for social change?

MM: [Laughing] Born into it! Born into it! Really no ... the whole term "social change" is probably something that I don't relate to at all. "Social action," "social change," these are buzzwords. They don't mean anything to me, you know? [Pause]

MC: What words, then?

MM: "Resistance" means something to me. "Survival" means something to me. "Recovery" and "reclamation" mean something to me. "Decolonization" means something to me. "Unlearning" ... the historical traumas. "Healing" and unlearning the residue of historical traumas means something to me.

"Social change" comes from a different, a different drawer. A different box.

MC: What about the word "activism," does it come from that same box?

MM: Probably. That one, though, it feels like there's a little more *movement* in it. Activism at least has some inference to agitation, interference ... intervention.

The work that I'm doing now, the piece that's going up, that's based on the story narrative of effigy mounds and earthworks. The purpose of it is to *re-activate* and to *re-animate* the original purpose of the mound complexes on this land. So, "activate," to me, means move. Activism is movement. And animation is about the spirit or the *animus*, of the work that I do, both as an artist and as an activist. And there's not a lot of boundary between those works. Not anymore. It means that the work moves the spirit. My work will move the spirit.

And my art is my activism. I am most effective as an activist in my art.

MC: Do you remember a moment when you first came to understand that this was going to be your path, your life's work?

MM: I remember watching Selma, Alabama, on TV.[2] We had a little turquoise Zenith television. It was the 60s. We lived in California. I remember watching the German shepherds and the water hoses. That was the first march I was ever on. We walked from San Jose to San Bernardino. I remember walking behind a prop: It was a coffin that had "Selma" written on it. I was nine, but it wasn't my first awareness of injustice.

It was the first time I remember the activism and the being activated. And I knew I was walking because of what I saw on our little turquoise television. Seeing kids running from German shepherds and the water hoses. Little girls my age with their braids. But I think that there was much earlier, perhaps unspoken....

MC: Do you want to tell me a bit about your parents?

MM: I'm the eldest. I'm the first-born child of two Holocaust survivors. One is a recognized genocide and Holocaust. One is an unrecognized genocide. So that tension always existed in our household. I was born seven-and-a-half years after my father was relocated in the US as a war orphan, from France, because all of his family was wiped out. So I was raised by someone who these days we would say was suffering from severe PTSD. I could tell my father back, I could recite back, the story of his escape from the Nazis as a teenager. I remember not even being as tall as the kitchen table, standing in front of my father and telling him back his escape story....

My father had a package of photographs that were things his mother gave him the last time he saw her. She wouldn't escape with him. She wouldn't leave Paris. Even though they knew that their neighbours were being taken away ... I would look at these pictures of relatives and know that they are all dead.

Where are they?
They're dead.
Well why?
There was a war.
Why was there a war? Why are they dead? Why were they killed?
Because they were Jews.

I also remember my mother, the way that she explained war to me. It was the year that Picasso's *Guernica* was visiting the Museum of Modern Art, and she took me there. I remember sitting in front of it with her. And I was little,

I was like three. It was huge. And all of its power, and grotesqueness, and violence. [Pause]

And those were probably really the moments.

MC: How did your parents come to be together?

MM: New York, New York. Um, Greenwich Village, artists, lefties, New York in the 50s. They were postwar folks who wanted to change the world, on the vanguard of the Civil Rights movement, even before the Civil Rights movement.

I know that one of the things my dad felt was that he had no roots. When he was sent to the US, one of the ways that he put down roots was to marry a Native woman and have children with her. [Laughter] There were a lot of, um, there were a lot of issues that neither one of them could really talk about … that they weren't aware of. They were aware, but it was a different time.

MC: I'm curious about your mom. Did she have a sort of consciousness, an understanding of the parallel, of the similarity of this trauma? The intergenerational trauma for you on both sides?

MM: No. She knew racism. But she did not until recently come to a place where she acknowledges that what she went through in her upbringing in Brooklyn was trauma, and multi-generational trauma. It was the same kind of PTSD. She also always sort of deferred … "Oh, it's different. Your father suffered, he went through the war, the Nazis." Anyhow, I think she was slower to come to her own.

Also, I remember my dad telling me that when he first came, right after the war, Jews weren't talking about what they went through in Europe. Nobody wanted to hear about it. The first person he told was his first-born. So I had that bundle from the moment I was born. So it's really hard for me to pinpoint, "This is when I became an outlaw."

And this is how I refer to myself: as an outlaw. Not an activist.

MC: [Laughter] That is an excellent term.

MM: I'm an outlaw. Even in the activist world, I'm an outlaw. Outlaw, outlier. I'm always, um, I'm always the kid in the crowd who shouts out that the emperor is butt-ass naked. [Laughter] And the villagers come after you with their pitchforks.

ON AGING AND THE CONTINUUM

MC: I'm curious about your thoughts on aging. What is this dynamic of aging, and how has it informed your outlaw-ness?

MM: Where I'm willing to put myself. I'm tired. This isn't my first rodeo now, you know? I'm 63. As critical as things in the world feel, around water, and pipelines, land … missing and murdered Indigenous women … This isn't my first rodeo. I'm tired of fighting the same things that don't move. The same issues that don't move.

I have to be really, really, really picky about where I put my energies, where I show up in person: what committees I sit on, where I support in other ways.… I focus on what I bring into my work because I know that is the gift Creator gave me, as a performer. This is where I'm most effective to communicate these things.

So what I'm willing to do has changed. I don't really know how to say it… In some ways, aging has brought the boundaries of what I'm willing to be involved in closer to centre, but it also means that it's deeper and more concentrated.

MC: As you age, do you think of your work more as creating, building, making, or is it the fighting, the dismantling piece?

MM: It's both. I'm teaching more, and I'm figuring out how to teach what I do intuitively. But it's both, you know. It has to be both at this point, because the existence of what needs to be torn down is predicated on the invalidation of what I need to build. The structures that exist, those colonial structures do not allow for my existence.

I don't have the privilege nor the luxury to not keep tearing down. And I'm also angrier. This has to do with aging too, and I haven't quite figured it out.… I have not mellowed. I am angrier now than I was. I have not been this angry for 40 years. I haven't been this angry since before I had a child to protect.

And so, continuing to do the work, I can't continue to do it the same way as when I was 17 or 18. But how to do it in the most effective way? I have no formula, there's no recipe. It's day by day. It's day by day, to be as ethical and as honest and as clear and as effective, and picking and choosing the battles, you know? Where will there be an impact?

MC: I'm interested in the comment you made about the anger your felt when you had a child to protect. Do you want to reflect on your activism when you were in the thick of parenting?

MM: I couldn't take my son, Bear, into a situation where he would be in danger. I remember deciding not to go on the Longest Walk. I could never justify putting him in a situation where he could be tear gassed. This baby on my back, I couldn't be in a situation with him where there's violence, where he could be harmed. Or where he would not understand.

He did go with me on a walk. It was 1982. It was the UN Special Session on Disarmament. So he was not yet four. And he walked. And I remember walking with him, and there were some warplane exercises. And he looked up, this little guy with long braids, he said, "Momma, are those planes for war?" I said, "Yeah."

He said, "Momma, are those planes gonna drop bombs?" And I said, "No, they are not; we're safe. They're only practicing, doing their formations in the sky, as practice."

"Momma, if those planes are practicing, they're practicing for war. So that's why we're walking."

So I had this amazing little child, who always got it. He always, always got it. And um, where he has taken that is ... sometimes I get really emotional [tears] ... I never cease to be amazed with him. The videos that A Tribe Called Red[3] did in September, I was in one of their videos, and I recognized that when it came out, I said, "Bear, you've been writing this since you were 14, you've been writing this story!" You know, now it's out there.

MC: That's amazing.

MM: So there were those times where I had to protect him. And I guess the flip side is that he complained miserably that he never got read a story by his mom without her ruining the whole thing by making it a political lesson. [Laughter]

"We couldn't just read *Charlie and the Chocolate Factory*. No, my mom had to talk about how those Oompa Loompas were oppressed!"

MC: [Laughter] I love that! I can relate to that!

MM: And I remember one time, he must've been around eight or nine, on a bus. We were going to visit his family at Six Nations. I was reading a newspaper and there was an article about refugees, and he asked me what was happening in the picture. I told him. And he said, "What's a refugee?" And I told him, "Well, you know a lot of people who are refugees. Grandpa was a refugee. He had to leave someplace where he wasn't safe because there was a war. He was not safe because of what he was." And our roommate at the time was Chilean. I said, "He had to leave Chile because they had a man there named Pinochet, and he was doing this, that, and the other."

He got really worried. "Is Pinochet gonna come to Toronto and take our roommate with him?" So we were having this very involved conversation on a public bus. At one point I looked up and everyone around us was listening, watching.

A woman said to me, "Wow! I never thought of having a conversation like that with a child!"

I don't know if I'm really answering your question?

MC: I do really know what you mean. I have two young children, five and nine. I also have very difficult conversations with them, sometimes in public, and these can be looked strangely upon. But sometimes I think that those conversations are part of the activism. Do you know what I mean?

MM: Absolutely! And there is a responsibility to have those conversations. Because by the time he was 15, I was married to a Mayan man from Chiapas, and we took him there. And he was a really grumpy, stinky teenager. And we arrived in Cancun, went through this strip, where he was looking out the window, and saying, "Wow! McDonald's! Druxy's! Gold's Gym. Why are these here?" So we had a conversation about why those are there.

And when we got to Chiapas, he got really sick. He was so ill. Part of it I think was that he ate a popsicle that was made with the water that was there. But the other part of it was just the shock. He was so articulate. He said, "Mom, I've never seen our people begging like this. I've never seen this kind of poverty. I've been on reserves, but I've never seen this. I've never seen children eating garbage on the street." He said, "I saw the ones panhandling in Toronto. I pass them every day; I have conversations with them. But there always seemed a reason … because they were homeless, or because they were addicted, or they were the chronics.…" He said, "Here you see a blind beggar with a tumour. *And they're all my people!*" And he was sobbing. He was sobbing and sobbing.

"These are my people, and it's all because of what we saw when we came into Cancun. They're doing this. This exists here because of Druxy's and

McDonald's." And I knew that I was the one that raised him to be able to make that connection all by himself.

MC: Smart, smart 15-year-old. My goodness.

MM: He was 15. He didn't calm down until we went to my former husband's traditional village, and he looked up and he saw corn growing off the sides of the mountains. At that point, he said, "Corn! I know where I am! There's corn, there's corn. It's okay, there's corn." So yeah, I think part of my activism—and he certainly has a lot of stories and complaints about it—but part of my activism in those years has resulted in A Tribe Called Red.

MC: That's pretty amazing.

MM: I am so amazed, and so proud, and so over-the-moon every time I hear him talk. Every time I hear him talk. You know, he is so sharp and articulate. And I feel, or part of me feels, "Okay, my work here is done." [Laughter]

MC: Except it's not.

MM: No, it's not. But those on-the-bus conversations have morphed to being text conversations. You know?
      I don't even know if that answers your question.

MC: Yeah, I think it does. I'm thinking about aging, but not just aging in later life. How this work changes over our lives, you know? That piece about parenting is huge.

MM: I'm on a continuum, I think. It's more of a continuum. And that's the legacy of my family as performers. It has gone through a lot of transformation. My grandfather danced for tourists, and my mom and her sisters accompanied him. My mom and her elder sister quit showbiz at six because they couldn't stand it. And when they were asked, "How did you know at six and four that what you were doing was nonsense? How did you know to feel uncomfortable with that?" I remember my eldest aunt, she looked at me and said, "Because it wasn't what we did at home!" [Laughter] These little girls knew.

Those little girls grew up to become Spiderwoman Theater. And they trained me and my cousin, Muriel, who's the director of the Safe Harbors Indigenous Initiatives in New York. And then out of that, out of the work that I do, then came Bear and A Tribe Called Red, and he's also a visual artist in his own right. He's a filmmaker in his own right, outside of A Tribe Called Red. But, in the last little while, all of his video work has gone into the collective.

MC: Well, in thinking about A Tribe Called Red and the continuum, I have to tell you that I've been doing this beautiful life-history work, with a woman who is 94 years old [Jean Koning]. She is a settler woman who has been, as she would say, "walking with First Peoples" for about 60 years. She is pretty amazing. You know, she was busy learning the language 50 years ago, learning to speak Anishinaabemowin. She lives by herself in a very small apartment, and I go sit and drink tea with her and talk. Anyway, last year she was asked by some of my students about her favourite music. And she said that to burn off steam she loves to put on A Tribe Called Red in her apartment. She loves to dance to it!

MM: Oh my god! [Excitement] Oh my god, that's amazing! I'll tell Bear.

Yes, it is a continuum. I see it not about me as an individual as much as being the third generation of a legacy of "show Injuns." [Laughter]

PERFORMANCE, LAND, PROCESS

MC: In your own journey with performance and with activism, have there been any particular turning points?

MM: Well there's always the tension between being hired as an actor in a mainstream theatre to do conventional theatre or film and creating my own work, which is where I think my real contribution is. There have been times when I have said, "Okay, that's it; I'm not doing this anymore." There are times when I knew I had to create work that told the stories that weren't being told. When we formed the Turtle Gals Performance Ensemble—Michelle St. John, Jani Lauzon, and I—it was because the stories from women's points of view were not being told.

More recently I have become interested in the form and structure of *how* our stories are told. I'm not interested in recreating the well-made play, dropping Indigenous content into that structure. Because the structure dictates what you come up with. I've used the search for understanding Indigenous structures and narrative forms to reclaim culture and language, and to find those structures, those shapes, those movement patterns that exist within Indigenous cultures....

I put Indigenous knowledges at the centre of my artistic practices. So they're not window dressing. They are what's essential. And I often have no idea what it's going to end up being like. I'm relearning ways that were denied, that were suppressed, that were ripped away. But because my work has become land-based over the last little while, I take comfort that the stories are still there in the land. As long as the land is there, nothing is lost. So how do I make myself the best receptor and transmitter as I possibly can?

It has something to do with my maturity and aging as an artist. Also, I think there was a moment during a land-based artistic research process, when I was with my co-writer, LeAnne Howe, in England. We went to a mound site in England; we were walking around this mound site, and they are different there. We were trying to get a feeling and understanding for what some of those differences could possibly be. I remember turning and looking at her, and saying, "You know, this is our life's work."

So, the recognition that the things that I'm researching and working on aren't going to end with the next show, the next production—you know, when everything is put away and returned, when closing night happens, our work continues. This work is my life's work. Right now I think this is blossoming and becoming substantial. The idea that finding dramaturgy from land, place, and iconographies that are aesthetically specific to each Indigenous culture— that's my life's work. It's not about creating the product, or the production. [Pause]

MC: It's about process?

MM: It is about process; it is about living. It is about living, knowing where I am. What is the history of where I'm standing? And the energies of the waters, and the land, and the ancestors that are still around us in this place.

And we're, we're invisible. We're invisible. Part of the work that I've been doing is making visible that which is invisible on so many different levels. Now, on multiple levels, those mounds are invisible on the land. They don't know that they're there. We are invisible on the landscape. Unless you know that we're there. Unless you know somebody.

INVISIBILITY AND WHITE FEMINIST FAILURE

MC: Do you want to talk a bit more about your sense of invisibility? About the Strawberry Ceremony you mentioned earlier, on February 14th in Toronto, for missing and murdered Indigenous women?

MM: I went to the Strawberry Ceremony for missing and murdered women again this year with slim hope, just really slim, hope—you know, after seeing the turnout for the women's marches[4] just a few weeks before: "Well, maybe we'll have more numbers this year." And there were not. There were not more allies, there were not more numbers. You know, it's all the same people that usually go. There were a few individuals that hadn't been before, but I really—it put me over the edge. You do not have our back. You will not put yourself, you will not put yourself, your body, in place to have our back. Okay, I got it. Got it.

Why are we invisible? We're not women enough? We're not dead enough? Isn't violence against women supposed to be a feminist issue?

MC: I think it is a feminist issue, for sure ...

MM: Not when it comes to Indigenous women. Women who are descended from settler colonialism have to confront their complicity and their ongoing benefit, and that isn't going to happen. They have to confront that we are not oppressed equally, that we are not oppressed by the same systems. The statistics that apply to white women in terms of where the violence is coming from do not apply to Indigenous women. For most demographics, the statistics show that they experience violence, sexual assault, murder from men who are within their own circles and community. That's just not true for Indigenous women.

I think that the feminist project has failed miserably when it comes to support, to solidarity with Indigenous women. That, and their own complicity to not want to confront that they still benefit from this system that is killing us.

MOVING INTO GRANDMA TERRITORY

MC: Where do we go next? What of the future? Where you do you see yourself moving?

MM: To the land! To the land! Land, language, and resurgence. To the revitalization of the cultural knowledge that is waiting for us to connect with it. To the land....

I have Isaac Murdoch's *Thunderbird Woman* tattooed on the inside of my arm. As an icon. As medicine. As therapy. So that when I raise my fist in the air, she faces out. It's on my body; she acts through my body.

But it's also through knowing when it's time for me to step back and stand behind the young ones. Stand behind the youth to say, with everything I've got, "Go. I trust you. I believe in you. Go!" And it doesn't mean that I feel that I'm useless, but we have to stand behind them.

MC: Yes, they need you.

MM: One of the women who has been a mentor to me, Madonna Thunderhawk, I heard her say something strong that has stayed with me, when she was interviewed at Standing Rock. "It's their time," she said, "You know, we had our time." And she was reminiscing that during the Wounded Knee occupation, "the Elders didn't call us out; they didn't shame us. They didn't tell us we were wrong. They always had our backs."

I think, for me, moving into that Grandma territory, my responsibility is really to hold up those young ones, and make sure that they, as much as they want to, are able to receive the stories of those of us who have been doing it for 40 years. That those memories and stories are passed on. Does that make sense?

MC: Yes. So much sense.

MM: And then, we let them go, and we have their backs.

NOTES

1. In 2007, Mojica founded Chocolate Woman Collective to develop the play *Chocolate Woman Dreams the Milky Way*, a performance created by devising a dramaturgy specific to Guna cultural aesthetics, story narrative, and literary structure. Her first play, *Princess Pocahontas and the Blue Spots*, was produced in 1990 and is widely taught in curricula internationally. She was a co-founder of Turtle Gals Performance Ensemble with whom she created *The Scrubbing Project*, the Dora-nominated *The Triple Truth* and *The Only Good Indian*.

2. The Selma marches were three historic protests in 1965 that were central to the Civil Rights movement in the United States. Protestors marched from Selma, Alabama, to the state capital of Montgomery, demanding that Black/African-American citizens be allowed to exercise their constitutional right to vote.

3. Mojica's son, Bear Witness, is one of three members in the hugely influential "native Producer and DJ crew" A Tribe Called Red (see www.atribecalledred.com).

4. The 2017 Women's March took place in cities across the globe on January 21, 2017, in support of women's rights, immigration reform, healthcare reform, environmental protection, a stop to pipelines, LGBTQ rights, racial equality, freedom of religion, among other causes. These rallies, which drew out over 2 million people across Turtle Island/North America, with the largest numbers in the USA, were precipitated by the inauguration of President Donald Trump. Mojica was referring to the march in Toronto, which drew out 500,000 people, and her dismay at the limits of white feminism and the failure of people to mobilize widely in Canada to end violence against Indigenous women.

CHAPTER 4

Settler Solidarities and the Limits of "Granny Activism"[1]

May Chazan

Every two years, Raging Grannies from across Turtle Island (Canada/United States) gather at their "Unconvention" to participate in activist workshops, listen to guest speakers, network, and stage political demonstrations. The Raging Grannies first organized in the late 1980s in Victoria, Canada, as peace activists protesting the appearance of US submarines carrying nuclear warheads in the Victoria harbour (Roy 2004). Nearly 30 years later, a diverse network of over 100 groups (or granny "gaggles") spans the continent (see www.raginggrannies.org). They protest wars, fracking, climate change, poverty, child care inaccessibility, denial of refugee rights, and inequitable conditions for Indigenous communities, among other injustices. In 2014, I participated in their Unconvention in Montreal as part of my broader research on aging and social movements. This experience significantly extended my understanding of their movement: It challenged me to think beyond their well-documented, flashy performance activism and to investigate their lesser-recognized, quieter settler-solidarity work.

The Raging Grannies' iconic "granny activism" has three central features: dressing in flashy costumes, singing satirical songs, and being irreverently uninvited (Kutz-Flamenbaum 2007). As Dana Sawchuk describes:

> Grannies dress in flamboyant costumes of skirts, shawls, and decorated hats while they flaunt their identities as feisty grandmothers instead of as "nice little old ladies." At their "rages," as their organized protests are called, they show up—invited or not—to city halls, shopping malls, nuclear power plants, armed forces recruiting centres, and anti-war and antiglobalization demonstrations to sing out their political messages to the tunes of songs from days gone by. (2009, 171–172)

My experiences at their Montreal Unconvention, however, revealed to me the need to consider both the iconic and the lesser-recognized activist practices that comprise their movement in order to gain a more nuanced understanding of who the Raging Grannies are and what they do. One moment in particular challenged me to shift my attention from these women's "wild hats, cheeky songs, and witty actions" (Roy 2004) to think about how their solidarity-building activities might extend existing analyses of their movement.

On the last evening of the gathering, some two dozen Grannies convened for a late-evening sharing circle. As it ended, Carole TenBrink, a white settler woman and poet in her 70s, hesitantly stepped forward to perform a piece of spoken-word poetry:[2]

I hear the First Nations and Indigenous Peoples of Canada.
They rise up, Idle No More.
And they want to speak to us.... We must *just listen*. It's time.
Listen   to their drums. Listen   to their chants.
I hear urgent voices saying...
We are the First Nations of the West Coast.
The Bella Coola, Squamish, Qualicum, Nanaimo, Musqueam,
Fraser River Salish, Malahat, Haida, Nootka, Tlingit and others.
You don't know us, do you, but we were here since the beginning of the beginning.
We rose out of the Dark. We go deep as the Pacific and today
we are a tidal wave, rising.
I hear more voices...
We are the First Nations of the Plains.
We are the Anishinaabe, Ojibwa, Blackfoot Kaina, Nakoda,
Assiniboine, Okanagan, Yakama and others.
You don't know us but we are old as wind, our spirits invisible to you.
Like wind that blasts and blares all the way across the plains,
today, we're rabble rousing...

She continued with her poem about resurgence. As she spoke, I reflected on how this gathering of predominantly white settler women—albeit women of different social classes, cultural backgrounds, and abilities—was being punctuated with an evocative portrayal of the Indigenous-led resurgence and decolonization movement Idle No More, which had begun garnering public attention across Canada some 18 months earlier (Barker 2015; Kino-nda-niimi Collective 2014; sy 2012).[3] I was intrigued by Carole's decision to explicitly name over 100 First Nations through the course of her poem—by her performed resistance to the erasure of most of these names from the collective memory of Canada's settler populations. I was struck by her repetition of the imperatives "listen" and "join us" throughout her performance, which she clearly intended to indicate her support for Indigenous struggles.[4] I was also aware that her initial hesitation to perform (and my initial discomfort with hearing) this poem revealed a paradoxical tension: between feeling compelled to speak out in such settler spaces about ongoing colonial injustices and the uncertainty of how to do so without reproducing colonial power dynamics. Similar tensions have been described elsewhere (e.g., Regan 2010). Carole's poem suggested that, for some Grannies, building support for Indigenous movements was a priority, and this was reflected in several other scenes from the 2014 Unconvention, including: the opening of the gathering by Stuart Myiow Sr. (an invited Elder of the Kahnawake Mohawk Traditional Council and Stone Iwaasa); the selection of Nakuset (an Indigenous community organizer, and executive director of the Native Women's Shelter of Montreal) to facilitate two prominent workshops; and a focus on Indigenous issues in the banners and songs of granny gaggles across Canada.

While a number of scholars have studied the Raging Grannies, focusing on the use of satire in their activism (Roy 2004), the implications of their activism for later-life learning (Narushima 2004), the potential health benefits of their engagement (Pederson 2010), and their strategic adoption of "grandmother" identities (D. Sawchuk 2009), none of these studies have examined the Grannies' solidarity efforts with Indigenous-led movements. This, then, is my launch point for this chapter.

Specifically, I investigate why and how members of various Canadian Raging Grannies groups are working to build solidarities with contemporary Indigenous movements in Canada. I ask: What is driving these women to support Indigenous struggles in Canada at this time? How do they position themselves within these relationships? How are they practicing (or seeking to practice) these solidarities? In so doing, I provide a more nuanced understanding of what is typically associated with granny activism, beyond their flashy and frequently uninvited performances. This chapter also unpacks the linkages between solidarity-building practices and what these mean for understanding solidarities among specific women in particular contexts (Brown and Yaffe 2014). Further, it challenges certain assumptions about feminist activists of the "baby boomer generation," typically women thought of as "second wavers"[5]: that is, assumptions that settler North American women born in the 1940s–1950s who identify as feminists typically practice essentialist identity politics and give little critical attention to how differences in power and privilege operate within their movements (Chazan and Baldwin 2016; Purvis 2004; Hogeland 2001).

RESEARCH CONTEXT

This research has taken place at a time when Indigenous-led movements have become widely recognized in Canada. While First Peoples across the continent have acted, persisted, survived, and resisted in so many politically, socially, and culturally significant ways from the earliest moments of European contact, the first decades of the 21st century saw the organizing work of Indigenous peoples gaining public prominence, in the Canadian media, among settler activists, in institutions, and elsewhere across the society. In addition to Idle No More, this organizing work has included campaigns calling for a national inquiry into missing and murdered Indigenous women (MMIW), widespread participation in the Truth and Reconciliation Commission (TRC), and numerous mobilizations around education, housing, drinking water, and other basic rights on First Nations reserves. These mobilizations have also been accompanied by prolific writing on anti-colonialism, decolonization, and resurgence (e.g., Corntassel 2012; Coulthard 2014; Simpson 2008, 2011), as well as critical scholarship on solidarity-building, including work on Indigenous/non-Indigenous alliances, settler consciousness, transnational feminisms, and solidarities across borders (e.g., Davis 2010; Mohanty 2003; Sundberg 2007).

This chapter draws conceptually from three salient themes within these writings. First, in asking why the Raging Grannies are seeking to ally themselves with Indigenous movements, it draws on work concerned with *motivations* for doing solidarity work. For example, it investigates the Raging Grannies' perspectives with reference to recent scholarship on solidarity-building based on moral and ethical responsibility. It also explores their motivations in light of critiques that solidarity based on moral responsibility can uphold existing social arrangements rather than working toward decolonization; many scholars and activists call instead for solidarity-building based on ideas of interdependence (Gaztambide-Fernández 2012; Walia 2012). Second, by investigating the connections between why and how the Raging Grannies are developing these alliances, I examine the theme of solidarity as *praxis*, seeking to theorize what "solidarity" means in this research, conceptualizing it as contingent on how specific relationships are practiced or performed in specific contexts (Brown and Yaffe 2014; Routledge 2012). Finally, the chapter delves into the theme of solidarity-building across *difference*, investigating whether and how the Raging Grannies grapple with issues of uneven power, privilege, and social position in their activist work. In so doing, it analyzes the Grannies' perspectives and practices alongside scholarship that explicitly portrays difference as the basis for Indigenous/non-Indigenous alliances and feminist coalitions (see, for example, Mohanty 2003; Snelgrove, Dhamoon, and Corntassel 2014).

I base my analysis of these central themes on a series of observations, focus groups, and interviews carried out with Raging Grannies between 2014 and 2015. In 2014, I engaged in participant observation at both the Unconvention in Montreal and the Peoples' Social Forum in Ottawa.[6] At the Unconvention, which brought together Grannies from across North America, I documented the content and format of workshops and sharing circles. At the Peoples' Social Forum, I documented key conversations and observations regarding Grannies' solidarity efforts. Following these gatherings, I analyzed 18 activist history interviews, which I had conducted over the previous year with Raging Grannies from across Canada; I focused my analysis on whether, why, and how women discussed engaging in solidarity work as part of their broader activist work. I examined a selection of Raging Grannies' websites from across Canada, noting that the majority, irrespective of province or region, indicated some level of participation in Indigenous-led rallies and/or other mobilizations. I then conducted a series of interviews and focus groups with a total of 14 Raging Grannies from four different groups in Ontario and Quebec, asking what motivated their solidarity-building efforts and how they were engaging in this work.

It is noteworthy that the Grannies involved in this research were predominantly, although not exclusively, white settlers living in Canada. Most were middle-class or working-class, university educated, and in their 60s and 70s. At the time of the research, many, but not all, were biological grandmothers, and they brought diverse activist histories and political perspectives to their activisms. Many, but not all, identified as "feminist" activists—and given their ages, social positions, and histories with feminist struggles, most would typically be considered "second wavers" (Laughlin et al. 2010). While there is no large-scale data on who joins Raging Grannies' groups, the characteristics of these participants also appear to reflect the wider movement, according to several long-standing Grannies, and as discussed in Chapter 1.

Grannies in this research were members of a number of different localized gaggles, which are loosely networked with no centralized organization; thus, different groups were focusing on different issues, depending largely on the interests of their members. Groups were engaging with Indigenous groups quite differently and with varying levels of involvement. Some had been involved in Indigenous solidarity work for some time; others were in the process of educating themselves in hopes of developing such relationships in the near future. Some regularly participated in Indigenous-led struggles; others were sympathetic but rarely engaged directly; still others had occasionally attended Indigenous-led rallies, but were unsure how to mobilize more fully. Grannies had varied experiences with and views of colonialism, in part as a result of their own diverse settler histories. Some were from European families that had settled in Canada several generations earlier, others were first-generation European-Canadians, still others were first-generation Canadians of European descent from other colonial contexts (such as India).

TO BE INVITED: VARIED APPROACHES TO "GRANNY ACTIVISM"

Despite the diversity within and among the Granny groups, there was resounding consistency in how they typically practiced their "granny activism." As noted previously, this typically involved outrageous outfits, humorous songs, and overall irreverence. As one Granny in my research said, "This is what makes us Raging Grannies." While the notion of being uninvited and the broader iconic image of "granny activism" reverberated throughout my research, what emerged most centrally in my conversations about solidarity-building was a tension: Many viewed their well-practiced strategy of theatrical irreverence as both quintessential to what they do and entirely inappropriate for engaging with Indigenous movements.

Unlike previous analyses of this movement, the theme of being *invited* was raised repeatedly in my focus groups. In Barrie, Ontario, for instance, one participant expressed: "It would be important to ask them [Indigenous leaders] what role they might want us to play, rather than us saying we could do this or would want to do that. We [the Grannies] cannot go along uninvited…. These individuals have had white people tell them what to do and when to do it for too many generations." In Ottawa, another participant explained, "We [the Grannies] are careful to follow their lead [the lead of Indigenous activists]. I really object to settlers going in and trying to tell the Aboriginal People what to do. I mean you work *with*, in solidarity, but in that situation we take their lead. We would never presume to try to go and sing at their rally unless we were invited because it's their rally, you know."

Several Grannies expressed their concern that their typical style of activism would be misunderstood or viewed as disrespectful. As one participant from Toronto articulated, "The challenge is not to be misunderstood. Our songs, our costumes, our whole way of doing things might be misunderstood, might be offensive." Another participant emphasized the differences she sees between solidarity with Indigenous movements and other activisms in which her group engages:

> Our relationships with Indigenous movements are different than other things that we protest against, because we really can't tell them what to do, we can't offer alternatives, all we can do is give them our support. Whereas,

when we're raging about the environment or so many of the other issues, we do talk about alternatives, we do talk about the things the government should do, etc. So it's quite different.

These Grannies differentiate, then, between what they do (or would think about doing) in building alliances with Indigenous movements and how they most often practice their activism. In the former scenario, they view their typical "granny activism"—being flamboyant and arriving uninvited—as inappropriate. Many felt unsure how to proceed, reflecting their deep self-awareness of their differences in power and privilege (echoing also Mohanty 2003; Snelgrove, Dhamoon, and Corntassel 2014). This contrasts with the stereotypes of older, feminist-identified, settler women as adhering to essentialist identity politics or having limited analyses of difference (Purvis 2004).

OUTRAGE, RESPONSIBILITY, INTERCONNECTION

Turning to the question of motivations, three central findings emerged in my conversations with Grannies about why they wished to engage in Indigenous struggles: outrage, responsibility, and interconnections. Most spoke passionately about their anger not only at Canada's colonial past but also (and perhaps most centrally) at Canada's colonial present. Enraged by ongoing racism coupled with state-sanctioned violence and discrimination against Indigenous peoples in Canada, many discussed the disproportionate levels of violence against Indigenous women and girls in Canada and the government's long-standing refusal to properly investigate those who have gone missing and those who have been murdered.[7] They noted that Canadian police and courts respond inadequately to such cases, while frequently upholding biased trials against those charged with committing violent crimes (see Razack 2002). One of the Grannies from Barrie highlighted this unequal valuing of lives:

> These women have been brutalized. Nobody [the government, the police] seems to be doing much in figuring out why. If they were white women, there would be an outcry. There would have been the government inquiry by now; but the government still won't even have an inquiry for these women. I think ... a lot of white people still think that what happens to Indigenous people doesn't really matter. I don't want to be counted among them.

Many also discussed the Canadian government's inadequate apology for the abuses of residential schools and its ongoing failure to act on commitments and promises. As one Toronto Granny noted, "The apology to First Nations was just so woefully inadequate and he [Prime Minister Harper] has so far come nowhere near the commitments and promises that need to be made. It's just appalling."[8] Some raised further concerns over the inequitable poverty experienced by many Indigenous communities, which they view as blatant disregard for First Peoples in Canada.

With this outrage often came a sense of personal responsibility, frequently tied to feelings of complicity, as has been discussed by Ravi de Costa and Tom Clark (2015) and others. Some, like the following Toronto Granny, described this personal complicity and responsibility by reflecting on their own families' settler histories: "My ancestors were some of the first settlers of Canada. One of my ancestors was the first European child born in the Moncton, New Brunswick area—to a guy who was a scoundrel, but that's beside the point. So the thing is, my scoundrel ancestors came over here and stole the land, so I owe something back."

Others coupled feelings of shame to their sense of responsibility, as reflected by this Montreal Granny: "My underlying response is really shame. It's the shame of … what we've done to these people. It's the shame of not knowing for years and years and years, of it being covered up … I know we can't overcome that shame, but we have a responsibility to at least acknowledge what we've done." Critically, scholars like Paulette Regan (2010), Rick Wallace (2014), and others call into question whether this kind of settler pain, guilt, and shame might inadvertently function to decentre Indigenous experiences, appropriate Indigenous pain, and enable settler complicity. In some cases, it does appear that participants were moving through the shame toward acknowledgement and using the guilt to propel themselves into accountable action.

Finally, some Grannies—though certainly not most—explained that they are driven by their belief in an interconnectedness between settlers and Indigenous peoples in Canada. Echoing some of the arguments put forward by Ruben Gaztambide-Fernández (2012) and others, this was evident in the words of this Granny from Alberta, shared with me at the Unconvention:

> The shame, the violence, the trauma, the history—it diminishes us all.… I know I benefit from the inequalities on the one hand, but I think we all—all of us, especially those of us who are most privileged—are stunted by what happened and what's still happening. The reality is that we're now all here together on this land. Our futures depend on each other; we all need to be part of … the decolonization.

Likewise, some focus group participants suggested that, as settlers, they feel dependent on Indigenous knowledges regarding sustaining life on Earth; that the future of the planet may well require a shift in world view toward what they understand as Indigenous knowledges. They thus understood their own and their offspring's survival as dependent on the First Peoples of this continent.

The Grannies in my research described their motivations for building solidarities with Indigenous movements as based on a range of feelings, including outrage, shame, complicity, and personal responsibility to take action. Some, furthermore, spoke about their sense of interdependency with Indigenous peoples and the need for decolonization to involve everyone in Canada.

QUIETER "GRANNY ACTIVISMS"

In reflecting on the question of how they go about (or would envision going about) practicing solidarity with Indigenous movements, the Grannies in this research revealed a variety of activities. These diverse solidarity-building practices—many of them more humble, quiet, and self-conscious than their usual antics—broaden what is typically associated with their movement.

In discussing their participation in formal Indigenous-focused protests or rallies, Grannies described playing a supportive role, avoiding the spotlight, not dressing in "Granny gear," and singing only if and when invited to do so. According to one Toronto Granny: "When we go to [marches for missing and murdered Indigenous women] now, we don't wear our Granny gear and we don't show up as Grannies or sing Granny songs. We may all go together, but out of respect … we step back and let them take the lead." Much of the solidarity activism that-Grannies described was spearheaded by individuals within their groups who had connections to Indigenous struggles through other organizations (such as Amnesty International, churches, and other religious organizations), personal relationships, or professional contacts. These individuals would often (although not always) draw their groups into related solidarity work. Many of the Grannies felt more comfortable with their efforts pivoting around openings offered by specific group members, rather than pushing their way into Indigenous movements without invitation.

Some Grannies were practicing solidarity by offering logistical and material support to specific Indigenous-led occupations or uprisings. Mirroring many aspects of Harsha Walia's (2012) reflections on "decolonizing together," they described the importance of doing only what was asked of them and following the lead of Indigenous communities. This Toronto Granny's story is illustrative:

> When the occupation happened in Caledonia, my husband and I contacted, through various levels of contacts, the Six Nations that were doing the

occupation there: How could we be of support? It turned out they could use a tent, and they would be happy if somebody came and cooked a meal. So we arranged it all in advance so all the security and everybody knew we were coming, and we were coming on a certain day and we would cook lunch. So we filled up the car with food and a tent and all kinds of stuff, and went out.... We cooked lunch and took it out to all the people who were guarding around the perimeter.... We did what *they* wanted. We didn't just arrive and say, "We're here as lady bountiful." We said, "What do you need," and had it all arranged a long time in advance that we would do this.

Many also suggested that practicing solidarity sometimes meant less prominent roles, such as educating themselves and other settlers. For instance, Carole viewed it as an act of solidarity to perform her poem (with which I opened this chapter), bringing attention to what she wrote were the 613 federally-recognized First Nations in Canada.[9] Likewise, the organizers of the Unconvention felt that it was part of their work to educate themselves and other Grannies by having (and paying) Indigenous speakers and workshop presenters.

The women in my research, then, discussed a myriad of solidarity practices. These included offering their time and resources to Indigenous-led protests; attending marches and rallies dressed in everyday attire and singing only if asked; educating themselves and others; joining campaigns facilitated by respected organizations; and working through their churches to redress past (and prevent future) harm. Their solidarity efforts incorporated small acts, often pivoting around individual members' personal connections.

DISCUSSION AND CONCLUSIONS

As this chapter shows, the Raging Grannies movement is changing over time and responding to the shifts taking place in activist movements across Turtle Island, including broader efforts to recognize, centre, and support the struggles of First Peoples across the continent in ways that try to avoid reproducing the ongoing workings of settler colonialism. The chapter also shows that the Raging Grannies are more diverse in their activist practices than has typically been recognized. Popular portrayals emphasize the flashy aspects of their iconic movement—their outrageous costumes, satirical songs, and irreverence. By documenting their solidarity-building efforts, however, it is also possible to reflect on the limits of their quintessential "granny activism" and acknowledge some of the lesser-known (quieter, humbler) aspects of their movement.

Driven by anger and shame at Canada's colonial present, and by feelings of interdependency with First Peoples across Turtle Island, the Grannies in this research described several solidarity practices: attending rallies in plain clothes, working for reconciliation within their churches, supporting existing campaigns led by other organizations, providing logistical support to Indigenous uprisings, educating themselves and others, and so on. These kinds of practices, they suggested, were less likely to reproduce the very colonial relations they wish to challenge or be misunderstood as disrespectful. Thus, investigating these solidarity efforts required thinking beyond more homogenous and static versions of who the Raging Grannies are and how they operate.

This chapter also contributes to efforts to develop and refine solidarity as a concept. Extending the works of Brown and Yaffe (2014) and others, it illustrates with grounded research that how solidarity is understood cannot be readily disconnected from how it is performed or practiced. The Grannies revealed that their motivations to build alliances were based on—above all else—their desire to change existing colonial power structures. These motivations were then inextricably linked to their practices: they set aside their typical "granny activism" approach for fear that entering Indigenous spaces uninvited, making their own voices heard, could reproduce colonial relations. Instead, they performed their solidarities in ways that they hope might have potential to decolonize their relationships through their very practice. By investigating the relationships between *why* they were seeking to work as allies and *how* they were performing these alliances, then, their solidarity can be seen as praxis—its theorization, in other words, is bound up in its contingent, relational, and performative practices.

Finally, by focusing on a movement composed of older women activists, this work adds to a growing body of feminist research on activist aging. Of particular importance, it challenges stereotypes of older, feminist-identified activists—women of the "baby boomer generation"—as stagnantly tied to essentialist politics and disengaged from contemporary analyses of difference (Hogeland 2001; Purvis 2004). In contrast, many of the Raging Grannies in this research were struggling to position themselves vis-à-vis Indigenous movements, clearly grappling with their differences in power and privilege, Canada's ongoing racism, and their own settler histories.

While I have specifically examined the perspectives of white, settler, Granny activists in this chapter, I acknowledge there is a significant need for research into how diverse Indigenous actors and groups interpret, understand, and experience the efforts of Raging Grannies and other predominantly settler movements, and a need for critical inquiry into how effective this praxis is in terms of decolonization. It would also be worthwhile to investigate how Grannies enact their solidarities outside of their Granny groups and in their daily lives, how (and whether) they are challenging dominant settler consciousness, and what lessons their practices might hold for settler Canada and Indigenous/non-Indigenous relations more broadly.

Recognizing the importance of future Indigenous-centred inquiry, what emerges from this research is a sense of possibility. Grannies bring varied perspectives, experiences, and histories to the work of solidarity-building. While some of their analyses and perspectives could be critiqued, their words and actions also suggest the possibility for a meaningful process to emerge from the leadership of Indigenous communities and to be supported by the praxis of older, engaged, and politicized settler women. These women have the time, desire, and capacity to take the social risks required to confront their own privilege. Their stories are hopeful that change is possible, echoing in many ways the preconditions set out by prominent Indigenous scholar Taiaiake Alfred: "Real change will happen only when settlers are forced into a reckoning of who they are, what they have done, and what they have inherited; then they will be unable to function as colonials and begin instead to engage other peoples as respectful peoples" (2005, 184).

NOTES

1. Parts of this chapter were adapted from an article I published in the journal *Social Movement Studies* in 2016, volume 15, issue 5, titled "Settler Solidarities as Praxis: Understanding 'Granny Activism' Beyond the Highly-Visible."
2. I have left the spelling of the First Nations groups in this poem as Carole wrote them.
3. Idle No More is the name given to a mobilization of Indigenous communities across Turtle Island that gained prominence in 2013. This mobilization made visible the immense poverty faced by many First Nations, Métis, and Inuit communities across Canada, while also illuminating the strength of these communities to preserve their cultures and maintain their integrity despite centuries of abuse.
4. From our conversations, I believe Carole intended her poem as a call to settlers to listen to Indigenous-led movements and First Nations' perspectives. By using "we" and "us," however, I am aware that there is a resonance of inventing or appropriating certain Indigenous voices. While I am uncomfortable with this, I offer this in all its messiness to illustrate the work and the thinking taking place in these settler spaces.
5. The "wave" metaphor has been used widely to describe the history of feminism in North America. While some variation exists, an overview of each feminist wave is generally viewed as: 1) the first wave (1880s–1920s) associated with winning the vote for middle-class white women; 2) the second wave (1960s–1970s) followed after a period of supposed inertia, characterized by widespread struggles for equality and the universalizing notion of

"sisterhood"; and 3) the third wave (1990s–present) associated with challenges from women of colour to the essentialism of the second wave, as well as with increasing transnationalism, and the analytic of intersectionality. Many scholars have critiqued the wave metaphor for being North-centric, for eliding feminists of colour before the third wave, and for perpetuating ageism and false divisiveness (see Tripp 2013; Springer 2002; K. Sawchuk 2009; Chazan and Baldwin 2016).

6. The Peoples' Social Forum was a national conference of social movement organizations in which the Raging Grannies participated in Ottawa in August 2014 (see Peoples' Social Forum 2014).

7. After many years of inaction, the Canadian government finally agreed to set up an inquiry in 2016. Still, at the time of the research very little government action had taken place.

8. At the time of this research, Canada's prime minister was Conservative Party leader Stephen Harper; by the time of writing, the country had elected a majority Liberal Government led by Prime Minister Justin Trudeau. According to many, however, this Granny's reflection on the inexcusability of the Canadian state's unfulfilled commitments to First Peoples resonates across both Conservative and Liberal Party administrations (see, for example Gehl 2017; Palmater 2017).

9. This is the number cited in Carole's poem; this number has been highly contested and there may well be more than this.

REFERENCES

Alfred, Taiaiake. 2005. *Wasáse: Indigenous Pathways of Action and Freedom.* Toronto, ON: Broadview Press.

Barker, Adam J. 2015. "'A Direct Act of Resurgence, a Direct Act of Sovereignty': Reflections on Idle No More, Indigenous Activism, and Canadian Settler Colonialism." *Globalizations* 12: 43–65.

Brown, Gavin, and Helen Yaffe. 2014. "Practices of Solidarity: Opposing Apartheid in the Centre of London." *Antipode* 46: 34–52.

Chazan, May, and Melissa Baldwin. 2016. "Understanding the Complexities of Contemporary Feminist Activism: How the Lives of Older Women Activists Contest the Waves Narrative." *Feminist Formations* 28(3): 70–94.

Corntassel, Jeff. 2012. "Re-envisioning Resurgence: Indigenous Pathways to Decolonization and Sustainable Self-determination." *Decolonization: Indigeneity, Education & Society* 1: 86–101.

Coulthard, Glen. 2014. *Red Skin, White Masks: Rejecting the Colonial Politics of Recognition.* Minneapolis: University of Minnesota Press.

Davis, Lynne. Ed. 2010. *Alliances: Re/Envisioning Indigenous-non-Indigenous Relationships.* Toronto, ON: University of Toronto Press.

de Costa, Ravi, and Tom Clark. 2015. "On the Responsibility to Engage: Non-Indigenous People in Settler States." *Settler Colonial Studies*, August 2015.

Gaztambide-Fernández, Ruben A. 2012. "Decolonization and the Pedagogy of Solidarity." *Decolonization: Indigeneity, Education & Society* 1: 41–67.

Gehl, Lynn. 2017. "Canada Is Carrying Out Cultural Genocide with a Smile." *HuffPost Blog* (September 2017). www.huffingtonpost.ca/lynn-gehl/canada-is-carrying-out-cultural-genocide-with-a-smile_a_23204482/

Hogeland, Lisa Maria. 2001. "Against Generational Thinking, or, Some Things that 'Third Wave' Feminism Isn't." *Women's Studies in Communication* 24: 107–121.

Kino-nda-niimi Collective. Eds. 2014. *The Winter We Danced: Voices from the Past, the Future, and the Idle No More Movement.* Winnipeg, MB: Arbeiter Ring Publishing.

Kutz-Flamenbaum, Rachel. 2007. "Code Pink, Raging Grannies, and the Missile Dick Chicks: Feminist Performance Activism in the Contemporary Anti-War Movement." *NWSA Journal* 19: 89–105.

Laughlin, Kathleen A., Julie Gallagher, Dorothy Sue Cobble, Eileen Boris, Premilla Nadasen, Stephanie Gilmore, and Leandra Zarnow. 2010. "Is It Time to Jump Ship? Historians Rethink the Waves Metaphor." *Feminist Formations* 22(1): 76–135.

Mohanty, Chandra Talpade. 2003. *Feminism without Borders: Decolonizing Theory, Practicing Solidarity.* Durham, NC: Duke University Press.

Narushima, Miya. 2004. "A Gaggle of Raging Grannies: The Empowerment of Older Canadian Women through Social Activism." *International Journal of Lifelong Education* 25: 28–42.

Palmater, Pamela. 2017. "Justin Trudeau Has Forgotten His Promises to Indigenous Canadians." CBC News (February 2017). www.cbc.ca/news/opinion/promise-to-indigenous-1.3972965

Pedersen, Jennifer. 2010. "The Raging Grannies: Activist Grandmothering for Peace." *Journal of the Motherhood Initiative* 1: 64–74.

Peoples' Social Forum. 2014. *Peoples' Social Forum Program / Programme du Forum Social des Peuples.* www.static1.squarespace.com/static/52faa83fe4b00ea56bbb527a/t/53f4ad5ae4b02de8411c3719/1408544090885/PSF_eprogNnn.pdf

Purvis, Jennifer. 2004. "Grrrls and Women Together in the Third Wave: Embracing the Challenges of Intergenerational Feminism(s)." *NWSA Journal* 16: 93–123.

Razack, Sherene H. 2002. "Gendered Racial Violence and Spatialized Justice: The Murder of Pamela George." In *Race, Space, and the Law: Unmapping a White Settler Society*, edited by author, 121–156. Toronto, ON: Between the Lines.

Regan, Paulette. 2010. *Unsettling the Settler Within*. Vancouver, BC: UBC Press.

Routledge, Paul. 2012. "Sensuous Solidarities: Emotion, Politics and Performance in the Clandestine Insurgent Rebel Clown Army." *Antipode* 44: 428–452.

Roy, Carole. 2004. *The Raging Grannies: Wild Hats, Cheeky Songs, and Witty Actions for a Better World*. Montreal, QC: Black Rose Books.

Sawchuk, Dana. 2009. "The Raging Grannies: Defying Stereotypes and Embracing Aging through Activism." *Journal of Women & Aging* 21: 171–185.

Sawchuk, Kim. 2009. "Feminism in Waves: Re-imagining a Watery Metaphor." In *Open Boundaries: A Canadian Women's Studies Reader*, edited by Barbara Crow and Lise Gotell, 58–64. Toronto, ON: Pearson.

Simpson, Leanne. 2008. *Lighting the Eighth Fire*. Winnipeg, MB: Arbeiter Ring Publishing.

Simpson, Leanne. 2011. *Dancing on Our Turtle's Back: Stories of Nishnaabeg Re-creation, Resurgence, and a New Emergence*. Winnipeg, MB: Arbeiter Ring Publishing.

Snelgrove, Corey, Rita Dhamoon, and Jeff Corntassel. 2014. "Unsettling Settler Colonialism: The Discourse and Politics of Settlers, and Solidarity with Indigenous Nations." *Decolonization: Indigeneity, Education, & Society* 3: 1–32.

Springer, Kimberly. 2002. "Third Wave Black Feminism?" *Signs* 27(4): 1059–1082.

Sundberg, Juanita. 2007. "Reconfiguring North-South Solidarity: Critical Reflections on Experiences of Transnational Resistance." *Antipode*, Journal Compilation 39: 144–166.

sy, waaseyaa'sin christine. 2012. "Everyday Cry: Feeling through Ogitchidaakwe's Hunger Strike" [blog post]. *Anishinaabewiziwin* (December 2012). www.giizismoon. wordpress.com/2012/12/27/everyday-cry-feeling-through-ogitchidaakwes-hunger -strike/

Tripp, Aili Mari. 2013. "The Evolution of Transnational Feminisms: Consensus, Conflict, and New Dynamics." In *Gender and Women's Studies in Canada: Critical Terrain*, edited by Margaret Hobbs and Carla Rice, 691–702. Toronto, ON: Women's Press.

Walia, Harsha. 2012. "Moving beyond a Politics of Solidarity towards a Practice of Decolonization." In *Organize! Building from the Local for Global Justice*, edited by Aziz Choudry, Jill Hanley, and Eric Shragge, 240–253. Toronto, ON: Between the Lines.

Wallace, Rick. 2014. *Merging Fires: Grassroots Peacebuilding between Indigenous and non-Indigenous Peoples*. Winnipeg, MB: Fernwood Publishing.

REFLECTION 4

Learning to Listen: A Half Century of Walking with First Peoples

Jean Koning

Jean Koning, who was 94 years old at the time of writing, is a white settler woman who has dedicated much of her life to supporting the struggles of First Peoples. In this piece,[1] she reflects on the most profound learning of her half century of work: the need to keep quiet and listen. Jean has walked with First Peoples in her work with the Anglican Church of Canada, through the Kawartha Truth and Reconciliation Support Group, and through her quiet listening, writing, and organizing in the various communities in Ontario in which she has lived. She is recognized by many as an important settler voice in the struggle for decolonization. Collections of her writings and records of her work are held in the Anglican Church of Canada's archives and in the Trent University Library and Archives. Jean's reflections echo and extend many of the themes of the previous chapters, engaging with what it means to work with First Peoples in a critical and deeply personal way. Adapted with permission from an entry on her blog, Koning's Komments, she explores why learning to listen is a radical act in the process of healing and reconciliation.

Boozhoo. Aanii.
Jean ndi-zhinikaaz.
Windsor ndoo-njibaa.
Peterborough megwaa ndoo-daa.
Zhaaginaashii-kwe ndaaw.
Gchi-gbeying ngii-wiiji-mosemaag Nishinaabeg.
Ndoo- gjitoon waa-zhi Nishnaabemyaanh.
Aapiji go ngchi-nendam miinwaa waabminaa.

I introduce myself in the Ojibwe language to honour the Anishinaabekwewag who have been willing to teach me their beautiful language, beginning with Elder Rose Peltier who gave me my first Odawa lessons in Wikwemikong almost 50 years ago. Since coming to Peterborough in 2004, I have been happy to be able to meet her grand-nephew, Beedahbun, who lives and works here. And that is but a small part of the story of how the circle of my life continues to bring me happy memories of the past.

There are many things I could tell you about the past half century during which I have been walking in solidarity with the First Peoples, and how long it has taken me to reach my current understanding of the meaning of my relationship with First Peoples brothers and sisters, but I shall speak of only one experience.

Until I stopped driving, about five years ago, I spent a lot of hours in my car, which I always found was a good time to think. One day, I was thinking about how much time I have spent with First Peoples. I thought of how sorry I am about the devastating effects that my church and my governments have had on their lives; of how I have tried to show that I am sorry by standing with them, and speaking out for justice on their behalf; of trying to help my people to understand just how badly damaged the relationship between us is.

And as I thought about all this, I suddenly had an "aha" moment.

I thought: But why do I think that I have to be the one to fix things? Why do I think that I have to be the one who cares for others by taking the lead, and telling other people what to do? If there is one thing I have learned during the years that I have been in relationship with First Peoples—it is that the First Peoples are totally capable of caring for themselves. They have leaders among them who have so much knowledge, so much experience, and so much wisdom that has been handed down to them from their Elders—they have everything it takes to give leadership to their people—and more than that, they have the ability to give leadership to me and to my people.

Now many of you may think that this is a no-brainer, but I admit that to me, it was a revelation. Maybe it comes from being the eldest in a family of four children, used to assuming leadership in that small community. Or maybe I'm just a slow learner, which I know in many ways I am. I'm still trying to learn how to manage my computer—not to mention learning how to speak in Ojibwe.

But for me, that moment was a turning point in my life. Since then, especially when I am in meetings where First Peoples are present, I remember to say to myself: Okay, Koning, keep quiet and listen. What are the First Peoples saying? How are they offering to take the leadership role? And can I put myself in the position of being willing to accept that leadership?

It has offered me a whole new way of life! But—and again I have to ask for mercy here—that role does not come easily to a privileged white woman like me who has so often assumed a leadership role whether I was asked to or not. My British ancestry hasn't helped, either—my Victorian grandmother imparted to my child's mind a lot of the "Rule, Britannia" history that she grew up with.

But I believe that this is one of the most important insights from my experience I can share with you today. However, for some of us—like me—it may have to be an intellectual exercise—one that we have to go through in our minds before it can reach our hearts. But when you get to that point, you will then be able to join in the water walks or Idle No More events to appreciate the way in which First Peoples are offering us leadership across Canada—going out among the people in the streets and shopping malls, and even at blockades and in protest marches—to sing and dance and to offer the hand of friendship that will allow us all to join the Circle—to restore health to Mother Earth and to one another.

I pray that you will not have to take as long as I have to reach your place in that Circle.

Thanks for listening,

Jean Koning

NOTE

1. This piece is adapted from Jean's blog, *Koning's Komments*, "Panel Presentation at Pre-Gathering of Elders—Enweying," March 10, 2015, www.koningskomments.blogspot.ca/2015_03_01_archlve.html.

PART III

EMBODYING

POEM III

This Mouth

Niambi Leigh

Born in Jamaica and living in Nogojiwanong, Niambi is a poet in their 20s whose work explores the intersections of race, emotions, and mental illness. Their poetry is lyrical, deeply felt, and always rooted in storytelling. Niambi's work reminds you that the act of breathing is an expression of strength.

This mouth still kisses my mother.
Lies fly through its teeth,
And it spews tweaked trauma poems.
this mouth keeps you warm at night.
lives between the lines,
metaphors makes this mouth easy to hide.
In darkness this mouth wrestles for smiles.
it sings sunshine when blue,
This mouth is bold truth unfolding, is thorny to touch,
It warms cold hearts, Laughs curse words and abuse.
This mouth manipulates, shakes and screams.
Every so often this mouth licks spoonfuls of honey,
sucked dicks for money,
This mouth tells truths that rhyme.
It disowns its mother often, wonders if its daddy has daughter issues,
And is the reason your husband and money are missing.
On saturdays this mouth starts war fires
On sundays sings church songs in pews.

This mouth has been through a lot.

Kissed but never kept, felt up and left regretting,

forgetting some kisses is hard.

this mouth tries not to remember, so this mouth doesn't sleep.

this mouth never had a chance.

shadows claw at lips curled in silent screams.

This mouth is hungry, chooses eating over breathing

it is bank account starved empty.

This mouth doesn't like itself.

but it is resilient

smiles sweeten its speech,

tongue tasting thoughts traced on pages past.

teeth gnawing at emotions no longer useful.

this mouth transcends, sees value in voices speaking true.

this mouth loves like early morning, laughs lilacs laid out,

dances dandelions in the wind.

this mouth, attached to this tongue, these teeth

brings you poems like these, finds freedom in works on stages

And is no longer ashamed of experiences survived,

It is thanks to this mouth that this human is still alive.

INTRODUCTION TO PART III

Embodying

Sally Chivers

This book celebrates many ways to act for social change that do not *require* tirelessness, pert and alert body-minds, and physical marches. In doing so, it opens up new conversations about embodiment and activisms. In Part III, activists and scholars write about forms of visibility that are even more choreographed than others featured throughout the volume. They think about the connections among aging, embodiment, and activism through explicit performances. Keeping in mind performance theorist Peggy Phelan's pivotal claim that it would be a mistake to assume that increased visibility renders increased power, the pieces in this section show that there is a creatively productive difference between what an audience perceives and who a performer is. These authors show how dangerous it would be to assume that what we "see" is what we get.

Embodiment—the negotiation between the body and the social world—indubitably shifts with age. This is where *Aging Activisms* comes in. This book declines the ableist move of declaring that aging is not a disability while, at the same time, refusing to conflate aging with disability. It is not about how aging with or into disability necessarily constrains or changes activisms. Instead, it raises questions about what activisms based on aging and by activists of all ages can learn from the disability movement and from critical disability scholarship. While not all the pieces in this section explicitly address what readers might conventionally think of as disability, they each in their own way offer an opportunity to think about what disability offers the social and cultural world when it unmoors the body from a medical framework that serves largely political and economic goals. Older adults can benefit from a way of thinking that reimagines bodily difference beyond notions of cure, as can we all.

In her activist performance poem, "I Am Not One of The," Cheryl Marie Wade (1992), aka "The Queen Mother of Gnarly," drolly describes her self-dubbed "crip" self (she lived with juvenile rheumatoid arthritis) in public as "a sock in the eye with a gnarled fist." She exposes not only what feminist film makers label the "male gaze"—a way of looking that assumes "females" are there for visual pleasure—but also the "normate gaze"—a way of looking that situates some disabled people as inviting rude public stares or fearful avoidance so as not to seem to ogle. As Rosemarie Garland Thomson (1997, 25–26) points out, Wade calls attention to how some people can never luxuriate in the possibilities of invisibility. Wade inhabits her adamant visibility to challenge the efforts of people who try to look away from bodily difference, including through euphemistic terms such as "physically challenged" and "differently abled." Wade's challenge, foundational to the North American disability movement, to fully behold her is echoed and taken up throughout this section. How do older people, often rendered invisible, embrace an embodiment that invites a gaze they may have once resisted? How do they transmogrify that unwelcome attention into a chance for reimagining the body-mind?

In part because of assumptions about visibility, the relationship between old age and disability is productively thorny. Old age is, of course, not equivalent to disability, despite what the popular press often tries to say that an aging population will cost the world in the first half of the 21st century. But the proliferation of active-aging discourse—the Fitbit (non)revolution—comes from and plays on a deep social fear that old age means living with disability. Thinking this through requires care because it would be harmful and inaccurate to deny that growing old is associated with disability, in the popular imagination and in lived experience. And to claim an inherent link between aging and disability would appropriate the experience of people with disabilities who have come to inhabit a positionality in the world as the result of social responses to their radical visibility.

The two chapters and two reflections in this section offer ways to connect explicit performances to uses of "the body as a vehicle of social agency," which is one definition of embodiment (Gilleard and Higgs 2015, 17). Their explorations of performance as a venue for social change immerse them in questions of explicit visibility.

Before writing Chapter 5, Nadine Changfoot, Mary Anne Ansley, and Andrea Dodsworth met through a project that sought to make and screen highly visual digital stories to counter marginalizing stories of disability. Their chapter focuses on their subsequent coming together in quieter, less visible ways as a form of support to each other in their activisms. Together they work towards what David T. Mitchell and Sharon L. Snyder (2015, 5) have called "*meaningful* inclusion," which presents disability "as providing alternative values for living" in deliberate opposition to neo-liberal gestures to forms of superficial inclusion that do not result in social change. The authors' less public relationship-building, the backstage of their activisms, became the foundation of their work for social change. In particular they could safely explore the differences in their positions in intimate ways, doing the important work of talking through what it means to act from the various intersections of disability, aging, poverty, racialization, and Indigeneity. The co-writing process reflected within and productive of their chapter is in line with this book's ethos of collaboration.

In Chapter 6, "The Raging Grannies versus the Sexperts: Performing Humour to Resist Compulsory (Hetero)Sexuality," Marlene Goldman, May Chazan, and Melissa Baldwin display how the Raging Grannies' flamboyant performances mock social expectations for old women to comply, quietly and off-to-the-side. The Grannies' subversive stagings of aging sexuality, for example, require a combination of deep self-reflection while holding a murky mirror up to a world that does not expect them to stand up and sing. The authors show how, through their performance of "Geriatric Sexpot," the Raging Grannies humorously assert their autonomy to decide for themselves whether, when, and how they will engage as sexual beings in later life. Their provocative, sassy performance challenges narratives of old age as asexual and aging as decline but without overplaying the sexual older woman. The lyrics mock the so-called "experts" who place pressure on older women to remain sexually active and desiring (heterosexual) intercourse well into "old" old age, challenging the flip side of the decline narrative: the ableist and sexist package of sex and desire as part of "successful aging." The Grannies connect these regulating discourses to the pressures they experienced throughout their lives, both to remain virgins and to engage in "free love." In this way, they bring a lifecourse perspective to their performance of subversion, resisting the regulatory power of compulsory (hetero)sexuality.

In Reflection 5, "Words, Work, and Wonder—Poeting toward Midlife," Ziy von B offers a deeply first-person and yet communal account of their experience growing into and through activisms, showcasing how the intimate performance of spoken word has a distinctly visible form, but one that relies on often invisible contributions by family and friends. Their work speaks to what disability activist performer jes sachse calls "art's objective" of "*movement through.*" As sachse (2016, 205) explains, "the feminist dream of utopia or 'the rev'—the revolution—is always already realized as conceptual actions disrupt the colonially embedded frameworks." That the onstage work needs the offstage work, and vice versa, as described in this reflection, aids this disruption while also illustrating the collaboration central to the form and content of this book.

In Reflection 6, "(In)Visible: Photographing Older Women," Maureen Murphy and Ruth Steinberg explain their glorious photographic art, which exemplifies the inextricability of art and visibility within this book. These pictures reconfigure the gaze at aging bodies that exceed the cultural frames expected of older women and non-binary people by reducing context, allowing viewers to map and transform their assumptions about aging and gender. They refuse the normate gaze while enticing the resistant glance. The photos also challenge limited understandings of what comprises politics for activism. They offer what has recently come to be called "artivism" to emphasize the importance of cultural forms to movements for social change.

Collectively, this section illuminates and bends the narrow frame into which we are all pressured to contort our body-minds to match the expectations of a sexist, ableist, racist, ageist world. Reading about the production and reception of Changfoot, Ansley, and Dodsworth's digital stories, following von B's activist story that incorporates spoken word poetry excerpts, imagining the Raging Grannies performing, and contemplating Murphy and Steinberg's photographs—such acts show how the conjunction of aging and performance is "characterized by a flow of energy, and a way of being alive, that negates fixity," as Petra Kuppers (2013) declares of disability performance. This flexibility animates *Aging Activisms*, infused with hope for social change through thoughtfully visible, embodied action.

RECOMMENDED READINGS

Kelly, Christine, and Michael Orsini. Eds. 2016. *Mobilizing Metaphor: Art, Culture, and Disability Activism in Canada*. Vancouver, BC: UBC Press.

Kuppers, Petra. 2011. *Disability Culture and Community Performance: Find a Strange and Twisted Shape*. New York: Springer.

Kutz-Flamenbaum, Rachel. 2007. "Code Pink, Raging Grannies, and the Missile Dick Chicks: Feminist Performance Activism in the Contemporary Anti-War Movement." *NWSA Journal* 19(1): 89–105.

Lichtenfels, Peter, and John Rouse. Eds. 2013. *Performance, Politics and Activism*. New York: Springer.

Marshall, Barbara L. 2002. "'Hard Science': Gendered Constructions of Sexual Dysfunction in the 'Viagra Age.'" *Sexualities* 5(2): 131–158.

Matlok-Ziemann, Ellen. 2014. "'Old Women that Will Not Be Kept Away': Undermining Ageist Discourse with Invisibility and Performance." In *Alive and Kicking at All Ages: Cultural Constructions of Health and Life Course Identity*, edited by Barbara Ratzenböck, Roberta Maierhofer, and Ulla Kriebernegg, 259–273. Bielefeld, Germany: Transcript-Verlag.

Phelan, Peggy. 2003. *Unmarked: The Politics of Performance*. London: Routledge.

Sandahl, Carrie, and Phillip Auslander. 2009. *Bodies in Commotion: Disability and Performance*. Ann Arbor: University of Michigan Press.

SUGGESTED MULTIMEDIA AND ONLINE RESOURCES

The Penelope Project: www.vimeo.com/21302830

GeriActors and Friends: www.vimeo.com/geriactors

Cracked: New Light on Dementia: www.youtube.com/watch?v=v-hS2CnCmjs

Project Re•Vision: www.projectrevision.ca/videos/

RECAA Flash Mob: www.recaa.ca/recaa-flash-mob/

Cheryl Marie Wade, poetry performances:
- "Here": www.youtube.com/watch?v=G-lsnkhTtLo
- "Culture Rap": www.youtube.com/watch?v=GYA0nd-_D_o

Ruth Steinberg, *What the Body Remembers*: www.ruthsteinbergphotographs.com/what-the-body-remembers-photos#0

Maureen Murphy, *(In)Visible*: www.maureenmurphy.ca/PROJECTS/INVISIBLE/

REFERENCES

Gilleard, Chris, and Paul Higgs. 2015. "Aging, Embodiment, and the Somatic Turn." *Age, Culture, Humanities: An Interdisciplinary Journal* 2: 17–33.

Kuppers, Petra. 2013. *Disability and Contemporary Performance: Bodies on the Edge*. London: Routledge.

Mitchell, David T., and Sharon L. Snyder. 2015. *The Biopolitics of Disability: Neoliberalism, Able-nationalism, and Peripheral Embodiment*. Ann Arbor: University of Michigan Press.

sachse, jes. 2016. "Crip the Light Fantastic: Art as Liminal Emancipatory Practice in the Twenty-First Century," in *Mobilizing Metaphor: Art, Culture, and Disability Activism in Canada*, edited by Christine Kelly and Michael Orsini. Vancouver, BC: UBC Press.

Thomson, Rosemarie Garland. 1997. *Extraordinary Bodies: Figuring Physical Disability in American Culture and Literature*. New York: Columbia University Press.

Wade, Cheryl. 1992 (reprinted 2014). "I Am Not One of The," *New Mobility*: 21. www.newmobility.com/2014/04/three-iconic-voices/

CHAPTER 5

Strengthening Our Activisms by Creating Intersectional Spaces for the Personal, the Professional, Disability, and Aging[1]

Nadine Changfoot, Mary Anne Ansley, and Andrea Dodsworth

While there are emerging areas of scholarship bringing to light activisms around both aging and disability, these continue within largely separate spheres, with work on aging activisms focussing primarily on older women, and disability activisms on younger or middle-age adults. Analyses of the Raging Grannies have gained attention (Roy 2007, 2004; D. Sawchuk 2009; see also Chapters 4 and 6), as have the activisms of highly organized seniors' interest groups with socioeconomic resources (Holladay and Coombs 2004)—what is sometimes termed "chequebook activism" (Williamson 1998). Yet, older women are activists in many other ways too, as this volume shows. They occupy diverse and multiple positions that include, intersect, and extend beyond the "grandmother role," and they include women on the cusp of being labelled as old. Older women's activisms that are on a more modest scale with smaller audiences (i.e., activisms that reach audiences in ways other than through participation in organizations, protests, rallies, and marches) are less recognized, perhaps being understood as (too) ordinary and thus "justifiably" glossed over. These diverse ways of working for change remain at the edges of activist scholarship.

Similarly, disability scholarship has tended to focus on the broad approaches of disability activism that involve making rights- and socially-based demands of the state (Prince 2012). Scholars have considered disability activisms organizing through non-profits (Hutchison et al. 2007), making claims based on the Canadian Charter of Rights and Freedoms (Peters 2003), and engaging in consultations to create the Accessibility for Ontarians with Disabilities Act (Kitchin and Wilton 2003). Christine Kelly and Michael Orsini's (2016) edited collection also brings to light important disability activism at the intersection of disability arts and culture. Still, disability activisms tend to tacitly assume younger disability-identified activists, reflecting that disability studies have yet to address aging fully. This implies that disability is independent of aging even though people with disabilities *age*, and people age *into* disability.

While there are emerging accounts of activisms at the intersection of aging and disability (e.g., Bartlett 2014), more are needed, particularly with attention to understanding the nuances of this work, or what are sometimes called the "backstage" components. Backstage components are the often-invisible physical and emotional dimensions of activisms, the components that sometimes require a slower tempo than the typically hectic pace of organizing and participating in public actions, protests, and rallies (Bartlett 2014) and other ways of acting (Butler 2014). By not providing multiple and diverse accounts of activisms at the intersection of aging and disability, existing scholarship leaves largely intact several limiting narratives. First, youth-centred disability narratives produce and reinforce understandings of disability as beginning in childhood and ending at middle age, or as having been overcome, cured, or eliminated (Rice et al. 2015; Changfoot and Rice, forthcoming). Second, such accounts preserve depictions of aging as grim downward decline, or as change that can and should be successfully navigated (Rowe and Kahn, 2015), in keeping with the ableist norms that inform "successful aging" discourses (Martinson and Berridge, 2015), as discussed in the book's introductory chapter. Third, these narratives propel the framing of activisms as primarily public acts and performances, with the risk of portraying these as rather effortless.

In this chapter, we bring to light our own processes of disability activism. In particular, we bring forward the behind-the-scenes (or the backstage) of our activisms, which have engaged with and been shaped by many dimensions of our contexts, including but not limited to our aging embodiments (as three women in our 40s and 50s). Nadine is an associate professor at Trent University. She is a person of Chinese-Canadian background living in the predominantly white, homogenous city of Peterborough/Nogojiwanong,[2] and she has the experience of caring for two parents with disabilities; her work involves partnering with people with disabilities, members of First Nations, older-adult identified women, and queer and trans individuals to create and screen their digital stories to wide audiences, generating knowledge for social change at the edges of the academy. Mary Anne is a Peterborough resident and Ojibwa woman who has lived with a disability—spina bifida—from birth. She is a single mother of two boys who live with disabilities; she lives on a government disability pension and is an activist and advocate for survivors of abuse, as well as for her boys. Andrea has lived with a wheelchair since she was 12 years old. She also lives on a government disability pension, while she works tirelessly in the City of Peterborough to make the community more accessible for people living with disabilities.

From our backstage process, we have learned the importance of what we refer to as "affirmatively becoming-with" one another as disability activists, something we see as vital for both our continued work and our community together. We understand becoming-with as a relating-together, where we needed to become much more attuned to considerations of disability and aging without separating these experiences. For us, this has meant understanding the personal needs associated with disability, aging, and each of our personal and professional contexts. It has meant working toward safer spaces and a slower tempo, which was needed at certain times, not only because of our different needs (e.g., advocacy schedules for Mary Anne and Andrea, university schedule for Nadine, and physical needs related to disability) but also because it takes time to develop a deeper understanding of our becoming-with together and our *affective* needs as they are informed by our bodily vulnerabilities (Butler 2014).

Our activisms, which we increasingly understand to be at the intersection of disability and aging, even while we do not explicitly name it as such, emerge from a collaborative academic-community research initiative called Project Re•Vision, and specifically from a sub-project within this called "Mobilizing New Meanings of Disability and Difference," which sought to shift perceptions of disability in health care.[3] As part of this project, we worked together in a five-day multimedia workshop to create two to three minute videos, which pair audio recordings of personal narratives with visuals (photographs, videos, artwork, and more). Nadine co-coordinated the workshop with a team of Re•Vision facilitators; Mary Anne and Andrea made their digital stories (videos).[4] After the workshop ended, we decided to continue meeting together to advocate for accessibility by screening Mary Anne's and Andrea's videos; we refer to our group as Women Building Inclusion.

While disability was initially centred in our activisms, we came to realize that we needed to consider aging, as part of what Bartlett (2014) refers to as "backstage preparations," in order to continue our activisms with a different tempo and messaging. Our disability activism has morphed into disability-with-and-into-aging activisms in subtle ways. Below, we introduce how we met and the different roles we have played in our work together. We note the productive tensions we have experienced, the importance of attending to both aging and disability in order for us to keep going, the steps we have taken, and our further involvement together in disability, aging, activisms, and research. There are also dimensions of our lived experience not brought into discussion here but that are of intersectional relevance. Specifically, racialization and Indigeneity have taken a backseat to disability and aging, in large part because the initial purpose for which we met emphasized disability without full consideration of these complex and multiply-experienced positionalities. We have become increasingly aware of how our centring of disability can subsume our experiences of Indigeneity and racialization, and perhaps even recreate certain racial hierarchies and impairments (Gorman 2016). While we do not entirely address this systemic pattern in this chapter, by recognizing here the need to address it in a fuller way, we are taking an incremental step to reckon with this power dynamic.

MEETING THROUGH PROJECT RE•VISION AND BUILDING OUR METHOD

In fall 2012, we met through a Project Re•Vision digital storytelling workshop held at the local YWCA in Peterborough/Nogojiwanong. Since making our videos, we have screened Mary Anne and Andrea's videos in presentations to health care students, faculty, staff, graduate and undergraduate students, and health care professionals, as well as elected provincial and federal representatives. In these presentations, Mary Anne and Andrea speak to their own videos, telling audiences of their experiences of living with disabilities and on ODSP (Ontario Disability Support Program); Nadine provides the Re•Vision research framework and recounts the process by which the videos were made. In preparation for the presentations, Nadine offers questions to Mary Anne and Andrea to consider; ultimately, Mary Anne and Andrea decide what to share. In our meetings, Nadine transcribes each person's thoughts verbatim and repeats aloud what she has written, often leading to further rounds of discussion and providing a larger context from scholarship in disability, gender and women's studies, aging, and political economy. Mary Anne—who identifies as a survivor of domestic abuse, as the leader of Survivors Network of Peterborough, and as someone who lives with spina bifida—contributes reflections and knowledge of domestic abuse and of the experiences of survivors. Andrea offers reflections and experiences as an accessibility advocate in city policy and planning, as a board member of the Peterborough Council of Persons with Disabilities, and as adviser to the Peterborough Downtown Business Improvement Association.

We would like to share and note three productive tensions that emerged in and continue to inform our discussions: 1) maintaining respect for each person's knowledge and experience, 2) translating our knowledge and lived experience into a scholarly context, and 3) working together while responding to and managing our differences and different tempos. The first tension that we have managed in the writing of this chapter is making sure we are all on the same page in terms of how each of our knowledges is presented. "I don't want to be a specimen," Mary Anne asserts firmly. She understandably does not want the experience of being the object of able-bodied stares and put-downs repeated in our work together. Nadine provides clarification on the principle that each of our knowledges are being brought to the chapter according to a disability-justice framework (Rice, Chandler, and Changfoot 2016). For us, working together, this means that we recognize differential abilities and needs in a respectful way that does not belittle or diminish abilities and needs but instead ensures that each person's contributions and experiences are *fully* represented. The second tension involves building trust among the three of us, as very diverse women. Mary Anne and Andrea placed a high degree of trust in Nadine, the academic among us, to translate our lived experiences into a scholarly context in order to make clearer the knowledge we created by working together. Nadine prefers to undertake this form of writing together rather than writing *on* or *about* Mary Anne and Andrea.[5] By collaborating in this way, we disrupt the hierarchy between university researcher and non-researcher in a way that also resonates with the overarching epistemological aims of the book and is echoed in Chapter 8. A third tension relates to the different tempos and cultures of university and non-university contexts brought into the space of our meetings. We have each found the translation of academic, survivor, and city activist practices important to address so that our activisms and *becoming-with* one another could develop our processes, our language of communication, and the presentations we give together.

In the next section, we each encapsulate our activisms briefly through first-person accounts. These provide context, attending both to our differential abilities as we continue to work together and to our decisions to open a deeper understanding of our circumstances and contexts, find a slower tempo when needed, and create a safer space to discuss our changing embodiments.

Andrea Dodsworth: Accessibility Activist since Age 12, 44 at Time of Writing

I have been an activist since I was 12 years old, and I became more aware that I had already been an activist when I met Rick Hansen.[6] I was experiencing a low point in my life because I was coming to terms with the knowledge that a wheelchair was always going to be part of my life, having been told this fact after surgery. I wasn't really prepared to accept my new piece of equipment into my life, just yet, but I learned and now ... it's almost like I'm married to it. Still, even before the age of 12, I *knew* I was an activist at heart. I had to fight against being removed from the "regular" classroom because my wheelchair did not fit "properly" under the desks. I was forced to undergo testing to prove that my disability did not affect my intellect. I won this battle. At the same time, "activist" was not how I thought of myself even though I knew deep down inside that I was: *I think I knew.* Meeting Rick Hansen, and his encouragement to me that I was and would continue to be an activist, created a *click.* He told me that I could [do it] … I think I knew. Because I had won my fight to stay in the "regular" classroom, I knew that I had a right to be in the world. I knew that life wasn't always going to be easy, but I would make it so that I could get around … I would make it so that it would be easier and I would leave my mark on the world someday. Because I have learned that every person has something to teach—I even found that on a poster one day and brought it home.

Even while I knew I was an activist, being recognized, encouraged, and affirmed by someone like Rick Hansen supported my self-understanding as a person living with a disability. I have known that I want to make accessibility increasingly a reality throughout my lifetime. I have learned that, no matter how long it takes me and how long I have had my disability, I can make it different in my life and other people's lives and it doesn't matter whether they have a disability or not. They're still going to be able to take something from what I have done or something that I left behind; there's always going to be my mark left behind. I may not see it now but other people might see it later because I have had other people tell me that I'm special in my own way even though I don't see it.

Mary Anne's Activism, 57 at Time of Writing

I have been a lifelong activist for myself and my family, addressing disability discrimination; I consider my current activism to have started in 2011 when I was asked to join the group Survivors Advisory Committee (SAC) of the Peterborough Domestic Abuse Network (PDAN). PDAN wanted a subcommittee composed of women who have experienced abuse to advise professionals working with survivors of abuse about what works and what does not work in terms of support. SAC did projects that included presenting information at tables at events. Initially, there were about 15–18 women. In the first year, the group nearly disintegrated because of internal difficulties. At one point, I was the lone member of the group along with the YWCA support person and the PDAN representative. I persevered to *regrow* the group because I believed in the vision of SAC and what it was doing. After the first year, I carried out interviews with women who wanted to join SAC to make sure they were a good fit to do the work of public education. Eventually, I left SAC to form Survivors Network Peterborough so that men could also join such a group.[7]

After presentations I gave of my experience of domestic abuse, men would approach me, expressing that they wanted to create awareness of surviving domestic abuse from a man's perspective. I decided with some members of SAC to create a new group where men would be welcomed. Similar to SAC, both women and men are interviewed to make sure there is a good fit for the work of raising public awareness. PDAN helped start Survivors Network Peterborough financially. I am currently chair of Survivors Network Peterborough. My activism also includes knowledge dissemination of my experience living with disability into aging, specifically spina bifida. Inseparable from my activism is my spirituality; it motivates me. I have a passion and a heart for those who have to struggle in life—be it physically, financially, emotionally. I feel I want to share my experience of mercy and grace because they helped me let go of a destructive anger that abuse can often leave behind. I also see the injustices in the world. I want to be able to help those who have been on the negative side of that, to try to make their lives easier in whatever I have to give. I know that I can't erase those injustices, but I can do my part.

Nadine's Activism, 52 at Time of Writing

I see myself as having been born into my late mother's desired flow of social change; Lily (my mother) wanted to make a difference for herself, her family, her community, and her new home of Canada into which she was both welcomed and not welcomed, arriving in Toronto in 1964, having left apartheid South Africa. In my own becoming, I see the influence of my mother's visions of a racially harmonious society and the elimination of poverty, especially for Indigenous peoples. I also saw and felt my mother's disheartenment, bitterness, anger, and disappointments from her own experiences of discrimination. She and my late father (Jack) lived with chronic illness; I lived inside and outside disability as carer and advocate starting in childhood.

While I supported my mom's activisms as a child as part of daily life, I became aware *I* was an activist when I was in my 20s. I have participated in protests and marches, been on strike, volunteered and served on boards of anti-poverty and race relations community organizations, and participated in anarchist endeavours that focus on quality-of-life needs, such as food security. I used to feel pressure over how activism should be done. I felt policed and judged for what counts as activism and also, regrettably, participated in that, something I no longer want to do. Now, I believe in, am increasingly open to, and am learning of the endless possibilities of activisms as diverse and unique as each individual and their experiences. My activisms comprise many parts, including education within and outside of the university classroom. Building relationships comes increasingly into focus as part of this work:

relationship- and trust-building takes time and requires attuning to each person's differential needs and abilities. Since 2012, I have viewed my activisms as increasingly intertwined with research, especially through Project Re•Vision and another project, Community First, which is studying how the university can maximize community outcomes for social change through community/campus partnerships.

DISCOVERING THE NEED TO ATTEND TO OUR DIFFERENTIAL ABILITIES

While presentations of our Project Re•Vision videos have been taking place each year since 2013, it became clear in late 2013 and early 2014 that the initial desire and intention to concentrate on screening the videos was not working. When it came to scheduling our "next" meeting, we discerned a palpable hesitancy through affective expressions of longer-than-usual pauses and silences, halting "hmm's" and "ha's" over each person's availability, and the lowering or shifting gazes away from eye contact.

It was "that time," as Judith Butler notes, when "we ha[d] to ask what it is that holds [us] together, what demand is being shared, or what felt sense of injustice and unlovability, what intimation of the possibility of change heightens the collective sense of things" (2014, 106). In "Bodily Vulnerability," Butler brings to light the importance of assembly in venues such as prisons or "slut walks," which are not yet recognized as activist spaces. She points out that bodily vulnerability influences the time and space for the conditions and character of assembly. She refers to smaller assemblies in which principles get elaborated that "can nevertheless produce—or renew—ideals of equality and interdependency that may well be transposed onto larger national and global contexts" (ibid., 107).

Here, we include in this idea of assembly our monthly meet-ups, which took place in accessible, publicly funded spaces and cafés during summer months, and most often in Andrea's home during winter months. Winter months posed challenges around mobility, especially with inconsistent or unreliable snow removal. We also developed greater awareness of bodily needs related to extreme cold and mobility supports, which meant afternoons were better meeting times. These gatherings may be seen (from an able-bodied positionality) to be significantly more modest than organized demonstrations or walks. Yet, they are a necessary condition for the work we do together because they become spaces for our intersectional explorations—the backstage of our activisms. Even so, we realized we were each stretched with our daily/weekly/monthly commitments, experiencing more volume and complexity in each our own lives, as a result of professional, advocacy, and personal commitments, and identifying that we each needed to take care of ourselves relative to individual aging-disability-bodily needs; we came to realize that further conditions needed attention for us to continue.

DEEPER UNDERSTANDING OF ONE ANOTHER'S CIRCUMSTANCES AND CONTEXTS

Taking stock of each person's activities and commitments brought to light a deeper understanding of the challenges we were each facing. Over the course of our meet-ups, Andrea was a member of the City of Peterborough's Accessibility Advisory Committee, a member of the City's Accessible Transit Advisory Sub-committee, the chair for the City's Built Environment Sub-committee, and was serving on the Peterborough Council for Persons with Disabilities. Andrea gives her time voluntarily to these committees, each of which meets at least monthly. Mary Anne was working through some intense organizational-building of the Survivors Network Peterborough, which involved ongoing discussions over difficult issues and working through how to resolve her role with the Peterborough Domestic Abuse Network. Nadine took on the role of acting chair of her department in winter 2014, became chair that summer, was co-leading two research projects, and, overall, was on a steep learning curve. Additionally, each of us also had significant time commitments regarding our respective families and/or individual well-being.

NEED FOR SLOWER TEMPO

In light of our loads, we questioned whether our monthly meetings, with the additional work, time, and effort they required, were perhaps better left aside. Yet, we enjoyed meeting, learning, and working together; we acknowledged a desire to keep meeting. The benefits of our presentations were tangible for each of us and meaningful for the difference we discerned from audience feedback. We recognized we needed different ways of *becoming-with* and being together at a slower tempo, especially during the winter.

In spring 2014, we decided to focus on our own specific needs rather than only giving presentations. In discussion, the kinds of responsibilities we held became clearer; we wanted to develop greater awareness of these and feel safer to speak openly. Nadine was concerned that an exclusive focus on advocacy and presentations would cause our desire to continue meeting to plummet, in light of the responsibilities and life challenges we each held. One of us proposed that the space become a place where each could check-in, in more full and whole ways than our previous focus had allowed. After consideration and input from each person, we found a consensus to reorient our meetings as a space of revitalization, a space for supporting one another in each our own responsibilities and activisms, and a space to allow advocacy opportunities to emerge more organically through our networks.

SAFER SPACES TO DISCUSS STEREOTYPES AND CHANGING EMBODIMENT

We also learned that we needed to create a safer space for sharing the experiences whereby we each sometimes feel challenged, shredded, frustrated, and anxious. We came to agree that our inner resources were becoming depleted from daily responsibilities and that our meet-ups would support building our inner selves to feel stronger in our roles. We continued to check-in at the beginning of our meetings and, slowly, we began to share more candidly what was on our minds and what was felt in our bodies and hearts.

We engaged in discussions around our bodily vulnerabilities and the challenges of our work with a deeper level of specificity and description. We began to understand the entrenched dimensions of disability and aging stereotypes and to talk them over in ways that allowed us to position our agency differently and more effectively. We thought through options, and supported one another in ways we did not feel were available in other spaces of our lives. Changes in embodiment related to aging with disability also became lively subjects of discussion. During our meetings, health topics would come up. We spoke of difficulties encountered when discussing bodily changes, including those related to (peri)menopause, with health care providers and family: our symptoms not being believed or being trivialized; our sense that certain options were neither made available nor facilitated; and an absence of compassion or counsel to adapt, which we took tacitly to mean, "tough it out." Sharing our stories, we would laugh and sigh over our changing embodiments and the responses to them.

SHARING TO STRENGTHEN CONVICTIONS, BE UNDERSTOOD, AND KEEP REACHING OUTWARD

In light of the changes we made to our meet-up goals, we each feel better. We feel more incentive and motivation. Sharing increases our comfort level and self-acceptance. Andrea notes: "It makes me feel good that I can share things.... [It] makes me feel like I'm doing good when I hear Mary Anne's and Nadine's input to what I've done and experienced." When we hear negative comments about the work we are doing, it helps to discuss the possible ableism, ageism, sexism, and racism underlying these comments. This allows us to better understand the power relations involved and to think of possible responses for the next time. As one of us noted, "I can stand up for myself," and another, "I feel stronger moving forward."

Having a space to share the affective and emotional dimensions of our experiences is important. Our own professional interactions for advocacy and resistance do not allow the time and space for sharing difficult experiences. Words do not come easily to describe challenging experiences, with their newness and shock, and time is needed to process and give words to the emotional impact. Sharing these kinds of experiences—experiences that are difficult to render into language—strengthens our capacities in the work we do. Mary Anne notes:

> We can understand one another on a level that you don't get professionally. When you're with people that have experienced being an outsider [and] not belonging, you know people understand you. You spend a lot of time and energy convincing people [as an advocate and educator]. I'd been going four to five years to monthly meetings of an advocacy organization for survivors and I felt they didn't really know me until I did the presentation where I shared the video I made.

Nadine notes that, because we have shared experiences of disability with one another since 2014 and we continue to do so, we feel confident in ourselves and in our togetherness. Discussing our differences and the affective and emotional dimensions of our advocacy and professional lives, and hearing acceptance and feeling compassion from one another, allows us to feel even stronger *to be ourselves*. This sharing is *itself* important knowledge creation, the behind-the-scenes to our presentations.

GROWING RECOGNITION OF THE VALUE OF DISABILITY EXPERIENCE AND KNOWLEDGE

For Re•Vision-specific presentations, Mary Anne and Andrea receive honourariums. When Nadine learned they are also invited to give presentations of their lived experiences several times per year, she asked whether they received honoraria; they said, "We receive a thank you," and they physically motioned receiving a pat on the back. While important to their audiences, the value of the knowledge that Mary Anne and Andrea hold remains largely unacknowledged, beyond its symbolic value. The realities of living on ODSP and below the poverty line are largely kept invisible from discussions of accessibility or survivorship. The Ontario government claws back any earned income above the allowable $200 per month. The system of ODSP maintains, indeed deepens, poverty and debility in neoliberal times[8] by denying quality of life, and access to employment and a decent living. As a result of our increasingly intimate knowledges of each other's lives, Nadine began to regularly advocate for honoraria for Andrea and Mary Anne, leveraging her own position as an academic and researcher to impress on others in similar positions to herself the importance of valuing these women not only symbolically but also monetarily.

Following our presentations, we have witnessed and been part of productive discussions, reaching for possibilities that suspend stable binaries of disabled and abled and the meanings associated with each. Nadine's capacity has become enlarged to envision scholarly partnership with Mary Anne and Andrea, to contend with access at a historically inaccessible campus, and to advocate for recognition of disability expertise and experience through negotiating honoraria from within the university.

Our collaboration has regularly brought Mary Anne and Andrea into spaces within the university, and particularly into communities of scholars who value their time, their lived experiences with disability, and their advocacy—including some communities that also see the importance of justly paying people for their time and expertise. For example, our collaboration has connected us with May Chazan's Aging Activisms project and brought us to co-authoring this chapter.[9] These experiences are creating new spaces of agency for Mary Anne and Andrea as engaged participants, while extending our *becoming-with* one another that increasingly includes in-depth conversations around the experience of aging with and into disability. In these conversations, we find ourselves more willing to open up and share with one another, and better understanding the relationship among aging, disability, and poverty. We increasingly understand and are able to discuss how social and economic systems erase aging, disabled, low-income, and poor women through barriers (e.g., the decreased reliability of prompt snow removal and mobility through the city during winter months, and the absence of roles for people with disabilities—employment—in the current economy). These intersectional experiences are made visible, explored, taken seriously, and heard by Nadine, who supports Mary Anne and Andrea in their advocacy and activism, as well as in their personal lives.

CONCLUSION

Our relationship started professionally, through research, and we wanted to continue to meet for advocacy purposes. In the first two years, our meetings were more formal in tone; in subsequent years, we have become closer activist-collaborators and friends. We have created a space that did not exist prior in our lives, a space for sharing experiences in an exploratory way, mindful of disability, and increasingly with attention to aging, as well as intersections of class, race, and Indigeneity. In our monthly meetings, we aim to centre our differences candidly, sometimes affectively, not always having the words to describe sensations and inchoate thoughts, but accept how important it is to bring the experiences that have been buried or hidden into sound and words. This has taken time and trust. We especially desire to create a meaningful sense of belonging for those parts of ourselves that remain excluded, hidden, or marginalized in communities in which we participate. We want to make a difference in our respective communities for our own and others' belonging. When we began to meet, we trusted that each of our respective activisms focused on making a difference even if, as Andrea says, the concrete or tangible differences might only be experienced and/or enjoyed in the future; not by ourselves, but by others.

We took part in the Re•Vision digital storytelling workshops each for our own reasons, yet a common connector was that we wanted our stories to be told in the pursuit of positive change. We did not know each other prior to the research, nor did we conceive that we would continue our relationship as collaborators, advocates, and friends, and that these would become entangled in productive ways and with productive tensions. We have seen ripple-out effects in our presentations to students, faculty, and health care professionals. Mary Anne and Andrea are increasingly recognized and affirmed for their respective differences by individual faculty, students, and staff in the university. They are becoming seen as more capacious and having more capacity, disrupting dominant stereotypes of disability and difference as pitiable or as "sites of no future" (Kafer 2013), and instead demonstrating a lifelong and continued history of agency and activisms. At the same time, we find ourselves increasingly considering aging in our meet-ups and in the other activities and projects we do together.

Our diverse experiences of the personal, professional, disability, difference, and aging connect us in our meetings and the activisms we share. New narratives arise and bring to light what cannot be said in each of our personal and professional contexts; sharing with one another creates an intersectional space that is safer, energizing, and, thus far, sustaining as we continue to navigate tensions noted above. From this safer space rises knowledge, self-understanding, and an activist pride, affirmation, and validation. This supports, emboldens, and re-energizes us for the work ahead, together and independently.

The backstage, or the behind-the-scenes, of our own individual activisms and our activisms together has required and continues to require relationship-building, ever-deepening understandings of each other's circumstances and contexts, a slower tempo, and safer spaces in which to share experiences of changing embodiments alongside stereotypes of disability and aging. Importantly, it is in this intentionally created space that intersectional exploration of disability, aging, domestic abuse, the personal, the professional, race, and Indigeneity has been possible and proudly sustained. We believe it is our intersectional exploration that enables more fully our *becoming-with* together and also sustains our continued activisms together. These intimate conversations about difference are rarely part of our presentations, perhaps speaking to the norms that denounce speaking of vulnerability in university spaces. However, these discussions strengthen our activisms both individually and together. In other words, they are *foundational*. We create this intersectional space to bring into words our multiple differences and positionalities, as differently abled, aging, racialized, and intergenerational women. Finding a way to incorporate race and Indigeneity more explicitly in our disability-aging activisms remains a challenge. Yet, this chapter's focus on the backstage brings us a step closer to this possibility.

NOTES

1. This work was supported by the Canadian Institutes for Health Research Grant #106597 and Social Sciences and Humanities Research Council of Canada Grant #895-2016-1024.

2. The city of Peterborough (Nogojiwanong—the place at the end of the rapids—traditional territory of the Michi Saagiig Anishinaabe) has a surrounding population of about 124,000 and is 125 km northeast of Toronto, Ontario. Trent University is located in Peterborough.

3. The mandate of "Mobilizing New Meanings of Disability and Difference" (CIHR funded, and led by Dr. Carla Rice, University of Guelph) was to produce multimedia digital stories (videos) directed by storytellers living with disability and difference, very broadly defined. Storytellers brought experiences of living with disability and difference into view on their own terms and in resistance to dominant disability stereotypes. Experiences of disability, difference, and affective and emotional dimensions of alienated labour are unwelcome in the public sphere. See Clare 1999; Changfoot 2016; Garland-Thomson 2009; and Rice et al. 2015.

4. Mary Anne, Nadine, and Andrea's videos can be viewed here: www.vimeo.com/album/4589042. Password: unsettlingactivisms. These videos are not intended for circulation.

5. Feminist scholars can reinforce privilege and marginalization when representing women, especially those not in the academy. See Brown 1997.

6. Rick Hansen set out from Vancouver, BC on his two-year Man in Motion World Tour (1985–1987) to raise awareness of the potential of people living with disabilities. He is a celebrated Paralympic athlete and tireless advocate for accessibility and inclusivity: www.rickhansen.com/

7.   PDAN did not allow men to join SAC at that time.

8.   Drawing upon Margrit Shildrick's (2015) phrase of "living on, not getting better," it can be argued that disabled persons "pay for the progress" of greater awareness and education of disability through debilitating barriers such as the $200 additional maximum.

9.   To date, Nadine and Andrea have made Aging Activism media capsules that can be viewed here: www.agingactivisms.org/nadine-media-cap and www.agingactivisms.org/andrea-media-cap-nogo

REFERENCES

Bartlett, Ruth. 2014. "Citizenship in Action: The Lived Experiences of Citizens with Dementia Who Campaign for Social Change." *Disability & Society* 29(8): 1291–1304. DOI:10.1080/09687599.2014.924905.

Brown, Maria T. 2009. "LGBT Aging and Rhetorical Silence." *Sexuality Research and Social Policy Journal of NSRC* 6(2): 65–78.

Brown, Wendy. 1997. "The Impossibility of Women's Studies." *differences: A Journal of Feminist Cultural Studies* 9: 79–102.

Butler, Judith. 2014. "Bodily Vulnerability, Coalitions, and Street Politics." *Critical Studies* 37: 99–119.

Changfoot, Nadine. 2016. "Creating Meaning: Creating Emancipatory Moments through Storying Outlawed Experiences and Relational Aesthetic." *Journal of the Society of Socialist Studies/Revue des études socialistes* (The Subaltern: Speaking Through Socialism) 11(1): 62–84.

Changfoot, Nadine and Carla Rice. Forthcoming. "Aging with and into Disability: Futurities of New Materialisms." In *Aging/Disability Nexus*, edited by Katie Aubrecht, Christine Kelly, Carla Rice. Vancouver, BC: UBC Press.

Clare, Eli. 1999. "Exile and Pride: Queerness, and Liberation." Cambridge, MA: South End Press.

Garland-Thomson, Rosemarie. 2009. *Staring: How We Look*. Toronto, ON: Oxford University Press.

Gorman, Rachel. 2016. "Disablement In and For Itself: Toward a 'Global' Idea of Disability." *Somatechnics* 6(2): 249–261.

Holladay, Sherry J., and W. Timothy Coombs. 2004. "The Political Power of Seniors." In *Handbook of Communication and Aging Research*, edited by Jon F. Nussbaum and Justine Coupland, 383–406. London: Lawrence Erlbaum Associates.

Hutchison, Peggy, Susan Arai, Alison Pedlar, John Lord, and Felice Yuen. 2007. "Roles of Canadian User-Led Disability Organizations in the Non-Profit Sector." *Disability and Society* 22(7): 701–16. DOI:10.1080/09687590701659550.

Kafer, Alison. 2013. *Feminist, Queer, Crip*. Indiana University Press.

Kelly, Christine, and Michael Orsini. 2016. "Introduction." In *Mobilizing Metaphor: Art, Culture, and Disability Activism in Canada*, edited by Christine Kelly and Michael Orsini, 25–53. Vancouver, BC: UBC Press.

Kitchin, Rob and Robert Wilton. 2003. "Disability Activism and the Politics of Scale." *Canadian Geographer* 47(2): 97–115.

Martinson, Marty, and Clara Berridge. 2015. "Successful Aging and Its Discontents: A Systematic Review of Social Gerontology Literature." *The Gerontologist* 55(1): 51–57.

Peters, Yvonne. 2003. "From Charity to Equality: Canadians with Disabilities Take Their Rightful Place in Canada's Constitution." In *Making Equality: History of Advocacy and Persons with Disabilities in Canada*, edited by Deborah Stienstra and Aileen Wight-Felske, 119–136. Concord, ON: Captus Press.

Prince, Michael. 2012. "Canadian Disability Activism and Political Ideas: In and Between Neo-Liberalism and Social Liberalism." *Canadian Journal of Disability Studies* 1(1): 1–34.

Rice, Carla, Eliza Chandler, and Nadine Changfoot. 2016. "Imagining Otherwise: The Ephemeral Spaces of Envisioning New Meanings." In *Mobilizing Metaphor: Art, Culture and Disability Activism in Canada*, edited by Christine Kelly and Michael Orsini, 54–75. Vancouver, BC: UBC Press.

Rice, Carla, Eliza Chandler, Elisabeth Harrison, Kirsty Liddiard, and Manuela Ferrari. 2015. "Project Re•Vision: Disability at the Edges of Representation." *Disability & Society* 30(4): 513–527.

Rowe, John W., and Robert L. Kahn. 2015. "Successful Aging 2.0: Conceptual Expansions for the 21st Century." *The Journals of Gerontology: Series B* 70(4): 593–596.

Roy, Carole. 2007. "When Wisdom Speaks Sparks Fly: Raging Grannies Perform Humor as Protest." *Women's Studies Quarterly* 35(3/4): 150–164.

Roy, Carole. 2004. *The Raging Grannies: Wild Hats, Cheeky Songs, and Witty Actions for a Better World*. Montreal, QC: Black Rose Books.

Sawchuk, Dana. 2009. "The Raging Grannies: Defying Stereotypes and Embracing Aging through Activism." *Journal of Women & Aging* 21(3): 171–185.

Shildrick, Margrit. 2015. "Living On; Not Getting Better." *Feminist Review* 111: 10–24.

Williamson, John B. 1998. "Political Activism and the Baby Boom." *Generations* 22(1): 55–59.

REFLECTION 5

Words, Work, and Wonder: Poeting toward Midlife

Ziy von B

With family lines stemming from Jewish communities in Poland and Lithuania, Ziy von B is grateful to be raising children, stringing together words, and nurturing relationships with and on Michi Saagiig Anishinaabe territory in Nogojiwanong. Ziy is a poet and grassroots community organizer who has also had the great privilege of directing inspiring organizations like the New Canadians Centre, the ReFrame Film Festival and the Kawartha World Issues Centre. Ziy is committed to transformation and healing through social justice, queer consciousness, and decolonization. Like the analysis of the preceding chapter, Ziy's reflection explores the intricate connections between the onstage, the offstage, and the backstage of their activisms.

INTRODUCTION

For everything that has brought us to this moment in time.
For the folks who created you
birthed you
and raised you.
And the folks who created
birthed
and raised them.
              All the way
        all the way
    all the way
back.

For every single star
whether a shout from the past
or still burning toward ash.

      For every unselfish raindrop
      that falls and dies
      then secretly, daily
      re-paints the sky.

            For the quiet exchanges
            of lungs and leaves.
            For the vulnerability of grief.

For the all but impossible life on earth.
For the four-leggeds, the fins and the fur.

For every word(-)casting light
whether whispered to the beat of bending flames
or (w)rapped around the crystal of a mic.

For every grass blade	ocean rock	mountain top
For each everglade	outcrop	aftershock
From black hole	to Ice Age	
Past cave folk	and old rage	
From tail's first wag	to human jaunt on two legs	
From first planted grain	to ravaging plague	
From every ounce of blood spilt		
	to each grain of white guilt	
From the first canoe		
	to the last stampede	
From the first atom splitting		
	to the second	
	you were conceived	
Through the tears of every tiny thing		
	that ever made you	
	want to pray.	

All the way
     all the way
         all the wily way
             to this.

This moment.
This confluence of forces

that finds us face to face
at this exact time
and precise place.
This
is sacred
space.
("Shehechiyanu," 2015)

I have often wondered what it was that drew me into social justice work—my outsider status as a nerd and a queer? My innate sense of justice? The sheer luck of proximity to activist work and movements? All of the above and more, I'm sure.

While I aim to work toward social justice and decolonization in many ways, the most visible form my work takes is spoken word poetry. First as a young teen, encouraged to share my writing, then as a young organizer, helping to start the Peterborough Poetry Slam Collective, and now as a parent who facilitates spoken word workshops for marginalized youth, and helps to hold space for open and supportive stages—I have been honoured to witness the healing and empowerment that can come from intimate performance. I find power in words to validate common experiences, to hold the complex emotions, doubts, and despair we are feeling as humans who strive for justice, to challenge notions and misconceptions, to honour the work of activists and trailblazers, and to suggest spaces of hope and vision. While I do write to call attention to specific events and movements—helping to raise awareness, for example, of indefinite immigration detention in Canada—my writing is also always personal. I write as a parent, as a lover, as a community organizer. Over time, my writing has followed themes that matter to me, that hold real weight in my day-to-day as I move through youth, through evolution in my queer and gender identities, through righteousness, through illness, through parenting.

PATHWAYS INTO ACTIVISM

When I had short hair, I'd walk down the street
A car would slow down, and I'd hear, "beep beep!"
Down the window would roll, and I'd make out, "Dyke!"
As they sped away, I'd say, "I guess they're right."
Yeah, I'm a dyke, baby, I'm a geographical phenomenon.
(excerpt from "Mo' Than a Mofo," 2001)

My earliest memories involve anger about injustice and a desire to make things right. At three, bringing tissues to my mother, hurt by my father's rage. At six, requesting a blank report card from the principal so I could evaluate my first grade teacher, adamant that the process should work both ways. At nine, initiating the Earth Kids Club to motivate my fellow students toward environmental protection. At ten, my teacher describing me, in writing, as "the questioner from hell."

In high school, my social struggles began to intersect with politics. Thanks to summer camp role models and a critical class on media, I rejected ideas about femininity, defending my right to shave my head—and not my armpits!—as I became more aware of sexism and oppressive beauty standards. I had a racialized boyfriend who was facing criminal charges. Although I lacked a nuanced analysis of racial oppression, I saw immediately the inequity between his opportunities and mine, and the complete dysfunction and oppressive processes of the so-called justice system. At the same time, I was grappling with my sexuality, as I began to notice my crushes on girls. Through the school's women's issues group, I started to see my differences as potential sites of empowerment instead of liabilities. Throughout all this, I was engaged in a constant power struggle within my family of origin.

I grew hungry for anti-oppressive initiatives. I got involved in addressing sexual harassment at school, raised funds for environmental initiatives, and was incredibly lucky to take after-school workshops with my first writing mentor, theatre artist Evalyn Parry. The outcome of the workshops was a zine (a handmade photocopied booklet) called *Girls in Space*, filled with our writing and art. I was encouraged to read my work aloud in public venues. I started writing a youth column for the local lesbian magazine, and had a co-op placement at a community radio station, CKLN, where I shared an office with the most diverse array of adults I had ever encountered. They ran shows on everything from feminist, Black, Indigenous, and queer resistance to mental illness, queer arts, police brutality, and the taxi industry. They called me on shit. They didn't censor themselves, or try to make me comfortable. I joined a working group called Women Against Corporate Globalization. I became a volunteer for the LGBT youth line, where intensive training gave me a grounding in queer theory and trans politics.

I first witnessed a big police confrontation at a march against the Organization of American States, in Windsor, where my uncle introduced me to the Council of Canadians. I was happily surprised to see so many seniors standing up for justice, and to witness that they in turn were inspired by us young folk.

DIRECT ACTION MEETS SPIRITUAL REFLECTION

Jewish mystics say
on the day when justice is truly done
the moon will shine as bright as the sun
we'll shed our shells and become
one
so I use orange
to colour my dream of that bloated moon
eclipsing the sky someday soon
but I live in the now
noticing how
the crayon labelled 'skin colour'
only comes in one shade...
(excerpt from "White Lies," 2000)

I chose to attend Trent University because of its openness. I knew I would live at Peter Robinson College, which was known to attract queers and political radicals.

I was stoked for all the social justice opportunities Trent promised. I worked at the alternative library for the Women's Centre, joined the Ontario Public Interest Research Group (OPIRG) and by January, I had locked myself in the vice-president's office as part of an occupation to protest the closure of the downtown colleges, the corporatization of the university, and the undermining of the democratic process. After a few days, we were dragged away by police in the middle of the night, strip-searched, interrogated separately, and kept in jail overnight. Months later, after fundraising thousands of dollars for legal fees, and digging up the evidence that implicated the university president in the way we were treated, we accepted a conditional discharge. I performed my community service hours at OPIRG. This was my most textbook activist moment; but it left our activist community depleted, energetically and financially.

Soon my activism began to shift in two ways. First, I began to look more into my heritage, studying perspectives on Judaism I didn't have access to as a child. I challenged an idea I'd internalized in which spirituality posed a threat to political activism. Through listening to and reading feminist Jewish leaders, I began to learn how to weave the two together, incorporating the concept of *tikkun olam* (returning the world to wholeness) into my activist framework.

Second, my world view was transformed by Indigenous Studies. In a lecture, Professor Paula Sherman critiqued "anti" politics, like the "anti-globalization movement," and spoke about the importance of being "for." Professor Leanne Betasamosake Simpson awarded me the lowest grade of my degree, while teaching me the most. I learned not only to question things like the hierarchy in our food-chain model, but my own cut-and-dried perspectives about activism. I learned the importance of building relationships, and of questioning cultural hegemony, even or especially within activist cultures.

CHANGING BODY, SHIFTING ROLES

It wasn't until I was sick
that you called me
'spunky'

As a casualty
you could see my vitality
sharp in contrast
to the absence I could leave
like fall leaves—we pass the same trees every day
It's only in autumn that we look up in awe
(excerpt from "Now That the Fight is Over," 2006)

At 25, after years of unnamed fatigue, I was diagnosed with Hodgkin's Lymphoma. A year of chemo, radiation, and recovery forced me to focus on my health, and re-evaluate my priorities. I made a commitment to pare down my obligations, and make more space for time with myself, time outside, time with those I love. While I can't say I don't still struggle with that balance, I am definitely better at saying "no," focusing my commitments, and celebrating quiet contributions. I live by the ancient Jewish teaching: "You are not required to complete the work, but neither are you free to abandon it."

Now in my mid-30s, parenting is my most important role and the crux of my activism. Seven years of sleep deprivation and the intensive demands of two small humans force me to be realistic about my responsibilities. Every day I am challenged by their questions about what we encounter in the world around us. How do you explain queerphobia, gender oppression, racialized violence, media tyranny … in ways that inspire creative solutions and not fear? How, in a world of inequity, body shaming, isolation, and competition, do you empower kids to trust their instincts, work collaboratively, and find peace and strength within?

In response to my children's expressions and interests, I am working to build better educational opportunities, address gender policing, and support more age-diverse events and movements. I have a much broader and longer view of activism. I know my most crucial role is to be steady and loving.

I have always been supported in my work by compassionate and generous people. My partner, who shares my values but prefers to stay in the background, takes care of me when I get so fixated on a project or performance that I lose sight of other essentials. She makes sure I eat, takes care of the kids, and gives me space to get work done. She sees this as her contribution to social change, which has helped me to rethink the way we value and share work. This has helped sustain my activism over time.

I am also motivated by community. My ideas only come to fruition when there are other dedicated folks working with me who have a shared vision, and hold me to account.

LISTENING... FOR THE FUTURE

And yet the sun is rising.
And yet the planet spins.
And yet the children—Anishinaabe, Syrian, Jew—trudge up the hill toward school.
And yet the duck sits idly on the Otonabee, drifting slowly tailward.
And yet, the oak leaves rustle in the iridescent breeze.
And yet the lips part, the ribs stretch, the heart beats.
As long as your veins are home to blood coursing, there is more to the story.
There is more to this story.
Keep on.
("And Yet," 2016)

Decolonization is now the framework I use to understand the world. All the various issues I've organized around—queerphobia, misogyny, environmental degradation, corporate greed, racism, immigration detention—are ongoing colonial processes. The resurgence of Indigenous ways of knowing, the recognition of sovereign Indigenous Nations, and the revitalization of Indigenous languages are crucial to any just future. I see my work as unlearning and listening. Unlearning the values of ego, production, efficiency, and ownership. Listening to as many Indigenous, Black and POC (people of colour) voices as I can, with an open heart and without rush. I am also working on deepening my connection to all life, transforming my view from one that trivializes or mocks such a commitment, to one that fosters loving relationships with flowing water, tenacious plants, and four-legged creatures. That love is the basis of our dedication to defend all life, and to support Indigenous-led movements against land exploitation and continued colonial control.

I see decolonization as the only way forward, and the only true source of hope, not just for sustained life on Earth, but for a story arc for humanity in which our ethics and interdependence strengthen despite greed and domination. While I have increasingly more questions than answers, I do know that the more present and grounded I can be as a partner, parent, neighbour, and collaborator, the more transformative potential there will be in our relationships, in our communities, and in our world.

CHAPTER 6

The Raging Grannies Versus the Sexperts: Performing Humour to Resist Compulsory (Hetero)Sexuality

Marlene Goldman, May Chazan, and Melissa Baldwin

In the fall of 2015, we had the pleasure of watching the Peterborough Raging Grannies perform at an event at Trent University in Nogojiwanong (Peterborough, Ontario).[1] Their songs ranged from a rallying call to end climate change to an anthem for rekindling democracy. The song that stood out for us the most, however, was "Geriatric Sexpot."[2] Chronicling "the experts'" views of women's sexuality from ages 60 to 100, "Geriatric Sexpot" gently mocks the idea that women's sexuality and desire are subjects or "problems" on which "experts" can speak with authority. As they sang, dressed in floppy hats, frilly aprons, and feather boas, the Grannies moved their bodies provocatively and exaggeratedly, at times bringing the audience to cacophonous laughter. Compared to their other songs, this performance sought to resist societal narratives around aging and sexuality in a much more explicit way. We wondered how the Grannies viewed this dimension of their activism; how they felt about (and while) performing "Geriatric Sexpot"; and what they hoped to accomplish through this performance. We also considered how their iconic Granny tactics—particularly their flamboyant "little old lady" (or LOL) parody—might illuminate the personal as political in old age.

The Raging Grannies are known across North America for the way they parody stereotypical images of LOLs to attract media and draw audiences in, and for how they then subvert this stereotype by their very presence as activists in public spaces. As Dana Sawchuk notes, they are infamous for dressing in "flamboyant costumes of skirts, shawls, and decorated hats while they flaunt their identities as feisty grandmothers, instead of as 'nice little old ladies'" (2009, 171–172). They show up "at their 'rages,' as their organized protests are called … invited or not, at city halls, shopping malls, nuclear power plants … to sing out their political message to the tune of songs from days gone by" (ibid.). With their flashy Granny getups, bold public performances, and satirical political songs, they intervene in several of the dominant aging narratives set out in the book's introduction: They contest ideas of activism as the domain of the young (Richards 2012); they resist narratives of aging women as apolitical, non-confrontational, and passive (D. Sawchuk 2009); and, more broadly, they challenge the idea that aging is necessarily synonymous with decline (Gullete 1997). There is a growing literature on the Raging Grannies (e.g., Roy 2007; Chazan 2016; see also Chapters 1 and 4), however, there is not yet a sustained examination of their activism as an assertion of their bodily and sexual autonomy as aging women, nor of how their performances resist dominant societal narratives of the desexualization of old age, successful aging, and compulsory (hetero)sexuality.

In this chapter, we take up this examination, drawing on a close reading of "Geriatric Sexpot," reflections from this 2015 performance, and an analysis of the group interview we carried out in a park in Nogojiwanong in 2016.[3] We begin with an exploration of the Grannies' well-known activist tactics of performance, irony, parody, and the communal singing of protest songs, as well as with a discussion of the regulatory narratives of aging as decline, successful aging, and compulsory sexuality. We then move on to examine how, in the case of "Geriatric Sexpot," the Grannies' performance strategies couple the unexpectedness of older women as political agents with the perceived impossibility of aging women as sexual agents. In this way, they politicize and challenge society's unwillingness to acknowledge not only older women's political power, but also their *power to decide whether, when, and how* they experience themselves as sexual. They bring humour to the often disregarded and certainly unfunny situation of the regulation of women's sexuality and desire, which many have struggled with throughout their lives. Their comedic tactics make their audiences sing along and laugh, opening the possibility for conversation about what is often unspeakable: aging women, aging bodies, desire, and sex.

The Grannies' iconic devil-may-care attitude, which many claim to have grown into with age, allows them to engage not only in performance activism for wide-ranging causes but also in staking out their sexuality on their own terms. Their approach facilitates a personal, intimate reclamation of their authority to decide for themselves what sexuality/sensuality means for them in later life—choosing for themselves the terms on which they express their sexuality, without regulation by the "experts." Our analysis draws on thinking about the roles of performance activism, irony, parody, and satire—particularly clowning—to make an argument about importance of this kind of humour to create spaces for needed but silenced and shame-laden conversations; to draw audiences in and change public perception; and to resist long-standing regulation of women's sexualities.

AGING AND PERFORMANCE ACTIVISMS

Much of the subversive, perspective-challenging potential of the Grannies lies in their musical (though *not* harmonious), humorous, and costumed performance activisms. Raging Grannies typically draw on well-known tunes and their unexpected performance of the LOL persona to compel listeners to not only heed their political messages but also question their own assumptions about aging. We open with a brief discussion of these theatrical tactics in their activisms broadly, as they also make possible the subversion performed in "Geriatric Sexpot."

Performance and singing are powerful agents for social transformation. Performance "allows for a process of exchange—between artists and audiences, between the past and the present—where new societal formations emerge" (Roman 2005, in Friedman 2013, xv), while political music has been a staple since the eighteenth century to "evoke or reflect a political judgement by the listener" (Dunaway 1987, 269, cited in Roy 2004, 46). Since the Raging Grannies first formed, singing has provided a way to direct the public's attention to pressing political concerns and to vent fear, anger, and distress (Roy 2004). In addition to releasing pent-up emotion, as each gaggle sings, their collective voice instigates a shift in the public's perception of the aesthetic gifts of older women.

This sense of collectivity enacted when Grannies join their voices evokes Kim Sawchuk and Aynsley Moorhouse's discussion of collaborative projects that "shift creativity from its traditional moorings within notions of individual artistic genius, grounding it instead in the act of *doing* with others" (2016, 188). As a facet of this "doing," singing allows the Grannies to resist invisibility in the creative realm: It helps to correct the "common misconception that creativity is restricted to 'artistic' subjects or belongs in the domain of children and young people" (ibid.). Not to be mistaken for musicians, the Grannies unabashedly admit that they are terrible singers: as Peterborough Granny Olive[4] proclaims, "We never let musicality stand in the way of our message."

Singing is only one of the transformative facets of the Grannies' performative techniques; their satirical lyrics and clown-esque enactments draw on humour's capacity to question norms and assumptions (Melo 2015; Routledge 2012). Relying centrally on parody, their humorous exhibitions enable them to engage in contradictory acts of "establishing and then undercutting prevailing values and conventions in order to provoke a question, a challenging of 'what goes without saying' in our culture" (Hutcheon 1998, 1). When Carole Roy researched the Raging Grannies in the early 2000s, those she spoke with readily admitted that they dress like "cartoon grannies, like the stereotypes of older women, by wearing quaint shawls and bonnets decked with all manner of flowers—artificial and otherwise" (Roy 2006, 33). By donning "old fashioned floral dresses, aprons, shawls, and extravagant hats," as Rachel V. Kutz-Flamenbaum argues, they "draw upon hegemonic gender norms to reassure and attract observers and potential adherents" (2007, 98). In this way, their self-reflexivity and reliance on parody index their identity as "nurturing, maternal, caring, passive, polite, and kind" as a consoling fiction—one that is subverted by the exaggerated, ridiculous features of their attire and by the flamboyant, comic, performative nature of their protests.

From the start, the Grannies understood the risks and benefits of drawing on the role of "the clown," "the wise fool," or "the court jester" to transform the public's thinking (Acker and Brightwell 2004, xi). While at times they have been accused of reproducing ageist LOL stereotypes, their performances of garish whimsy defy their erasure as older women—not only in the creative realm but in society and in social movements more broadly. As one Granny from Roy's research insisted, the "only way we're going to get anyone to notice us and pay attention is to dress ridiculously" (2004, 29).[5] Another recalled, "Once, we were invisible. Like all older women, we were expected to fade into the background along with our looks, our health, our income and our importance to society" (Acker and Brightwell 2004, xi). Thus, it was largely to counteract the stereotypical "decline narrative" (Gullette 1997) that the Grannies hit on the idea of dressing "like clowns" (Roy 2006, 141).

The Grannies' subversive power comes not only from parody but also from how they couple parodic humour with the bold political commentary contained in their satirical lyrics and their unapologetic insertion of themselves into public spaces. The result is a powerfully performed irony: the unexpectedness of LOLs as *political* agents and as visible public protestors. The Grannies' costumes arrest the attention of the public, shift the experience into the realm of play, and prompt the audience to "lean in," allowing their humorous songs to drive home their political message.

AGING, SEXUALITY, AND THE POLITICS OF REGULATION

The performance of "Geriatric Sexpot" offers a prescient, political challenge to ongoing societal attempts to control women's sexuality. Our analysis of this song, as it was performed and reflected upon by the Peterborough Raging Grannies in 2015, engages with ongoing conversations within critical aging and sexuality studies, specifically around three interrelated discourses: desexualized aging, successful aging, and compulsory (hetero)sexuality. The lyrics of "Geriatric Sexpot" repeatedly refer to "the experts'" views of sexuality and aging—we take this to mean not only individuals with some claim to expertise in geriatric sexuality, but also these regulatory discourses broadly (discussed further below), and the combined practices and messaging of the media, the beauty and anti-aging industries, and the health and medical sectors.

In "Geriatric Sexpot" the Grannies challenge both ageism and its twin, "successful aging," a widely used but highly critiqued discourse in contemporary public health frameworks (as discussed in the book's introduction, connected with the similarly dominant framework of "active aging"). Successful aging equates success in later life with youthfulness and able-bodiedness, thereby discriminating against people aging with and into disabilities; it also places responsibility for health in later life on individuals, with little to no attention on how systems of power operate to condition experiences of aging and embodiment. Where sexuality is concerned, successful aging, for women, is predicated on the necessity of maintaining "sexiness" and desire for heterosexual sex well into old age. As Barbara L. Marshall observes, the contemporary and reductive association of "heterosexiness with successful aging has offered new forms of cultural imagery around which consumer marketing has rallied and which health promotion has embraced" (2017, 17). In the context of the prevailing "sex for health" discourse (Gupta 2011), thanks to new drugs such as Viagra, Cialis, and now Addyi[6] for women, women are expected to enact traditional, heterosexual sex until death. While the impetus to distinguish successful aging from unsuccessful aging may appear to be anti-ageist, it remains a co-conspirator with ageism since, in accordance with the definition of the latter, one is still "shaped into something that is always less than what one really is" (Cooper 1988, in Roy 2004, 197).

This "heterosexiness" asserted by successful-aging discourses remains part of the broader regulatory influence of *compulsory sexuality*. As Kristina Gupta and others argue, compulsory sexuality (associated with a movement of "sex-positivity") is a regulatory framework that imposes sexuality as normal, necessary, and good. Within this framework, both the hypersexualization and "desexualization of particular groups can be used as a method of social control" by marking these groups as something other than "normal" (Gupta 2015, 141). Thus, "those considered 'normal' face strong pressures to be sexual, and those who seek access to the normal must establish themselves as sexual subjects" (ibid., 142). Critics of this framework warn of the "limitations of viewing sexuality as a path to liberation" (ibid., 132), because sex-positivity can also function to regulate behaviour by defining what is normal, healthy, and good.

Until recently, ageist expressions of this system of control worked to *desexualize*, and thus pathologize, old age (Marshall 2002; Gupta 2015). As Marshall (2012) has argued, in an effort to paint aging in a positive light and resist narratives of decline and frailty, successful-aging discourses launched a potent bid against "decline" by sexualizing old age, making active sexuality a key tenet of aging well. This binary of success and decline takes (hetero)sexual functioning/activity to be a marker of success, and asexuality a marker of decline (Sandberg 2013a). Performing (hetero)sexuality has "unsurprisingly become almost a metaphor for health itself in later life" (Marshall 2017, 14). While successful-aging rhetoric that encourages specific forms of sexual activity might, at the outset, appear liberatory, this discourse is not being generated by older women: Instead, a narrow conception of "healthy sexual activity" is imposed upon them as an expectation to be fulfilled. With this in mind, Marshall (2012), following Foucault, cautions us to critique both the *de-* and *re-*sexualization of old age as *part of the same regulatory framework* that defines and hierarchizes subjects according to the sexual.

While Gupta asserts that compulsory sexuality is not limited to heterosexuality, successful-aging rhetoric works to limit old age to a compulsory heterosexuality. Marshall (2017) argues that aging successfully "is equated with enactments of normative, gendered heterosexuality." In certain ways, the heteronormativity of later life is asserted through a preoccupation with sexual "functionality." As Stephen Katz and Barbara L. Marshall show, anxieties around dysfunction, the new pathology, have invigorated concern over maintaining the "ability to perform heterosexual intercourse adequately and consistently" throughout the aging process (2004, 64). Functionality for men is most commonly associated with the physical ability to maintain an erection, while for women it is most often tied to the *desire* to engage in intercourse; thus both ability and desire are gendered, medicalized, and stigmatized (Sandberg 2013a). This focus on functionality, which dominates discussions of sexuality and aging, presumes and upholds heterosexual, penetrative intercourse as the standard and the goal of sexual activity (Calasanti and King 2005). The privileging of intercourse not only leaves little room for sexualities beyond the hetero, but also eclipses sensuality, pleasure, eroticism, intimacy, touch, sensation, and other experiences and practices that exist outside of this rigid script of penetrative intercourse.[7] Functionality narratives also rely on and reify the compulsory able-bodiedness that pervades successful-aging discourses (Sandberg 2008). Again, these norms of a reinvigorated sexual old age have not been established by older agents themselves. Instead, "medical experts" decide what is "successful," imposing a narrow hetero/ableist understanding of functionality as "'normal,' 'natural,' and 'healthy'" for sexuality in later life (Katz and Marshall 2004, 53).

"Geriatric Sexpot" sits amid these tensions—at odds with the asexual-old-age/sexy-senior binary—as we explore through the remainder of the chapter. By parodying this unasked-for and narrowly defined sexualization of their old age, the

Grannies are attempting neither to resexualize nor desexualize themselves as aging women but, instead, to mock a sexualization that has been imposed on them. The song neither buys into nor refutes this sexualization—it simply makes visible that it has been imposed by the "experts."

CONTEXT: THE PETERBOROUGH GRANNIES AND "GERIATRIC SEXPOT"

Raging Grannies write their lyrics to popular tunes in the public domain,[8] sharing these for wider use with an understanding that individual groups will rewrite the lyrics and even change the melodies to meet localized agendas (see www.raginggrannies.net). Because songs are written and rewritten, it is often difficult to trace the history of any given tune. Musicologists Ron Eyerman and Andrew Jamison observe that "in social movements, music and other kinds of cultural traditions are made and remade, and after movements fade away as political forces, the music remains as memory and as a potential way to inspire new waves of mobilization" (1998, 1–2).

"Geriatric Sex," the song from which "Geriatric Sexpot" emerged, appears to have been written by the Victoria Grannies to the tune of "Lili Marlene." In Peterborough, the song has been adapted for "Geriatric Sexpot" and sung to the tune of "There Will Always Be an England." The original romantic war tune of "Lili Marlene" conjures notions of women's bodies and sexuality as a kind of battleground. However, the Peterborough group insisted that the tune of "There Will Always Be an England" evokes a different kind of irony. One of the longest-standing members remarked that she loved using a tune that was both "an old colonial standby" and a "liberation tune" because of its ironic and dual nature, implying perhaps that women's sexuality is simultaneously liberated and colonized or repressed.

The "Sexpot" version is sung by at least two other groups (Ottawa and Calgary), although the Peterborough group has changed a few key lyrics. The Peterborough Grannies shared their lyrics with us with a number of words stroked out and changed:

Oh I'm 80 and I ought to
There's no time to put things off
No excuses like, "I'm breathless," or
"Exertion makes me cough!"
For, I'm told I've still got fires that I didn't know I had
And I would tell my ~~husband~~ *lovers* this, but
When I wake ~~him~~ *them*, ~~he~~ *they* gets mad!

From the way this group explained it, it seems these changes made were in effort not to reproduce heteronormative and monogamous assumptions about older women's sexuality. As Granny Olive told us, this makes the song "much more queer friendly" and pushes it beyond narrow ideas of marital sex, instead allowing for multiple, non-gendered lovers. This change is clearly part of their resistance to societal prescriptions; as another Granny said, they are demanding others "not to put us in pigeon holes."

FROM SEXPERTS TO GRANNIES AS SEXUAL AGENTS: LYRICS, PERFORMANCE, HUMOUR

"Geriatric Sexpot" begins with the phrase, "We're 60 and we're sexy." In the 2015 performance, the Peterborough Grannies sang this opening line while shimmying their shoulders and gyrating their hips, all the while maintaining pointed eye contact with audience members. The unexpectedness alone of this performance of "sexiness" by older women serves to catch the audience off guard and undermines stereotypes of older women as washed up, undesirable, and uninterested in sex. Put differently, the song's humour makes it possible—in a society saturated with ageist, sexist beauty norms—to conceive of the desirability of aging bodies. From start to finish, "Geriatric Sexpot" resists older women's desexualization by playfully reclaiming sexuality and sexiness.

However, by the second line, this resistance becomes significantly more complicated. As the lyrics unfold, the song does not make a simple claim to aging bodies as sexual, sexy, or desirable. Instead, it stages a resistance to how experts prescribe a certain kind of sexual activity, and indeed to "heterosexiness," as necessary for older women to age well. The song mocks "the experts" and their imposed ideals about how older women should look, feel, and experience themselves as sexual beings as they age. The lyrics assert, for example, "We're 60 and we're sexy/ At least that's what we hear/From programs seen on TV/And talk shows on the air." Through repetition and sass, the song proceeds to ridicule this set of external expectations around older women's desires and ideals.

Although the song mocks the "experts," its subversive power lies in the fact that it never actually corrects them. Instead, it refuses to make universal claims about aging and sexuality. In essence, the lyrics expose the absurdity of depicting a homogeneous experience of, or ideal around, aging and sexuality. Equally critical to their interventions, by refusing to correct, the Grannies resist coming under this kind of regulation themselves. The lyrics subtly reveal the "experts'" complete disregard for how older women actually feel and what they want, offering a simultaneous resistance to the desexualization of older women *and* to their resexualization by way of the regulatory power of compulsory (hetero)sexuality. As Granny Kit said, "It's about not buying into the box that people want to put us in," whichever box that may be.

The song ends with the Grannies' strongest and most explicit refusal to conform to imposed standards, cheekily performed to bring the audience to uproarious laughter:

Now I'm 90 and I'm naughty
And there's nothing new to me
I've been having sex since 60 and I'm tired as can be
But I'm telling you a secret
Tho' it's one that you must keep
When I get to be 100
I am damn well going to sleep!

Here, the Grannies inform the audience in no uncertain terms that, as sexy and naughty as they are told they are and are supposed to be, they will ultimately be the ones to decide how to express their sexuality, even if it takes them until the age of 100. The verse stakes out turning 100 as the turning point when, finally, they have license to say "no" to these scripts. Offering up this turning point as a "secret" alludes to the ongoing silence around (older) women's sexuality. By stating their defiance to the script, they raise the possibility that not having sex, but instead choosing to sleep, could be part of a package of aging well. The public performance of this often-quietly-held anxiety is unexpected after their lengthy performance of sexiness through the ages; the discomfort it raises evokes laughter and, with it, deep contemplation of how difficult it is for women—even women who are seasoned activists—to transgress the narratives of compulsory sexuality and the attendant, gendered discourse of "functionality" (which, for women, defines "functional" as maintaining a sex drive).

The role of performance, spectacle, and irony in "Geriatric Sexpot" recalls our earlier discussion about how these strategies work as part of the Granny's activism around other issues. But these tactics also open up other possibilities: They make possible elderly women as political agents. Equally critical, they produce possibilities for non-scripted sexualities for older women as sexual agents. Finally, they are also integral to the Grannies' abilities to adopt new perspectives on their own sexualities. For example, during the interview, Granny Kit confessed to her delight in the freedom to "vamp" while singing "Geriatric Sexpot." As she explained, "We get to *pretend* we're sexy." In accordance with irony's capacity to install meaning in the guise of play, Grannies Jude and Olive corrected her, saying, "No, we *are* sexy."

Recalling the doubled meaning of their eccentric grandmotherly outfits, both options remain available. The cognitive dissonance of "nurturing, quaint" grannies, in their getups, performing and "vamping" about their supposed sex drives perverts and theatrically exposes the absurdity of the expert discourse, while making their sexuality visible and unavoidable.

"Geriatric Sexpot" initially presents as a challenge to the desexualization of older women, using clown-esque parody to make visible the Grannies as sexual beings—a reclaiming of their bodies as desirable. As the performance proceeds, however, we understand that it is not simple resistance to their desexualization. Rather, it serves as a resistance to regulation: to being put in a box, to having "experts" (whether media, the beauty industry, or the medical profession) tell them how they should be or feel or what they should do as they age. Using humour and cheekiness to shift the register of this conversation, they defy regulation: they challenge the desexualization and the resexualization—both of which are integral to compulsory sexuality as a regulatory framework—of older women's bodies. Older women themselves should decide what is sexy and how, when, or whether they will have sex.

PERSONAL AS POLITICAL: SEXUALITY ACROSS THE LIFECOURSE AND IN LATER LIFE

Performance, song, and humour not only draw the audience in and make possible this sophisticated critique but also, importantly, open possibilities for the Grannies to speak amongst each other on this largely unspeakable topic. During our group interview, the Grannies chortled at the song's description of the persistence of their desire across the lifecourse and described their witty lyrics as "gorgeous." Humour and their ability to laugh—a constant, joyous feature of our interview—clearly made this group feel more comfortable broaching the subject of sex. Our group interview, which asked these women to offer their interpretations of "Geriatric Sexpot," turned quickly into an intimate, detailed, and courageous discussion of how they have experienced sexuality across their lifecourses. Noting their eagerness to delve into their personal experiences, we asked the eight women involved how aging and sexuality are generally talked about in their social circles and with their doctors. To our surprise (given their bravado on stage), for most of the women in this group, this was the first time anyone had ever opened this up as a conversation. Granny Jude marvelled, saying, "I don't think I've *ever* had a conversation about sex and aging," to which the others nodded in agreement. For many, the topic of sex was taboo—even in conversations between women and their doctors. They reported a dearth of accurate information about older women's sexuality being disseminated by the media, fashion magazines, and doctors. "There's *zero* information," Granny Grace said; "We just hear about diapers, dry vaginas, and the need for lubrication." The shared performance of the song, and particularly the laughter and hilarity surrounding it, made the conversation that then ensued possible.

During our discussion, the Grannies explicitly connected the personal to the political—and this song to their other activist performances—by reflecting on sexuality and sexual regulation not only in later life but across their lifecourses. On the one hand, the Grannies admitted that "Geriatric Sexpot" is distinct from their traditional political ditties. On the other hand, they insisted that, since "sexual repression is political" and their song tackles this repression, it is also "deeply political."

Each woman spoke about her sexuality differently. Many, however, connected the regulation they were challenging in "Geriatric Sexpot" (associated with successful-aging narratives and compulsory sexuality) to the repressive attitude toward sexuality that was prevalent when they were coming of age—for this group, the 1960s. As they explained, this conservative attitude was often tied to religious beliefs about the dangers of female sexuality and the related view that women's sexuality had to be constrained within a heterosexual, marital relationship. Some recalled being told that women were not allowed to have sex purely for pleasure; instead, they had to please a man—their husband. They also insisted that the song playfully responds to the sexist medical information they received, particularly as young women, about their sexuality. Granny Dee remembered being asked by her family doctor if she intended "to hold her boyfriend's hand. If not," he informed her, "then you'd better go on the pill." At that time, though, she had no idea what the "pill" was. She went on to describe having an IUD inserted without being informed about the process and subsequently going into shock. Other Grannies connected bodily regulation with psychological control. For instance, reflecting on the repression and the shaming she endured, which aligned women's sexuality with sinful transgression, Granny Eve described its cumulative impact as "psychological circumcision." This observation recalls Adrienne Rich's assertion that compulsory heterosexuality works through both physical control and "control of the consciousness" (1986, cited in Kafer 2003, 79).

At the same time, others critically connected these controlling ideologies to the 1960s and 1970s "free love era": Even when attitudes shifted and women were no longer considered to be "damaged goods" if they were not virgins, the regulation persisted but took on a different form. Although the women's liberation movement in the 1960s had a positive impact for some women, Granny Grace explained that the situation did not change much: Whereas, before, there was pressure to *refrain* from sex to be socially accepted, during the 1970s she felt pressure to *have* sex to be "hip." Whether repressed by religion, or expected during the 1960s, women's sexuality was still being externally controlled. As Granny Kit explained, "All of this sexual [liberation] stuff around women [in the 1960s–1970s], it was a huge way to control women too.... There were ways of behaving, there were ways of thinking that, as you mentioned, that you had unconsciously internalized. I swear to God, it's only *last week* that I got rid of some of that shit." These reflections clearly resonate with the earlier-discussed idea that repression/liberation, and, relatedly, sex-negativity/sex-positivity, are two sides of the same coin or part of the same regulatory system that ultimately functions to control women's bodies and desires (Marshall 2012).

Contrary to the narrative of decline, and in keeping with their sass on stage, many of the Grannies reported that aging had lessened their inhibitions, allowing them to make choices about sexuality on their own terms. Several Grannies asserted that, if anything, aging had *increased* their sex drive, raising the question of whether their increased desire might be linked to their increased sense of choice. Generally, they agreed that, as they age, they feel less constrained by social norms and more able to reject reified sexual scripts. They recognize the absurdity of compulsory sexuality and the sexist and ageist health/beauty ideals that saturate the media. Agreeing with Sandberg (2013b) and others who argue that regulatory discourses of sexuality often decontextualize sex from the social and relational dimensions of intimacy and pleasure, some of the Grannies shared how they have come to think about sex differently in later life. They no longer understand *intercourse* as a sole or central expression of sexuality or intimacy, or sex as necessarily tied to looking sexy or performing certain acts. Rather, deciding the terms under which to have pleasurable sex (marital or not), or whether to have intercourse at all, was only one component of owning their sexuality. Their freedom as older women also came with the realization of themselves as *sensual* beings.

Granny Eve eloquently explained that sometimes what she desires from a partner is the sensual experience of going dancing; if later she wants an orgasm, she is happy enough to masturbate. She later spoke of abstaining from sex if it did not promise to fulfill her in certain ways, saying, "The older I get ... I feel better about me. And I look at men and think, if I'm going to have a sexual encounter, I want to enjoy it or else *why bother?*"—an assertion which was met with hoots and hollers of approval. As we repeatedly observed, the most vocal Grannies in this group are certainly not asexual; they are sexual and sensual. But they are also defying compulsory sexuality. They do not think of themselves as having to prove their sex drive or have sex in order to enjoy themselves, stay healthy, and make a contribution to society as they age.

CONCLUSIONS

As our conversations with the Peterborough Grannies and their "Geriatric Sexpot" song suggest, being pressured to have certain kinds of sex, maintain a sex drive, and remain sexy in later life are oppressive narratives, akin to the equally regulatory narratives of virginity-as-good and free-love-as-hip that governed their sexualities earlier in their lives. Instead of trying to dismantle the master's house using the master's tools,[9] which, in this case, would entail engaging in earnest scientific discourse—the Raging Grannies strategically opt instead for parodic humour and embodied performance. Rather than mimic the model of the lone, male genius, and pen a scientific treatise on the topic of women's sexual desire, the Grannies as a group sing about their aging and sexuality. These women navigate these repressive discourses fueled by some of the freedoms they feel in later life. At the same time, the fact that many said they had never talked about sex and aging this way, and that they felt that the only information they had access to was about "diapers" or "Viagra," makes "Geriatric Sexpot" even more important. This unique form of humorous feminist performative activism allows them to speak about the unspeakable, and permits their audiences to listen to the unlistenable.

NOTES

1.   The Raging Grannies began in 1986 in Victoria, Canada, as a group of peace activists protesting the presence of nuclear submarines in the Victoria harbour (Roy 2004; see also Chapters 1 and 4). Granny groups across the continent then began mobilizing at different times and around multiple social and environmental issues. In Nogojiwanong/Peterborough, the local Raging Grannies group formed in the mid-1990s in response to the neoliberalization of Ontario's provincial legislation. Their first interventions took place during the "Days of Action" (1995–1998); they sang anti-poverty and anti-racism messages and were closely aligned with the labour movement. Over the years, the Peterborough group has raged on many issues; they currently focus mostly on climate justice, democratic reform, and environmental sustainability.

2.   "Geriatric Sex" was written by the Victoria Grannies and sung to the tune of "Lili Marlene." The Peterborough Gaggle changed some of the words and set it to "There Will Always Be an England." Their lyrics (with edits marked) are as follows:

"Geriatric Sexpot"

Tune: There'll Always Be an England

I'm 60 and I'm sexy, at least that's what I hear

From programs seen on TV

And talk shows on the air

The magazines, print articles, by some authority

Are telling me, at 60—I'm as sexy as can be!

I'm 70 and sensual

Though it really doesn't show

Geriatric experts tell me, I'm mature and all aglow!

They say hidden wells of passion

Are just bubbling up in me

And at 70 I've hit my peak—of sensuality!

Oh I'm 80 and I ought to

There's no time to put things off

No excuses like, "I'm breathless,"

"Exertion makes me cough!"

For, I'm told, I've still got fires that I didn't know I had

And I would tell my ~~husband~~ *lovers*, but

When I wake ~~him~~ *them*, ~~he~~ *they* gets mad!

Now I'm 90 and I'm naughty

And there's nothing new to me

I've been having sex since 60 and I'm tired as can be

But I'm telling you a secret,

Tho' it's one that you must keep

When I get to be 100

I am damn well going to sleep!

3. As a Canadian literary and age-studies critic, Marlene's interest in the Raging Grannies' activism lies in contextualizing their ironic tactics within the transformative, embodied potential associated with social protest that relies on clowning and popular music. As a feminist scholar who studies aging and activisms drawing on community-based approaches, May brings to this analysis long-standing research relationships with Raging Grannies and an extensive knowledge of their movement. The primary research for this chapter was carried out by May and Melissa; the writing was a joint endeavour. We also acknowledge valuable input offered by Barbara L. Marshall, a well-known scholar in the area of aging and sexuality.

4. We use pseudonyms for all research participants.

5. The Grannies' primary focus on dress recalls the etymological definition of the word "clown," which dates to its use in 16th-century England. At the time, "clown" referred to those who did not behave or dress like gentlemen, but instead donned "clownish or uncivil fashions" (Davison 2013, 1). As scholars observe, clowning is one of "the oldest forms of live performance, and has taken the form of the trickster, jester, fool, harlequin, and

buffoon" (Routledge 2012, 432). As Paul Routledge affirms, the playful antics of the clown "draw players out of the bounds of everyday life, liberating them from the usual laws and regulations" (ibid., 433).

6. Addyi was reluctantly approved by the FDA in 2015. See www.newviewcampaign.org, which documents feminist resistance to the medicalization of sexuality.

7. Linn Sandberg, studying older heterosexual men, contends that intimacy, which is often obscured through a preoccupation with understanding functionality, "may be a way ... to navigate between current binary discourses of asexual old age and 'sexy seniors'" (2013b, 261). Sandberg also "suggests that it is not enough to queer age studies by focusing on LGBTQ elders, arguing that we must 'explore the production and maintenance of normativity on relationships, embodiment, intimacy and what constitutes the good (later) life'" (Marshall 2017, citing Sandberg 2015). See also Sandberg and Marshall (2017) for extensive discussion of queer/queering aging.

8. The Grannies choose older songs that will not put them at risk of charges of copyright infringement.

9. We borrow this phrase from Audre Lorde's formative chapter, "The Master's Tools Will Never Dismantle the Master's House," which first appears in her 1984 book *Sister Outsider: Essays and Speeches*.

REFERENCES

Acker, Alison, and Betty Brightwell. 2004. *Off Our Rockers and into Trouble*. Victoria, BC: Touchwood Books.

Calasanti, Toni, and Neal King. 2005. "Firming the Floppy Penis: Class and Gender Relations in the Lives of Old Men." *Men and Masculinities* 8(1): 3–23.

Chazan, May. 2016. "Settler Solidarities as Praxis: Understanding 'Granny Activism' beyond the Highly Visible." *Social Movement Studies* 15(5): 457–470.

Cooper, Baba. 1988. *Over the Hill: Reflections on Ageism between Women*. Freedom, CA: The Crossing Press.

Davison, Jon. 2013. *Clown*. Basingstoke, UK: Palgrave Macmillan.

Dunaway, David King. 1987. "Music and Politics in the United States." *Folk Music Journal* 5(3): 268–294.

Eyerman, Ron and Andrew Jamison. 1988. *Music and Social Movements: Mobilizing Traditions in the 20th Century*. Cambridge, UK: Cambridge University Press.

Friedman, Jonathan. 2013. *The Routledge History of Social Protest in Popular Music*. New York: Routledge.

Gullette, Margaret Morganroth. 1997. *Declining to Decline: Cultural Combat and the Politics of the Midlife*. Charlottesville, VA: University of Virginia Press.

Gupta, Kristina. 2015. "Compulsory Sexuality: Evaluating an Emerging Concept." *Journal of Women in Culture and Society* 41(1): 131–154.

Gupta, Kristina. 2011. "'Screw Health': Representations of Sex as a Health-Promoting Activity in Medical and Popular Literature." *Journal of Medical Humanities* 32(2): 127–140.

Hutcheon, Linda. 1998. *The Canadian Postmodern*. Oxford, UK: Oxford University Press.

Kafer, Alison. 2003. "Compulsory Bodies: Reflections on Heterosexuality and Able-bodiedness." *Journal of Women's History* 15(3): 77–89.

Katz, Stephen, and Barbara L Marshall. 2004. "Is the Functional 'Normal'? Aging, Sexuality, and the Bio-marking of Successful Living." *History of the Human Sciences* 17(1): 53–75.

Kutz-Flamenbaum, Rachel V. 2007. "Code Pink, Raging Grannies, and the Missile Dick Chicks: Feminist Performance Activism in the Contemporary Anti-War Movement." *NWSA Journal* 19(1): 89–105.

Marshall, Barbara L. 2017. "Happily Ever After? 'Successful Ageing' and the Heterosexual Imaginary." *European Journal of Cultural Studies* 21(3): 363–381. DOI:10.1177/1367549417708434.

Marshall, Barbara L. 2012. "Medicalization and the Refashioning of Age-related Limits on Sexuality." *The Journal of Sex Research* 49(4): 337–343.

Marshall, Barbara L. 2002. "'Hard Science': Gendered Constructions of Sexual Dysfunction in the 'Viagra Age.'" *Sexualities* 5(2): 131–158.

Melo, Carla. 2015. "Are We All in the Same Boat?: Staging the 'Invisible Majority' in the Streets of Toronto." *Canadian Theatre Review* 161: 33–37.

Rich, Adrienne. 1986. "Compulsory Heterosexuality and Lesbian Existence." In *Blood, Bread, and Poetry: Selected Prose 1979–1985*, 23. New York: Norton.

Richards, Naomi. 2012. "The Fight to Die: Older People and Death Activism." *International Journal of Ageing and Later Life* 7(1): 7–32.

Roman, David. 2005. *Performance in America: Contemporary US Culture and the Performing Arts*. Durham, NC: Duke University Press.

Routledge, Paul. 2012. "Sensuous Solidarities: Emotion, Politics and Performance in the Clandestine Insurgent Rebel Clown Army." *Antipode* 44(2): 428–52.

Roy, Carole. 2007. "When Wisdom Speaks Sparks Fly: Raging Grannies Perform Humor as Protest." *Women's Studies Quarterly* 34(3/4): 150–164.

Roy, Carole. 2006. "The Irreverent Raging Grannies: Humour as Protest." *Canadian Women's Studies* 25(3/4): 141–148.

Roy, Carole. 2004. *The Raging Grannies: Wild Hats, Cheeky Songs, and Witty Actions for a Better World*. Montreal, QC: Black Rose Books.

Sandberg, Linn. 2015. "Towards a Happy Ending? Positive Ageing, Heteronormativity and Un/Happy Intimacies." *Lamda Nordica* 4: 19–44.

Sandberg, Linn. 2013a. "Affirmative Old Age—The Ageing Body and Feminist Theories on Difference." *International Journal on Ageing and Later Life* 8(1): 11–40.

Sandberg, Linn. 2013b. "Just Feeling a Naked Body Close to You: Men, Sexuality and Intimacy in Later Life." *Sexualities* 16(3–4): 261–282.

Sandberg, Linn. 2008. "The Old, the Ugly and the Queer: Thinking Old Age in Relation to Queer Theory." *Graduate Journal of Social Science* 5(2): 117–137.

Sandberg, Linn, and Barbara L. Marshall. 2017. "Queering Aging Futures." *Societies* 7(3), 1–11. DOI:10.3390/soc7030021

Sawchuk, Dana. 2009. "The Raging Grannies: Defying Stereotypes and Embracing Aging through Activism." *Journal of Women and Aging* 21: 171–185.

Sawchuk, Kim, and Anysley Moorhouse. 2016. "At the Edge of Meaning." *Modern Drama* 59(2): 177–192.

REFLECTION 6

(In)Visible: Photographing Older Women

Maureen Murphy and Ruth Steinberg

As Maureen Murphy and Ruth Steinberg declare, "There comes a time in a woman's life when she transitions from 'visible' to 'invisible.'" For these two women, it arrived in their late 50s, with their greying hair and softening bodies. They felt that aging had rendered them invisible and irrelevant. They also knew that their experience was not unique—that many older people feel relegated to the sidelines in public discourse, and that this sense of fading may be disproportionate in the experiences of older women of colour, older women with disabilities, and older women from LGBTQ-IA2S+ communities. Choosing to resist this erasure, Maureen and Ruth photograph older women. In this reflection, they offer a series of stunningly beautiful and painfully honest photographs, making older women's faces and bodies boldly visible.

RUTH

I love creating portraits. I love the conversation that precedes the shoot, the time of getting to know my subject so that I can better present her visually in the finished photograph. I don't presume, however, that in those brief moments of conversation and photography that I truly *know* the sitter; what I capture, in mere fractions of seconds, is the face that my subject chooses to reveal in that place and time. As renowned photographer Sally Mann (2015) said, "Photographs economize the truth; they are always moments more or less illusorily abducted from time's continuum."

So if a photograph is a fiction, why not make it easier for the viewer to conjure up the life of the sitter by offering clues to their imagined plot line? Older faces offer those details that a younger face cannot: how the skin folds and creases, where lines cluster, how a face *settles* into an expression after years of smiling or frowning, worrying or laughing. The set of the shoulders, the unguarded expression, how she sits, and the (dis)comfort in her body: These observations provide a glimpse of what the sitter's life experiences might have been. As a photographer, I must be sensitive to these details and nuances if I am to make a portrait that viewers stop and look at, and then return to look at again. The *truth* of the narrative is unimportant—the *presence* of the subject is what matters to me in portraiture.

I do not have a preference between older or younger sitters; both contribute to my understanding of myself. Older sitters invite me to look at my own life, to see the path ahead, to make decisions about how I might choose to live the remainder of my years. Younger sitters fill me with optimism, or regret about the path not chosen; each offers me something of value.

My photo selection includes photos from *What the Body Remembers,* a series of nudes of women aged 55 years and older. I have borrowed the title from the novel of the same name by Shauna Singh Baldwin; I like the suggestion that the physical and emotional experiences of life are remembered by their imprint on the body.

We are not accustomed to seeing nudes of older women in our films or our art; women "of a certain age" are not considered sensual or vibrant or passionate or heroic. This brings up important questions for me: why do we believe aging *eliminates* our capabilities and our appetites? Why are we so loath to look at the changes that time and life render to the body? And why can't we acknowledge that *our own* bodies will thicken and wrinkle, our posture less upright, than when we were young?

I find the aging body beautiful and compelling and I'm drawn to its exploration through photography. I am grateful that the women who posed for this series were open to explore this topic with me.

MAUREEN

This year I will be 70—am I one of those women whom society deems "invisible" as I age? I don't think so. I am among the many older women who are fully engaged in life. We are painters, photographers, politicians, musicians, singers, activists, students, athletes, along with being grandmothers, lovers, mothers, and friends.

We run, earn degrees, argue about politics, take 900 kilometre cycling trips, play bridge, and chain ourselves to the legislative buildings and other halls of power. One of my goals in photographing women is to examine and challenge perceptions of those who think we are (or should be) invisible. I want to celebrate the many ways we challenge this stereotype and encourage others to live their lives out loud. We have not passed our expiry date; we still contribute to society and to the lives of others.

I photograph older women because the faces are interesting: filled with experience and character. Older women can let down the barriers about how they look. I want to celebrate the beauty of older women—laughter lines, wrinkles, and all. They have laughed, cried, sung, danced, cursed, and loved for a lifetime and more—it shows in their demeanour, their expressions, their actions, and even in their inaction. The challenge is to capture who they are—not necessarily how they look.

I am fortunate enough to be connected to dozens of women who are "visible" in many ways and who are willing to sit in front of my camera and have their stories told through photography.

THE PHOTOS

We both have a deep appreciation of older women: their faces, their bodies, their perspectives, their beauty, and their engagement in life. They love the process and the experience of taking these photographs and come away with a richer knowledge and greater appreciation of their own lives.

The photographs on the following pages are a celebration of older women. The first selection is from Ruth's project *What the Body Remembers*. The second selection includes portraits from Maureen's project *(In)Visible* as well as some of Ruth's portrait work.

REFERENCE

Mann, Sally. 2015. *Hold Still: A Memoir with Photographs*. New York: Little, Brown and Co.

What the Body Remembers

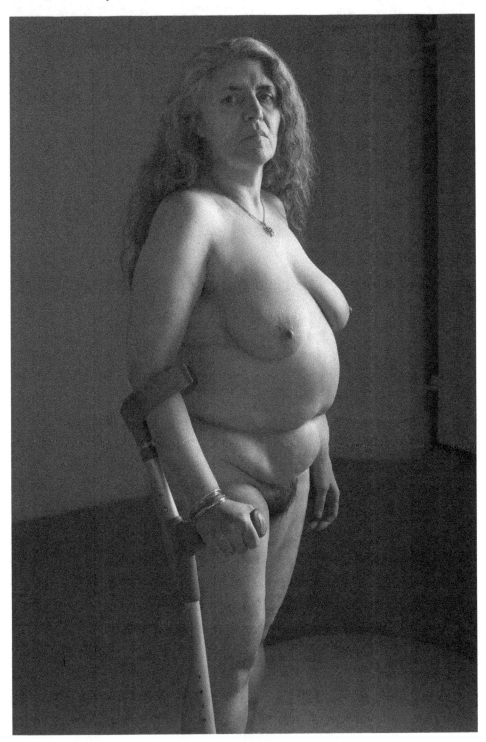

Source: Ruth Steinberg, *What the Body Remembers*

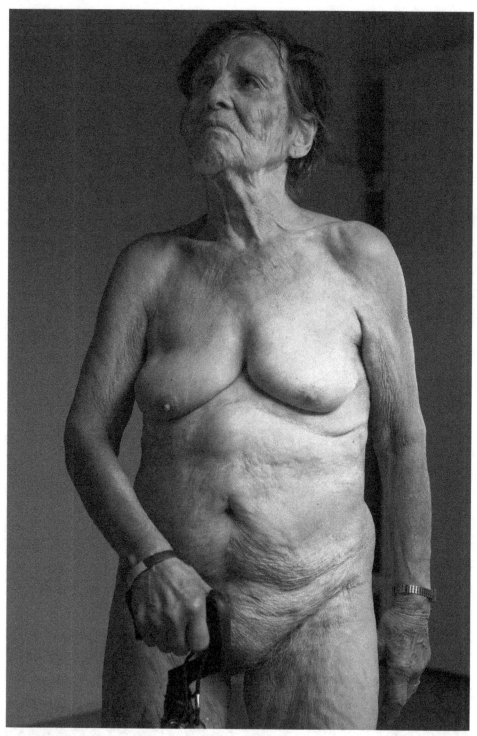

Source: Ruth Steinberg, *What the Body Remembers*

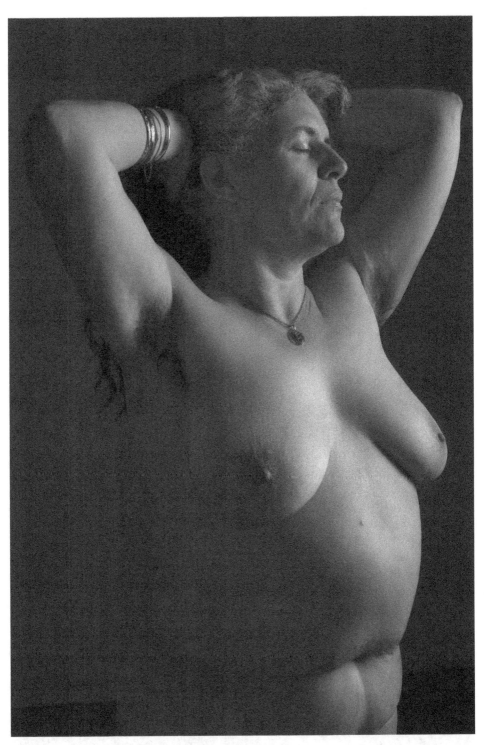

Source: Ruth Steinberg, *What the Body Remembers*

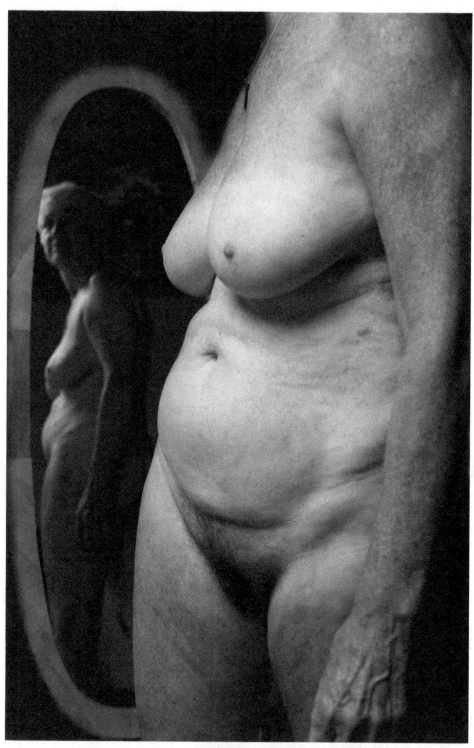

Source: Ruth Steinberg, *What the Body Remembers*

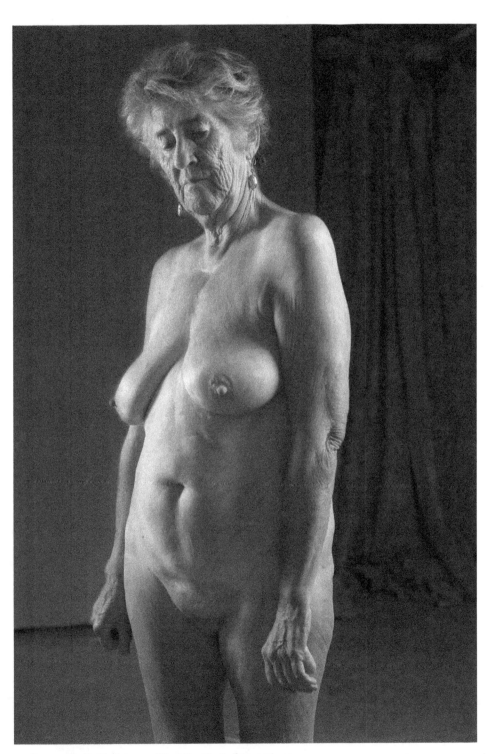

Source: Ruth Steinberg, *What the Body Remembers*

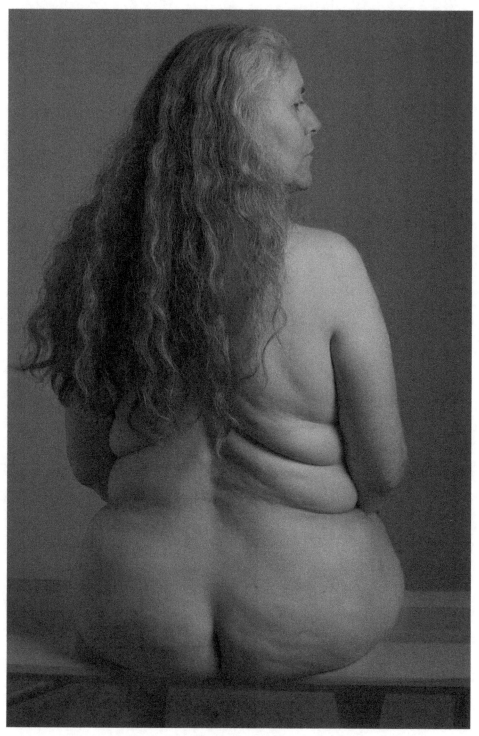

Source: Ruth Steinberg, *What the Body Remembers*

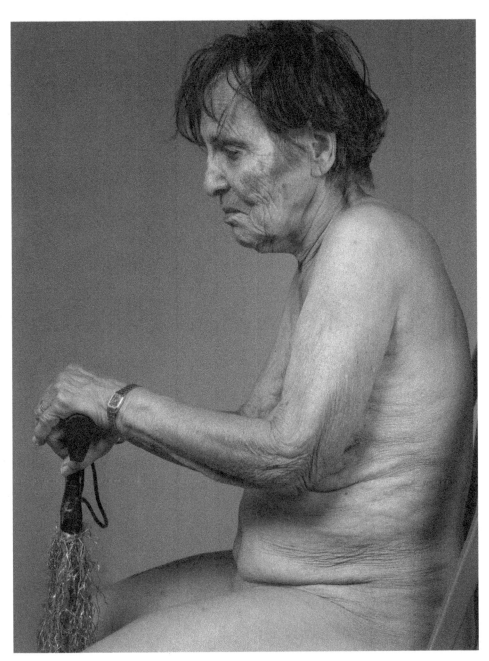

Source: Ruth Steinberg, *What the Body Remembers*

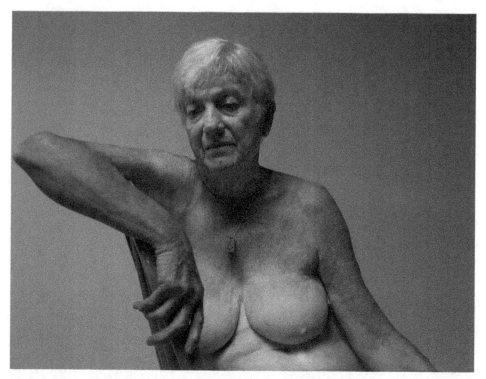

Source: Ruth Steinberg, *What the Body Remembers*

Portraits

Source: Maureen Murphy, *(In)Visible*

Source: Maureen Murphy, *(In)Visible*

Source: Ruth Steinberg, portrait

Source: Ruth Steinberg, portrait

PART IV

REMEMBERING

POEM IV

Lip Point for Bearded Womxn[1]

waaseyaa'sin christine sy

waaseyaa'sin christine sy's words and bio can also be found elsewhere in this volume, on pages 22 and 74. In this piece she offers a sobering and satirical reminder that we are the ancestors of the grandmother activists to come, seven generations from now.

🌀

Board Meeting Minutes (Fiscal Moon, 2078)
Hinky corporate suits toil
whisper fervent words
over glossy boardroom tables,
pray to politicians, shareholders
and two barely animate amphibians
blinking in their terrarium,
"Make the fish come back,
make the fish come back.
We're sorry."
The only thing the lizards
could decipher
through the begging-words
was, "We're broke."

oral history (no moon/not earth, 2254)
your great nokom from seven generations ago always said you were her fortune. in 2078, when the giigoonhsag were on the verge of collapse—thirty years after experts predicted

they would die off—she hover-boarded to the Pacific Ocean, to a place called the Bay of Umbilical Cords and Placentas. here, she got naked and waded into neap tide at setting sun. it's said she floated supine into the future holding a tool in either hand: a knife and a curette. your nokom was a contrary, being facetious in the most serious of times. as she lingered in the refractions of the radiated emerald waters and fluorescent mango sun she is said to have relished what it did to her skin: "i look like a shimmering plum. it's amazing how much more becoming polluted air and light can make an old woman's prune skin appear. too bad i'm on another gig at the moment or i'd try to package this up and make a buck."

E-News Archive (Salmon Moon, 2078)
First person accounts indicate that all along the Pacific Coast of the Americas, old womxn of variable shapes, colours, sizes, and mobilities have been seen entering the ocean. Early reports indicate this is the first round of mass-suicides-as-demonstration against continued Corporate and State investment in global and intergalactic progress and development. Witnesses indicate hearing the womxn repeat a variety of words in different languages. The words reportedly refer to different kinds of fish. The womxn are carrying knifes and what appear to be surgical tools. Also, reported but not yet confirmed: all the womxn are bearded.

lip point for bearded womxn, a ceremony (no moon/not earth, 2254)
ceremonies to honour Grandmothers
who entered dilapidated oceans
found every festering feruncle
in the salt water of our ancestral life
Grandmothers whose curettes incised
poisonous wounds in caverns, crevices
and those swimmers still living, whose
beards absorbed the drainage, whose knifes
liberated their aching bodies from buoyant,
tangled weight, leaving bloodsalt&water—
a wash for the living
ceremonies to honour Grandmothers
who saved the Fish and Us
ceremonies to honour Grandmothers
who saved the Fish and Us
because hinky corporate suits didn't,
even when their prayers were answered

NOTE

1.   An earlier version was first published online at *CV2: Contemporary Verse 2, The Canadian Journal of Poetry and Critical Writing*, www.contemporaryverse2.ca/en/poetry/excerpt/lip-point-for-bearded-women.

INTRODUCTION TO PART IV

Remembering

Laura Madokoro

Novices to archives as both craft and institution often puzzle over why the word *archives* is conventionally presented in the plural. Why, for instance, do we say we are visiting "the archives" instead of "the archive"? Debates about whether or not to pluralize the word are long-standing. While either format is grammatically acceptable, it seems particularly appropriate and even urgent to insist on the pluralization of the word, given the issues raised in the reflection pieces and chapters that follow. The term *archives* speaks to a number of conjoined issues: contents, subjects, and institutions. It therefore makes sense to think of a repository and its materials in the plural. However, the pieces in this section point to an even more pressing reason for thinking of archives in the plural: the multiple subjectivities embraced by people we might simultaneously refer to as creators, users, and archivists as they work, in a self-conscious fashion, towards being remembered.

Traditional understandings of the record-continuum or record life cycle (a somewhat ironic phrase, given the topic of this collection) posit clear breaks and boundaries between those who create records, those who preserve them, and those who use them in historical research. As the contributors to this section show, these clearly delineated roles have been, and continue to be, called into question, particularly by those who have not felt, and still do not feel, themselves reflected in the materials massed in conventional collecting institutions (e.g., libraries, state archives, museums). The activisms of older women and non-binary individuals are notably absent from conventional archives, although they sometimes appear as a result of a political role they have occupied. For instance, a former politician or head of state who happens to be an older woman might expect her fonds to be preserved at a state archives. Yet, unlike the "ordinary extraordinary" activists in this collection, such highly public individuals rarely curate or shepherd their own records to preservation; they are simply assumed to be worthy of historical memory, and institutional labour is in place to assure such preservation.

The pieces in this section offer a very different approach to archiving, as they demonstrate an openness towards rethinking not only who is remembered but how this remembering takes place. Indeed, the following pieces point to the need to break down structural barriers and artificial categories of responsibility, while also revealing a variety of ways in which the very idea of a record-continuum can be reconceptualized. In the words of Jenn Cole, Pat Evans, Sharon Swanson, Melissa Baldwin, Maddy Macnab, May Chazan, and Gabriela Aceves Sepúlveda, we see the results of innovative thinking about activisms, memory, and archiving, as well as novel possibilities for the varied sources being created and identified for preservation.

Reflection 8, Jenn Cole's contribution, epitomizes the enlarged scope of possibilities by documenting the experience of conversing with her grandmother and the ideas that were shared as a result. In Cole's work there is a clear purpose to the intergenerational transfer of knowledge, the idea of a "return home." Equally importantly, Cole sees the process of knowledge sharing as a kind of archiving, and the process of sharing and archiving therefore becomes critical to a larger history and to women's sense of place in this history and on this land. This theme reappears in a number of pieces in this section, showing how process is central to both archiving activisms and activist archives; it is through the process of remembering, sharing, translating, and communicating that participants affirm for themselves what is at stake. As Cole observes, she is "taking the long way home" because remembering is important. Indeed, remembering is even critical, especially when as Cole writes, "the stakes of loss are both personally and politically grave."

Reflection 7, by Melissa Baldwin and Maddy Macnab, also documents a kind of journey, but here the focus is on new territory rather than the return described by Cole. In describing the intent and some of the surprising outcomes of their radio show, *Aging Radically*, Baldwin and Macnab highlight their desire for inter-generational connections. What becomes clear in their piece, which describes both recorded on-air moments and the equally significant interactions off-air, is that archives in the context of evolving intergenerational relationships must be broadly focused. In the case of the *Aging Radically* radio show, Baldwin and Macnab were surprised that one of their interviewees wanted to interview them in turn. They reflect, "As much as our exchanges went both ways, intentionally sharing more of ourselves might have deepened these intergenerational dynamics." Their reflection affirms that archives—in this case in the form of interviews and off-air interactions—assume multiple meanings for participants and listeners in the present, as well as in the future, and that encounters with the archives have a potentially transformative effect.

This idea of archives as transformation, which is a common thread in this section, is particularly pronounced in Chapter 8, which is co-authored by GRAN members Pat Evans and Sharon Swanson, as well as May Chazan and Melissa Baldwin. Here the authors are explicit about their assumptions as they began to entertain the creation of a GRAN archives, as well as about the change that took place in their thinking once they began their collaborative endeavor. They are also honest about what is at stake in terms of "what should be remembered" and how difficult it is to be invested in the production of historical memory. To quote, "As our image of archives as inert records faded, it was replaced by a vision that was far more exciting, if also, at times, daunting."

The importance of intergenerational collaborations is on further display in Gabriela Aceves Sepúlveda's piece—Chapter 7—on the personal archives of the Mexican feminist artist Ana Victoria Jiménez. In tracing the context in which Jiménez first produced photographs of feminist activists, next archived them, and then "reactivated them" in recent years, Aceves Sepúlveda demonstrates the multiple ways in which "women as agents of the archive" work towards the production of historical memory that is in keeping with their evolving activisms. Jiménez's archives is especially interesting given that its contents, and its very existence, spans decades of activism, enabling Jiménez to offer evolving perspectives on what was, and what remains, at stake in the production and preservation of historical memory.

In rethinking the nature of archives, activisms, and intergenerational connections, the authors in this section place great emphasis on the importance of being remembered through the creation of activist archives, broadly defined. This attribution of the power and influence of archiving and being archived might strike some as somewhat exaggerated. Yet in a world where information is fleeting, where facts are parlayed into convenient truths, and where activists of all stripes are seeking to make tangible contributions, it seems that, if anything, the value of being recorded—and of participating in this process—needs to be emphasized even further. What the contributions in this section demonstrate is the iterative process that is unleashed when activists participate in the documentation and preservation of their activities and when archiving becomes a core element of an activist vision. The knowledge that someone else might read about or learn about one's activities has a profound impact on the self-awareness and deliberateness of decision-making, of action, and of words that result. Archives affect activisms, activisms affect archives, and both are entirely transformed as a consequence.

RECOMMENDED READINGS

Ajamu X, Topher Campbell, and Mary Stevens. 2010. "Love and Lubrication in the Archives, or Rukus!: A Black Queer Archive for the United Kingdom." *Archivaria* 68: 271–294.

Bly, Lyz, and Kelly Wooten. Eds. 2012. *Make Your Own History: Documenting Feminist and Queer Activism in the 21st Century.* Sacramento, CA: Litwin Books.

Caswell, Michelle. 2014. "Seeing Yourself in History: Community Archives and the Fight Against Symbolic Annihilation." *The Public Historian* 36(4): 26–37.

Cvetkovich, Ann. 2003. *An Archive of Feelings: Trauma, Sexuality, and Lesbian Public Cultures.* Durham, NC: Duke University.

Eichhorn, Kate. 2013. *The Archival Turn in Feminism. Outrage in Order.* Philadelphia: Temple University Press.

Flinn, Andrew, Mary Stevens, and Elizabeth Shepherd. 2009. "Whose Memories, Whose Archives? Independent Community Archives, Autonomy and the Mainstream." *Archival Science* 9: 71–86.

Gumbs, Alexis P. 2011. "Seek the Roots: An Immersive and Interactive Archive of Black Feminist Practice." *Feminist Collections* 32(1): 17–20.

McLeod, Dayna, Jasmine Rault, and T. L. Cowan. 2014. "Speculative Praxis towards a Queer Feminist Digital Archive: A Collaborative Research-Creation Project." *Ada: A Journal of Gender, New Media, and Technology* 5. Online interactive document: www.adanewmedia.org/2014/07/issue5-cowanetal/

SUGGESTED MULTIMEDIA, ARCHIVES, AND FILMS

Aging Radically Podcasts: www.agingactivisms.org/agingradically

Feminist Freedom Warriors, "A digital video archive documenting cross-generational conversations about justice, politics, and hope with feminist scholar-activists": www.feministfreedomwarriors.org/

Hemispheric Institute Digital Video Library: www.hemisphericinstitute.org/hemi/en/hidvl

Janet Marie Rodgers: Native Waves Radio podcasts, www.soundcloud.com/user386441415, and spoken word and performance poetry, www.soundcloud.com/janet-marie-rogers/

Museo de Mujeres, MUMA: virtual exhibition, www.museodemujeres.com/es/exposiciones/101-mujeres-y-que-mas

Mónica Mayer: Visit the Archive of Ana Victoria Jiménez (blog, in Spanish), www.pintomiraya.com/redes/archivo-ana-victoria-jimenez.html

Mobile Homecoming, "Intergenerational Family Building, Experiential Archive, and Amplifying Generations of Lesbian/SGL/Queer Black Brilliance around the Country": www.mobilehomecoming.org/

Older Women Live podcasts: www.actproject.ca/act/older-women-live/

Rise Up!: A Digital Archive of Feminist Activism: www.riseupfeministarchive.ca/

CHAPTER 7

Activist Archiving and the Feminist Movement in Mexico: Collecting Art and Ephemera as Political Practice

Gabriela Aceves Sepúlveda

On May 9, 1971, a group of 15 women gathered at the Monument to Mothers located in Jardín del Arte in Parque Sullivan, at the crossing of Reforma and Insurgentes Avenues in Mexico City (Jiménez 2010). They carried banners and distributed flyers and balloons printed with the question: *"Somos Madres ¿Y qué más?"* (We are mothers and what else?). Their objective was to demand a change to mass media's manipulation of Mother's Day celebrations and its objectification of women. This was the first in a series of demonstrations organized by a new wave of feminists who established more than a dozen feminist collectives in Mexico City that demanded the eradication of discrimination against women in all levels of society.

Ana Victoria Jiménez (b. 1941, Mexico City) was among the 15 women who participated in the 1971 demonstration. From that moment, Jiménez, then a typesetter by day, photography student by night, and member and militant of the National Union of Mexican Women (UNMM), used her camera to document many of the demonstrations that would follow. Jiménez also preserved pamphlets and posters that, with her photographs and documentation of her own artwork, constitute a one-of-a-kind visual archives of the history of the new wave feminist movement[1] in post-1968 Mexico.

In 2009, Karen Cordero Reiman (b. 1957, New York), a feminist activist and art historian, and Mónica Mayer (b. 1954, Mexico City), a feminist activist and artist, began to reactivate Jiménez's archives (Mayer 2009, 2010). In March 2011, Jiménez's personal archives—containing more than 3,000 photographs and 500 documents on new wave feminist activism and feminist art practices—was donated to the library of the Universidad Iberoamericana (IBERO) in Mexico City, a private academic institution (Cordero 2010). Its acquisition was a significant milestone in the recovery of the histories of post-1960s feminist movements. Moreover, for

Jiménez, reactivation of the archives meant revisiting her earlier activisms from the perspective of someone entering older age.

This chapter draws on interviews and archival documentation to discuss how Jiménez's archival practice has shaped her political subjectivity and informed her social activism over the course of four decades. It reveals both the power of her daily acts of recording and keeping documentation of her activism and the importance of institutionalizing her one-of-a-kind collection of ephemera (pamphlets, flyers, posters, etc.) and photographs, which commemorates several decades of feminist demonstrations and art. Tracing Jiménez's activism through the lens of her archival practice proposes a more nuanced narrative of the histories of Mexican new wave feminism, one that casts it not as an exclusive movement of middle-class university-educated women but rather as an intergenerational movement of those who, across their different backgrounds, ages, and forms of education, were concerned about inequalities within the movement and about how different oppressions implicated women of different classes.

CONTEXT: ACTIVIST ARCHIVING, AGING, AND MEXICAN FEMINISMS

Throughout this chapter, I frame the discussion of Jiménez's archival practice as a daily activity that crucially shaped her identity as a feminist activist. This activity emerges at two different but interconnected moments: First, during the ongoing creation of her collection, when Jiménez was between 30 and 60 years old and, second, at the point when she came to understand her collection as an archives in the context of its transfer to the private university in 2011. This transfer came about as Jiménez entered what is commonly referred to as old age, over 65 years old. How did aging influence Jiménez's transformation of her collection into an archives? How did this transformation change Jiménez's activism? What other connections and conditions made possible the revaluation of Jiménez's collection as an archives? In order to answer these questions, I also consider her activities as a feminist art intervention across generations. I discuss how her friendship with Mónica Mayer, who is 13 years younger than Jiménez, was a major influence in the reactivation of Jiménez's archives and how together their archival activisms continue to produce reverberations. Rather than signposting an end to Jiménez's activism, the transformation of her collection into an archives brought recognition to her ongoing concern for women's rights, casting later life as a productive and meaningful stage rather than a pathology (Dolan and Tincknell 2012).

I use the waves metaphor to distinguish between 1970s feminisms and pre-1970s feminism, following its use by Mexican feminist scholars and activists (Bartra et al. 2000). In Mexico, the term "new wave" rather than "second wave" is used to denote a shift from suffragist and labour claims of early feminist activists in the 1930s to demands for sexual and reproductive rights in the 1970s (ibid.). Within Mexican new wave feminism, there are three distinctions. The term "historical feminists" is used to refer to the first generation of 1970 activists who were middle-class and university educated. The term "second generation" is mostly used to refer to feminist activists who were active in the 1980s when the movement reached out to rural and urban activists from lower classes. The term "third generation" is used to refer to activists who started to organize in the 1990s when the movement became more open to Indigenous women activists (Bartra et al. 2000). These distinctions, however, are problematic as they tend to uphold ideological and generational divides.[2] As I will show in this chapter, Jiménez's archives, activism, and work as an independent publisher, editor, and artist indicate both how these distinctions were not clear-cut and how she was able to bridge generational, class, and ideological divides to carve her own identity as a feminist activist.

In a broader sense, this chapter also seeks to explore how feminist archival practices outside the United States, Britain, and Canada produce alternative historical narratives and enable political agents. Since the 1970s, activists, academics, and artists have questioned the traditional conception of the archives as a repository of texts no longer in use, giving rise to what is known in academic circles as "the archival turn" (Stoler 2002, 83–100). As a result of this turn, historians approach archives through different modes of reading, which allow them to uncover silenced voices, untangle hierarchies of historical production, and scrutinize gender biases in archival practices (Stoler 2009; Burton 2003; Spivak 2006). Likewise, performance and queer theorists have expanded the notion of the archives to include embodied practices (such as oral traditions, re-enactments, domestic practices) as powerful and valid archival mechanisms in the process of knowledge transfer from generation to generation (Taylor 2003; Muñoz 1996; Schneider 2011). In an attempt to "queer the archives," others are interrogating the ways in which the traditional archives condemn feelings and sexual experiences that are not easily documented (Danbolt, Rowley, and Wolthers 2009; Cvetkovich 2003). These diverse configurations of the archives have played a critical role in questioning the authority of those who determine what is historically valuable and in dismantling dominant structures that have erased diverse ways of being and oral traditions from history. However, as Kate Eichhorn argues in her book *The Archival Turn in Feminism*, more still has to be done to understand the role of women as agents of the archives (2013, 2). More than looking for women's voices in the archives, Eichhorn seeks to understand the role of women in enabling the creation of archives.

Eichhorn (2013) locates a feminist archival turn in the activism, cultural production, and scholarship of US feminists born since the late 1960s. While this chapter engages with Eichhorn's interest in the archival turn in feminism, it challenges her US-centric and ageist perspective, which considers only so-called "third wave" feminists as agents of the archives. By showing how the archives has been a central concern for non-US feminists born before 1969, this chapter contends that a broader geographical and temporal lens is needed to expand our understandings of women as agents of the archives. It argues that this lens should consider intergenerational dynamics among activists, as Jiménez's story shows to be the case in Mexican feminism. Equally, it posits our present concern with the archives and archival practice not only as a drive to understand the past but also "as a strategy to engage with some of the legacies, epistemes and traumas pressing down in the present" (Eichhorn 2013, 5). As a potent activist practice, and as is evident in Chapter 8, more and more older women activists are turning to archiving as a way to commemorate their activisms, bring awareness to social justice, and intervene in the writing of history.

THE BIRTH OF AN ARCHIVES AND 1970S MEXICAN FEMINISM

Jiménez's archival practice developed at a crucial time for international women's rights battles and in the midst of a violent decade in which the Latin American region struggled with the consequences of the Cold War. In the aftermath of the massacre of students in 1968 in Mexico City, the administrations of Presidents Luis Echeverría Álvarez (1970–1976) and José López Portillo (1976–1982) showed little tolerance for dissent. They used violence to dispel street demonstrations and brutally suppress rural unrest and urban radical activity. However, both presidents also approved a series of reforms that opened up opportunities for the participation of women in public office and created political conditions that strengthened competing feminist agendas. Most notably, and in the context of the First United Nations International Women's Year Celebration (IWY 1975) celebrated in Mexico City, Echeverría reformed Article 4 of the Mexican Constitution, granting equal rights legislation for women (1974), and both presidents supported a nation-wide family planning campaigns (1974–1982) promoting the use of contraceptives. Feminist collectives took advantage of this political moment and elaborated a project on voluntary-motherhood legislation that was presented to Congress in 1979 (Lau Jaiven 1987; Zapata Galindo 2007). While Congress did not pass the legislative proposal, and while their demands were generally rejected by a predominantly Catholic and conservative society, the activities of feminist activists combined with the populist endeavors of Presidents Echeverría and López Portillo to put women's issues on the agenda for public debate.

By the early 2000s, a renewed interest in the 1970s feminist art movement was taking hold; recognizing this is pivotal to understanding the context in which Mayer and Cordero began negotiations to institutionalize Jiménez's archives. Younger generations of female artists were beginning to look back at the work of their predecessors as they used art to denounce oppression. By then, many early new wave feminist activists were labelled as historical feminists and were entering old age; many held important posts as academics, professionals, and politicians (Bartra et al. 2000). Among these, many were continuing their activisms and beginning to write the histories of Mexico's new wave feminist movement. Initially, most of these efforts concentrated on articulating the histories of this movement through an appraisal of its successes and failures in formal politics—particularly related to passing legislation on abortion or ending violence against women (Bartra et al. 2000; Lamas 1990). Bolstered by certain ideological divides, most of these efforts left out younger voices and did not include the cultural and artistic side of the movement. By 2012, in the context of the commemoration of 40 years of the new wave feminist movement, activists and scholars were beginning to articulate a more inclusive vision of the histories of feminism in Mexico (Acevedo and Lamas 2012). As "feminisms" came to be discussed in the plural, cultural practices and younger generations of activists were included as part of the movement's historical narrative (ibid.).

Mayer and Cordero were also working in the context of changes to public access to archives and renewed interest in understanding Mexico's social movement histories. At the time of Mayer's and Cordero's efforts to institutionalize Jiménez's archives, Mexicans were tacitly granted public access to documentation of Mexico's Dirty War of the 1970s and the 1968 student movement. Some records from the Mexican bureaus of secret intelligence were declassified and transferred to Mexico's National Archives (AGN) in 2002. Records documenting feminist activism were filed in the same boxes in the AGN.

A few years later, amidst these varied commemorative efforts (new wave feminism, feminist art histories, and 1960s social activism, including the student movement), the reactivation of Jiménez's collection shed light on the connections between previously disconnected histories of social activism, feminism, and art

(Aceves 2013). Moreover, as I discuss further, Jiménez's archives not only gives visibility to the life history of an older woman activist who defies representations of older age as a passive stage in life; it also reveals the role of older women in political organizing across decades and generations.

ANA VICTORIA JIMÉNEZ'S ARCHIVAL PRACTICE AS AN INTERGENERATIONAL POLITICAL INTERVENTION

During our conversations, Jiménez framed her political activism and her interests in collecting, photography, and feminist art according to her shifting and some-times conflicting views on feminism. These views combined her early affiliations with left-leaning organizations, the legacies of post-1920s feminism, and her in-volvement with 1970s feminist collectives. This attempt to cover the entire history of women's movements was key to her representation of herself as an archival per-sona: a persona who tried to encompass as many facets of the movement as possible, while simultaneously consciously aware of classifying, collecting, and periodizing difference. This effort provides coherence to her archives and, most importantly, frames her activism as an ongoing activity that does not end with recognition or old age. As I will explain, Jiménez's constant need to bridge the intergenerational and ideological divide amongst feminist activists, as well as her current concern for elderly women's rights, positions aging as an undercurrent in much of her work. Her activities denote a desire for older age to be demystified and made visible as a socially and culturally productive stage of life.

Jiménez came of age politically in the 1960s when she became a member of the National Union of Mexican Women (La Unión Nacional de Mujeres Mexicanas, UNMM), an alliance of women's organizations, activists, and workers' unions established in 1964, mostly affiliated with the Communist Party. Before becoming a member of UNMM she had been affiliated with the Communist Youth League and had been marginally involved in the 1968 student movement (Jiménez 2010). From 1969–1970 Jiménez was the representative of UNMM at the International Democratic Federation of Women in Berlin, and for some years she collaborated in the production of the union's bulletins (ibid.). It was at this time that she began to collect graphic ephemera and to take photos of the demonstrations and events organized by the UNMM.

Her interests in collecting and photography can also be found in her career in the graphics industry. In the early 1960s, she studied graphic arts at the Union of Linotype Press Workers (El Sindicato de los Artistas Gráficos) and soon after began to earn a living as a typesetter in a print shop (ibid.). But it was not until

1974, as Jiménez entered her mid-30s, that she was able to study photography more formally. She quickly established herself as an editor and desktop publisher, publishing books on the history of the UNMM and its members as well as some artists' books (Jiménez 2010).

Jiménez's perspectives on feminism began to transform in 1971 after she joined the feminist collective Mujeres en Acción Solidaria (MAS) and later Movimiento Nacional de Mujeres (MNM). Through her affiliations with MAS and MNM, Jiménez became acquainted with a diverse group of women who were concerned with issues of gender equality and sexual rights. Throughout the 1970s, Jiménez participated in more than a dozen feminist demonstrations and belonged to various feminist collectives. She became engaged not only in a new set of issues—including abortion, sexual rights, and concerns about the ways women were represented in the media—but also a different way of performing protest and making demands about those issues in public. Unlike UNMM or Communist Youth League demonstrations that she had attended previously, these new feminist demonstrations, according to Jiménez, were "much more upbeat, with more of a sense of the visual, with a particularly distinct way of expressing demands in their banners and signs" (2010). This difference, she told me, is what inspired her to take photos and collect ephemera more rigorously.

Beginning in 1978, and influenced by her collaborations in Rosa Martha Fernández's[3] film productions and her participation in various feminist art groups (Aceves 2013, 2014), Jiménez's activism and her interest in photography were increasingly driven by a concern with feminist art as a way to recover the histories of feminism and promote intergenerational dialogue. This interest was expressed through her participation in a group of militant artists established by Mayer that resulted in an art exhibition entitled *Muestra Colectiva Feminista* (1978), and through her involvement in the organization of Suzanne Lacy's *International Dinner Party* (1979) in Mexico City on February 14, 1979 (Jiménez 2010).[4] As part of *International Dinner Party*, Jiménez and Mayer's mother, Lilia Lucido de Mayer (also a feminist activist), organized a dinner in Lucido's home to honour Adelina Zendejas (1909–1993, Mexico), Amalia Castillo Ledón (1898–1986, Mexico), Elvira Trueba (1899–1993, Mexico), and Concha Michel (1899–1990, Mexico). These four women were all important in the post-1920 period and had fought for social causes; they were, as Jiménez would call them, *"nuestras madrinas"* (our godmothers) (Olcott 2005). It is worth emphasizing here that this event bridged and commemorated different generations of women's activism. By honouring her *madrinas*, Jiménez positions herself not only as part of this important genealogy of Mexican women activists but also in relation to the pioneering generation of

US-based feminist artists. Her ongoing negotiation between different generations of women's activism and her interest in documenting her relation with *las madrinas* is indicative of her need to provide coherence and continuity to her own political commitment to women's movements. As I discuss, this also points to the ways in which Jiménez's archival and artistic practice became the bedrock that gave meaning to her multi-faceted feminist activism.

In 1985, Jiménez joined the feminist art collective Tlacuilas y Retrateras (1983–1985) with six other feminist artists and activists. At the same time, she continued to take photographs and keep records of each demonstration she participated in. As new wave feminist collectives disbanded, Jiménez continued to participate in other forms of social activism and document demonstrations such as the women garment workers' movement in 1985 and the electoral campaign of 1988 in Mexico City, to name just a couple. This wide range of interest shows that, at its core, Jiménez's activism was concerned with bringing an end to women's oppression across social classes. Also, rather than diminishing with age, Jiménez's interest in social justice continued to expand.

After Tlacuilas y Retrateras dissolved in 1986, Jiménez's involvement with artistic initiatives waned, but she continued to be prolific in publishing activist memoirs and in writing the history of the UNMM, using her personal archives as a major source. At this time, she also turned her activism towards aging. From 1988 to 2003, Jiménez organized a series of seminars to bring awareness to issues affecting aging women and to dispel myths about later life (Jiménez 2017).[5] This concern towards aging was inspired by the work of Betsie Hollants (b. 1903), a Belgian feminist activist who established CIDHAL (Coordinación de Iniciativas para el Desarrollo Humano de América Latina), a Christian feminist community education centre and library established in Cuernavaca, Morelos in 1969. CIDHAL was the first organization dedicated to the documentation and dissemination of information on issues affecting women in Latin America. Both CIDHAL and Hollants were crucial influences for Jiménez's archival practice. In our conversations, Jiménez recognized CIDHAL's community library, publication efforts, and archives as the only other existing feminist collection and an antecedent to her collection (Jiménez 2010, 2017).

Jiménez's career as an independent publisher, along with her work with elderly women, not only speaks to her activism, but also to her ongoing capacity to reinvent ways to intervene in different forms of oppression. Hence, in the context of these ongoing activities, it is clear that the transformation of her collection into an archives did not put an end to her activism but, instead, as Mayer and Cordero say, only reactivated it (Mayer and Cordero 2015).

JIMÉNEZ'S ARCHIVES AS ART

In this section, I discuss how Mayer's engagement with Jiménez's archives, and particularly her recognition of the archives as a work of art, was an important catalyst that brought attention to the historical importance this archives. At the time when Mayer and Cordero began to revise Jiménez's collection and look for an institution to house it, art critics and visual artists who had also been working in the 1960s and 1970s were engaged in archival contestation (Enwezor 2007; Merewether 2006; Pollock 2007). In particular, conceptual-based artists whose ephemeral practices remained only through documentation also began to advocate for the preservation and institutionalization of their work. The reception to these endeavours was mixed.[6]

Despite some contention, Mayer and her partner, artist Victor Lerma, became important advocates for and agents of artists' archives. In 1988, they established Pinto Mi Raya, an independent online repository of newspaper and magazine articles on Mexican contemporary art. Considering their archives and archival practice as works of art in their own right, Mayer describes Pinto Mi Raya as "applied conceptual art." This is a concept that Mayer and Lerma coined to define: "conceptual art projects that, besides focusing on an idea, their purpose is to have a practical application; that is, they need to be functional. And, as we have repeatedly stated, the objective of Pinto Mi Raya has been to lubricate the art world; to detect its problems and propose solutions" (Mayer 2006). Thus, Mayer conceptualizes their activities as an art practice that is not only based on ideas but also proposes practical solutions to problems. She broadens the definition of art to an act of collecting and distributing information (Mayer 2009).

Mayer has curated several exhibitions, focusing on reactivating archives, including *Mujeres ¿y que más?: Reactivando el archivo de Ana Victoria Jiménez*, co-curated with Cordero in March 2011, which celebrated the transfer of Jiménez's archives to IBERO. Since then, Mayer has organized various community art events incorporating Jiménez's archives across Mexico, Latin America, and the United States to bring awareness to women's rights and violence against women. Due to the visibility of these activities, in 2016 both Mayer and Jiménez received an official recognition for promoting women's empowerment through arts (INMUJERES 2016). The alternative pathways traced through Jiménez's archival practice and relationship with Mayer merged feminist art and archival practice as integral to activism; these currently inspire and give voice to younger generations of activists who are continuing to demand an end to violence against women.

CONCLUSION

While Jiménez does not consider her archives as a work of art (Jiménez 2010), it not only includes her photographic and performance-based work but also documents important practices that, until recently, were not fully acknowledged in historical narratives. Jiménez's collection of photographs and ephemera (flyers, posters, photocopies) was crucial to the construction of her identity as a feminist activist and artist. It has also become an important resource for scholars who now consult her collection to write the histories of feminist organizing in post-1960 Mexico. By claiming distance from established politically committed artists and from diverse trends of feminisms (while at the same time claiming alliance), she constructed a sense of self that moved fluidly from a background in communist militancy, to new wave feminism, to editor, to independent publisher, to writer, to photographer, and to performance artist. Her networks, while similar to those of many other artists and activists, most often operated outside already-established channels of party politics, sanctioned art movements, or upper-class relations. This distancing speaks of an archival interest for classifying, collecting, and periodizing difference. Equally, it speaks of Jiménez's archival persona as one that tried to encompass as many facets of the new wave feminist movement as possible. Jiménez's archival practice positions her as continuing the work of her 1920s *madrinas* and of post-1968 feminists and women activists.

The combined commemoration efforts that led to the reactivation of her archives gave visibility to the life history of an older woman activist who defies traditional representations of aging as a passive, ailing, or self-loathing stage in life (Dolan and Tincknell 2012). Rather, Jiménez casts aging as a stage that provides continuity to women's activism. In looking at Jiménez's life history through her archival practice, aging emerges as a continual undercurrent. Her work depicts her concern for bridging the intergenerational and ideological divides between activists and for demystifying and making visible later life as a socially and culturally productive time, through her own activism and through her ongoing interest in writing and archiving the histories of feminist activists.

NOTES

1.   I use the term "new wave" to follow Mexican terminology and bring clarity to the argument. It is worth noting, however, that Jiménez and others were engaged in feminist work throughout these decades. As such, the use of the term "new wave" does not mean that the actors were "new" to activism. It should also be noted that the use of the waves metaphor to distinguish

ideological differences and phases of activity and inactivity to explain different historical periods within the histories of feminism has been under scrutiny by numerous scholars. For some, the wave metaphor obscures ongoing intergenerational connections amongst activists (Chazan 2015; Sawchuk 2009). For others, it follows a US- and British-centric lens that fails to acknowledge different histories of feminism across the globe (Tripp 2006). And yet for others, the waves metaphor is still useful as a means to subvert the histories of hegemonic feminism through a lens that considers race (Dua 1999). For debates with regards to the naming of 1970s feminism in the Mexican context see "Tres décadas de neofeminismo en México" in Bartra et al. 2000, 45–81.

2.   It is worth noting that the paradoxical relation between lesbian and feminist activists is not accounted for in this classification. For contradictions within the feminist movement regarding relationship to the lesbian movement, see Mongrovejo 1999.

3.   Rosa Martha Fernández (b. Mexico City, 1942), is a film director and feminist activist. In 1975, she established Colectivo Cine-Mujer, the first feminist film collective in Mexico.

4.   Lacy's *International Dinner Party* was a global project to honour feminist artist Judy Chicago's first exhibition of *Dinner Party* at the San Francisco Museum of Modern Art (Aceves 2014). Lacy's version of the *Dinner Party* project consisted of hosting dinners held on the same evening of Chicago's opening in as many places as possible to honour women in their own regions. At each dinner, women collectively wrote a statement that was sent back by telegram to Lacy who, at the opening, presented a 20-foot black and white map of the world on which each dinner was marked with a red inverted triangle.

5.   These seminars were held at Centro de Investigacions Económicas at UNAM (Univerisdad Autónoma de México) and were part of the activities organized by VEMEA (Vejez en Mexico Estudios y Acción), a community organization created to bring awareness to issues affecting older women and dispel myths about this life stage. VEMEA was established 1984 by Hollants after she left CIDHAL (Cervantes 2004).

6.   For instance, in speaking about interest in recovering the archives of Latin American artists who worked under 1960s–1970s dictatorships and violent populist regimes, art critic Sue Rolnik has argued that, rather than addressing a concern for recovering the memory of that tumultuous period, these efforts respond to a redefinition of the geopolitics of the art world, whose aim is to neutralize politics through visibility and access (Rolnik 2010). Correspondingly, in terms of the proliferation of feminist art exhibits around the world, Griselda Pollock (2007) advanced concerns that the recent attention to feminist art, what she calls "the musealization of the movement," could end up erasing the movement's radical criticality. While both Rolnik's and Pollock's arguments might be accurate in speaking about some of the perils of commodifying archives—that is, their circulation as objects of value within the art market and their increased value as "marginal objects"—and of the possible loss of the radical edge of marginal movements, their argumentations disregard the ways that wider accessibility can, at the same time, elicit

oppositional responses and nuanced readings. Andreas Huyssen, who has discussed extensively the contemporary desire for memorialization, argues that critical assessments of the institutions created by this desire have to consider how "there is always a surplus of meaning [in these practices and institutions] that exceeds ideological set boundaries, opening spaces for reflection and counter-hegemonic discourses" (1995, 15).

REFERENCES

Acevedo, Marta, and Marta Lamas. 2012. Cuarenta Años de Feminismo en México, Conferencia del Feminismo en México. Mexico DF.

Aceves Sepúlveda, Gabriela. 2013. "'¿Cosas de Mujeres?': Feminist Networks of Collaboration in 1970s Mexico." *Artelogie* 5.

Aceves Sepúlveda, Gabriela. 2014. "Mujeres que se Visualizan: (En)gendering Archives and Regimes of Media and Visuality in Post-1968 Mexico." PhD, History, University of British Columbia.

Bartra, Eli, et al. 2000. *Feminismo en México, Ayer y Hoy*. Mexico DF: Universidad Autónoma Metropolitana.

Burton, Antoinette. 2003. *Dwelling in the Archive: Women Writing House, Home and History in Late Colonial India*. New York: Oxford University Press.

Cervantes, Erika. 2004. "Betsie Hollants." *cimacnoticias.com.mx*, July 19, 2004. www.cimacnoticias.com.mx/node/38298.

Cordero Reiman, Karen. 2010. Interview with Karen Cordero Reiman. Edited by Gabriela Aceves Sepúlveda. Mexico City: unpublished.

Chazan, May. 2015. *The Grandmothers' Movement: Solidarity and Survival in the Time of AIDS*. Montreal, QC: McGill-Queen's Press.

Cvetkovich, Ann. 2003. *An Archive of Feelings: Trauma, Sexuality, and Lesbian Public Cultures*. Durham, NC: Duke University.

Danbolt, Mathias, Jane Rowley, and Louise Wolthers. Eds. 2009. *Lost and Found: Queerying the Archive*. Copenhagen: Nikolaj Copenhagen Contemporary Art Center.

Dolan, Josephine, and Estella Tincknell. Eds. 2012. *Aging Femininites: Troubling Representations*. Newcastle upon Tyne, UK: Cambridge Scholars Publishing.

Dua, Enakshi. 1999. "Canadian, Anti-racist, Feminist Thought: Scratching the Surface of Racism." In *Scratching the Surface: Canadian, Anti-racist, Feminist Thought*, edited by Enakshi Dua and Angela Robertson, 7–31. Toronto, ON: Women's Press.

Eichhorn, Kate. 2013. *The Archival Turn in Feminism. Outrage in Order*. Philadelphia: Temple University Press.

Enwezor, Okwui. 2017. *Archive Fever—Uses of the Document in Contemporary Art*. New York: Center for Photography, Steidl.

Huyssen, Andreas. 1995. *Twilight Memories: Marking Time in a Culture of Amnesia*. New York: Routledge.

INMUJERES. 2016. "XIV Entrega de la Medalla Omecíhuatl." http://data.inmujeres. cdmx.gob.mx/14-entrega-medalla-omecihuatl/

Jiménez, Ana Victoria. 2010. Interview with Ana Victoria Jiménez, edited by Gabriela Aceves Sepúlveda. Mexico City: unpublished.

Jiménez, Ana Victoria. 2017. Electronic Interview with Ana Victoria Jiménez, edited by Gabriela Aceves Sepúlveda. Mexico City and Vancouver: unpublished.

Jiménez, Ana Victoria, and Francisca Reyes Castellanos. 2000. *Sembradoras de Futuros. Memoria de la Unión Nacional de Mujeres Mexicanas*. México DF: UNMM.

Lamas, Marta. 1990. "El Feminismo Mexicano y La Lucha Por el Aborto." *Debate Feminista* 1(2): 29–33.

Lau Jaiven, Ana. 1987. *La Nueva Ola del Feminismo en México: Conciencia y Acción de Lucha de las Mujeres*. México, DF: Fascículos Planeta.

Mayer, Mónica. 2006. "Archivos de Arte y Arte Sobre Archivos." *La Pala*.

Mayer, Mónica. 2009. Interview with Mónica Mayer, edited by Gabriela Aceves Sepúlveda. Mexico City: unpublished.

Mayer, Mónica. 2010. Interview with Mónica Mayer, edited by Gabriela Aceves Sepúlveda. Mexico City: unpublished.

Mayer, Mónica, and Cordero, Karen. 2015. "Mujeres ¿Que Más?: Reactivando el Archivo de Ana Victoria Jiménez," archivoavj.com

Merewether, Charles. 2006. *The Archive*. London: Whitechapel.

Mongrovejo, Norma. 1999. "Sexual Preference, the Ugly Duckling of Feminist Demands: The Lesbian Movement in Mexico." In *Female Desires: Same-Sex Relations and Transgender Practices across Cultures*, edited by Evelyn Blackwood and Saskia Wieringa, 308–335. New York: Columbia University Press.

Muñoz, José Esteban 1996. "Ephemera as Evidence: Introductory Notes to Queer Acts." *Women and Perfomance* 8(2): 5–16.

Olcott, Jocelyn. 2005. *Revolutionary Women in Postrevolutionary Mexico*. Durham, NC: Duke Universtiy.

Pollock, Griselda. 2007. *Encounters in the Virtual Feminist Museum: Time, Space and the Archive*. London: Routledge.

Rolnik, Suely. 2010. "Furor de Archivo." *Estudios Visuales; Ensayo Teoría y Crítica de la Cultura Visual y el Arte Contemporáneo* 7.

Sawchuk, Kim. 2009. "Feminism in Waves: Re-imagining a Watery Metaphor." In *Open Boundaries: A Women's Studies Reader*, edited by Lise Gotell and Barbara Crow, 58–63. Toronto, ON: Pearson Prentice Hall.

Schneider, Rebecca. 2011. *Performing Remains: Art and War in Times of Theatrical Reenactment.* London: Routledge.

Spivak, Gayatri Chakravorty. 2006. "The Rani of Sirmur: An Essay in Reading the Archives." *The Archive*: 163–169.

Stoler, Ana Laura. 2002. "Colonial Archives and the Arts of Governance: On the Content in the Form." In *Refiguring the Archive,* edited by Carolyn Hamilton et al., 83–100. Cape Town, South Africa: David Phillips Publishers.

Stoler, Ana Laura. 2009. *Along the Archival Grain: Epistemic Anxieties and Colonial Common Sense.* Princeton, NJ: Princeton University Press.

Taylor, Diana. 2003. *The Archive and the Repertoire: Performing Cultural Memory in the Americas.* Durham, NC: Duke University Press.

Tripp, Mari Aili. 2006. "The Evolution of Transnational Feminisms: Consensus." In *Global Feminism: Transnational Women's Activism, Organizing and Human Rights,* edited by Myra Marx Ferree and Aili Mari Tripp, 3–23. New York: NYU Press.

Zapata Galindo, Martha. 2007. "Feminist Movements in Mexico from Consciousness-Raising Groups to Transnational Networks." In *Feminist Philosophy in Latin America and Spain,* edited by Maria Luisa Feminas and Amy A. Oliver, 1–19. Amsterdam, New York: Brill Rodopi.

REFLECTION 7

Activist Aging on the Airwaves: Radical Reflections on the Community Radio Show *Aging Radically*

Melissa Baldwin and Maddy Macnab

In this reflection, Melissa Baldwin and Maddy Macnab, two settler Canadians and aspiring scholar-activists in their 20s, discuss the first year of their radio show Aging Radically, which they started on the community station Trent Radio in the fall of 2015.[1] They discuss how, as co-hosts, they were motivated to develop the show to amplify some of the voices and stories of older women working for change in Nogojiwanong (Peterborough), to foster intergenerational dialogue about activism, and to create a recorded archives of these live, on-air conversations. In this piece, they reflect on this radio project and the spaces it opened up, on and off the airwaves.

"I don't want to age gracefully … I want to age radically!" These are the playful lyrics to the theme song for our community radio show, *Aging Radically*, which aired on Trent Radio, 92.7 FM, in Nogojiwanong. Though our theme song was a bit tongue-in-cheek, it did express our intentions for the show. In this piece, we reflect on our first year of *Aging Radically*, which aimed to amplify the voices of women older than us[2] who work for change and to foster intergenerational dialogue about activism. Ranging in age from 40 to 93, our guests were engaged in different social movements and held many different perspectives on their "activist aging." To capture our on-air conversations beyond the broadcasts, we recorded and archived the show.

Aging Radically came about serendipitously. Maddy was new to Nogojiwanong; enamoured with the immediacy and intimacy of audio storytelling, she wanted to start a radio show. Melissa had been living and working in Nogojiwanong, generating life histories with older women activists and finding tremendous meaning in these relationships (see Chapter 1). When we met, Melissa shared her observation that the vibrant core of older activists in Nogojiwanong—especially women—were often left out of local conversations about social change. We spoke about the possibilities and limits of intergenerationality in our own lives, realizing we were both eager for more relationships across generations. Through our first episode, memories of our own intergenerational family relationships became part of the show's archives. Melissa shared her remorse that she could no longer hear stories from her own grandmothers, while Maddy was able to honour her grandmother by sharing a recording of her voice. Holding the memory of these relationships close, we were excited to explore new intergenerational connections beyond our families.

During each show, we asked guests the same four questions about their current social change work and their thoughts on aging. We loved that we had no idea whether anyone was listening as we delved into these conversations live on air. Though the show started as a way to amplify and archive the "on air" moments, we were soon equally taken with the quieter "off air" moments. In this reflection, we share some of the stories broadcast on the airwaves alongside those less audible connections and ideas that have remained with us long after leaving the studio. Beyond providing an opportunity for our guests to be recorded and remembered, we became part of a dynamic process of remembering our pasts and imagining a shared future. We co-created a politicized intergenerational space that shook up ageist and sexist assumptions and lifted up social change practices that are not always understood as activism.

CHALLENGING MEANINGS OF "ACTIVISMS"

Our conversations on the show raised the question of what counts as activism. Our guests did not always position themselves as "activists"—nor did they have to. Liz Stone, who runs Niijkiwendidaa Anishnaabekwewag Services Circle, spoke about resistance in her Anishinaabe family:

> So, growing up in the Indigenous community, whether it was urban or rural or whatever it looked like at that time, there was just things that we did as a culture, as everyday life … Part of the reason why we didn't name it "activism" or "practicing our rights" or anything like that was because it was just a matter of living. Right?
>
> So, big issues were hunting and fishing. That was, huge issues. So we weren't, as Indigenous people, allowed to hunt and fish anywhere. Even in our own territories. So something that we did, we'd have a family picnic or a

community picnic, where people would come from all over the place, our family members or friends of the family, and we would make a point of, going to, say, a national park. And fish. The men would go out and fish, and the women would set up a nice barbeque or picnic area or whatever. And for us, it was never about, we never talked about practicing our rights or making a point or making a claim or anything like that. It was about, every year the family got together. And we went and did this.

We had weddings in national parks, ceremonies, we had gatherings. I just always knew that when we went through those turnstiles where park people were collecting money or whatever, that we weren't going to pay any money. That we weren't going to make reservations for certain areas or whatever. That, you know, my grandfather was going to drive us in and say, "This is who I am and this is our territory, so this is what we're doing," and drive through. Then there would be, the whole family would drive through collectively, or the whole group would drive through collectively. It never really dawned on me that we were doing anything but being a family and practicing our ways, our family ways, you know what I mean?

In narrating her political life in her own terms, Liz took hold of the studio, weaving it into a space for contesting the Eurocentricity of conceptions of "activism." Liz gently questioned our own framings of the space, and challenged what it means to be radical.

BEING HEARD ACROSS GENERATIONS

Other guests, such as local settler Canadian journalist and activist Melodie McCullough, challenged norms implicitly simply by speaking and being heard as older women who work for social change. On air, Melodie shared that coming on our show was outside of her comfort zone. She was not used to publicly narrating her reflections on social change, nor on aging. Afterward, via email, she reflected on the significance of joining us on air:

I found it quite liberating—I felt very special to be included as one of your chosen guests. It was a chance for me to reflect on some things that I hadn't really thought about before in connection to aging, such as how I got to where I am now, and my views on aging and still being active and an activist. When it was over, I realized how much my mother's aging process had influenced me.... So I've probably had her in the back of my mind as a role model, and the radio program helped me realize my contrasted experience and how much I value my own abilities to do stuff at this age.

For Melodie, telling her story and being heard by us across generational difference is what made this moment significant. The radio show became a space where Melodie could reflect intentionally on what it means to her to be an "aging" woman and an activist. This "off air" exchange was one of many moments that escaped recording, but was key to how we heard and remembered Melodie's activism.

ON THE OTHER SIDE OF THE MIC: INTERGENERATIONAL EXCHANGE

In many ways, the conversations themselves became a site of social change. In the intimate, politicized, and intergenerational space of the studio, we began to explore what intergenerationality can look like beyond what we typically access. We have carried these explorations outside the studio and into our daily lives. These explorations have led us each to notice intergenerational relationships that we already have, bringing more intention to them, and relishing what is nourishing and radical in them. We find ourselves seeking out intergenerational formations in our own community organizing, increasingly drawn to movements or campaigns where intergenerational connections are happening, while also seeking out the quieter, less explicit relationship work, listening, sharing, and learning of social change work and thinking deeply about how we might organize in a way that fosters these connections.

The intimacy of sharing personal stories and political practices across age shapes our ongoing relationships with our guests, and we have gone on to organize alongside and with many of these radical women. This has struck us as radical, rare, and different from our family experiences of intergenerationality. What we set out to capture through recorded conversations became something very different. Certainly, the recordings form an important part of how we "remembered" these local activisms, but equally important was the process of witnessing their stories and imagining a shared future. Our experiences have pushed us to continue these conversations and seek out new ones, across age and other differences. They have spurred us to reflect on our own ongoing experiences of aging. They encourage us to continue remembering and imagining the many forms that social change work has taken and might yet take in our lives.

NOTES

1. You can listen to episodes of *Aging Radically* at www.agingactivisms.org/agingradically.
2. In our first season, we specifically set out to bring women activists who were older than us into the studio. In our second season, we expanded our show to include activists of different ages and genders.

CHAPTER 8

Intergenerational Interventions: Archiving the Grandmothers Advocacy Network

Pat Evans, Sharon Swanson, May Chazan, and Melissa Baldwin

This chapter reflects on an intergenerational, academic/activist collaboration to create an archives of the Grandmothers Advocacy Network (GRAN), a cross-Canada movement of older women. The story of our collaboration, and of GRAN's archives generally, offers insight into the importance of activist archiving—for ensuring that activists' struggles for social justice are recognized and can endure. It also underscores the significance of archives and archiving for older women; while critical to all social movements (Flinn and Alexander 2015), the process of creating, keeping, and preserving records is especially important to older women, whose activisms rarely feature in historical accounts of social change (Charpentier, Quéniart, and Jacques 2008; Richards 2012). In telling this story, we reflect on three unexpected shifts we experienced through working together to create GRAN's archives: (1) a shift in our understandings of archives, from our initial vision of a collection of dusty boxes full of records to our growing appreciation that archives navigate social memory through active, deliberative, and selective practices; (2) a shift in our understanding of ourselves as activists of different ages/generations; and (3) a shift in how we perceived and experienced conventional generational roles.

Writing this chapter mirrors the collaboration that surrounded GRAN's archives project. Pat Evans, former GRAN co-chair (2013–2015) and co-editor of this book, and Sharon Swanson, GRAN Leadership Team member (2014–2016), have led the archives project since it began in 2013. May Chazan, book co-editor, is an academic whose research with GRAN (and other activist organizations and groups) dates back more than a decade. Melissa Baldwin, book co-editor, is a graduate student who has been working with May on research projects since 2013 and helped lay the groundwork for the GRAN archives project.[1] We are in our 70s, 40s, and 20s, respectively; we work across both differences in experience and similarities in our values and feminist leanings—similarities and differences that cannot be understood solely through our contrasting biological ages. As one of the two GRAN members who led the archival initiative, Pat took the lead in writing this chapter, consulting with Sharon in the process; this approach roots our work in feminist epistemologies that challenge the too often assumed authority of the researcher over lived experience. May and Melissa contributed to the chapter by drawing connections to existing scholarship that helped to ground our archival understandings and approach, while also offering their own similar and contrasting reflections.

This chapter departs from the tendency in writing about archives to focus on tangible products (that is, specific records or collections). Instead, we highlight what such a focus often obscures: the *processes* and the social relations through which archives are created.[2] We draw on Ashmore, Craggs, and Neate, who examine the "hidden collaborations and socialities" surrounding the creation and use of archives, suggesting that the social and emotional dimensions of collaboration can significantly influence the contours of an archives itself (2012, 81). In other words, we focus on archiving as a *process* that involves making decisions, negotiating relationships, and navigating feelings for the purpose of preserving memories or remembering (Caswell and Cifor 2016). In contrast to the usual erasure of the relations that shape archives, our collective archiving journey, with its surprising shifts in understanding, has been intricately intertwined with our evolving personal and professional relationships with each other. Our very vision of what an "archives" is, and of what "archiving" can entail, has been transformed through the process of "working-with" each other (ibid., 88)—this recalls the notion of "becoming-with" offered by Changfoot, Ansley, and Dodsworth in Chapter 5 of this volume. With these relationships always present, we reflect on the three above-noted shifts we experienced along our journey, attempting to place them at the intersection of critical archival studies and critical aging studies.

First, informed by critical archival work and specifically what has been termed "the archival turn," our approach shifted significantly over the course of our work together to take in the complexity, contingency, and politicized nature of archives and archiving.[3] Building on postmodern critiques that unsettle the foundations of what has been deemed credible knowledge, this scholarship frames archives as dynamic, partial, and unfinished rather than static and complete. Such scholars note that archives reflect and are produced through power relations, as they are created deliberately by particular people at particular times (Dunbar 2006). These scholars situate archivists as active creators/mediators of social memory, rather than as passive and objective collectors/reporters of uncontested histories. From this perspective, archives are always evolving and directed towards the future (Juhasz

2006; Eichhorn 2013). Through our project, which involved May and Melissa bringing pieces of archival scholarship into discussions with Pat and Sharon, our initial image of the GRAN archives-to-be as a series of static, rarely-opened boxes transformed into a reality that was far more dynamic, nuanced, and complex. As our thinking changed, we engaged with a different conception of the story of GRAN, how it might be recorded, who would be involved in its telling, and how we might document and make explicit our process.

Second, throughout our work together, we reflected—individually and collectively—on our subjectivities[4] as "activists" of different ages, fostering different understandings of our positions and practices. This resonates with work elsewhere on activist archiving, in which activists reject the idea of "being archived" as passive objects; instead, they position themselves as "archiving," as active agents of their own collections and authors of their own accounts (see Caswell 2014; Bly and Wooten 2012). We bring to our work an explicit aging lens: thinking about how dynamics of age, aging, and intergenerationality implicate our subjectivities and relationships, and recognizing this analysis as an extension to existing scholarship. While much critical archival work continues to depict older women as end-of-life donors of records or as subjects of past contributions (Chazan, Baldwin, and Madokoro 2015), we explicitly frame the GRAN archives as an example of older women creating their own archives, documenting their own stories, and focusing on their ongoing political organizing.

Third, we experience our archival processes as a site for intergenerational relationship-building. As such, our collaboration challenges certain normative generational scripts, or dominant ways of understanding and performing relationships across age/generation: As discussed in the book's introduction, such dominant scripts are based on heteronormative, colonial, and patriarchal world views, not on critical approaches to aging, the lifecourse, intergenerationality, or, as Mojica terms it in Reflection 3, "the continuum." In this chapter, we explore how we have worked together as co-learners, co-activists, co-archivists, and friends in an intergenerational configuration none of us have previously experienced outside of familial contexts. This dynamic extends to much of the archival literature, which reflects limited critical analyses of intergenerationality.[5] Drawing on themes from scholarship on intergenerationality to sharpen our thinking, we recognize that, within a society that is largely "age stratified" (Hogeland 2001, 178), it is rare for people of different generations to get to know each other, learn alongside each other, or work together for similar causes, as we do in this project. As Stephen Farrier (2015) contends, intergenerational dynamics are often intelligible only within a framework of heteronormative (and we would add "colonial") familial scripts,[6] which typically dictate rigid generational (and gendered) roles. Although this allows very few possibilities for relationships across generations to be conceived of or practiced in *unscripted* ways, our project opens up such possibilities.

We take up these three core themes against the background of the why's, what's, and how's of GRAN's archival project. Our discussion explores several pivotal questions, which we will return to in the final section of this chapter: How might archiving extend older women's agency and facilitate their "owning" of their activisms? Does archival work have the potential to transform dominant narratives of older women and to alter their understandings of their own activisms? What are the possibilities and particularities of intergenerational and community/activist collaboration?

GRAN AND ITS ARCHIVES

GRAN is a network of older Canadian women who advocate for policies that strengthen the human rights of women and children in southern Africa, with particular attention to grandmothers caring for children in the context of the HIV/AIDS epidemic. GRAN works closely with other movements and organizations with similar goals, informed, where possible, by the critical advocacy work undertaken by African women in their own countries. Operating as a virtual network with no physical headquarters, members from across the country participate in advocacy through local gatherings and through web-based action alerts. Though the most significant organizational work is done virtually, members meet face-to-face every two or three years for a national meeting. As noted in Chapter 1, most GRAN members are between 60 and 80 years old, and are white, middle-class, relatively well-educated, and grandmothers.

GRAN's roots date from 2007, with the founding of the National Advocacy Committee (NAC) of the Stephen Lewis Foundation's (SLF's) Grandmothers to Grandmothers Campaign. Since 2011, it has operated as an independent advocacy organization (see Edwards, Wallace-Deering, and Watson 2011 for the early history; also Chazan 2015, 2017). Members of NAC/GRAN first mobilized around issues of global access to medicines, advocating for changes to Canadian policies that hinder equitable access in the Global South. Since then, the focus has expanded to include advocacy goals of ending violence in the lives of women and girls and ensuring quality education for all (see GRAN 2014).

In 2009, one of the original founders of NAC/GRAN suggested compiling an archives. For several years, however, the project was sidelined by the urgency of advocacy work and the time and effort necessary to build a cross-country movement. As activists often focus more on *doing* rather than preserving for posterity, this is not surprising or unusual (Román 2006 cited in Danbolt 2010). The real impetus to the project occurred in 2013 when May and Melissa, as a part of their ongoing research, met with GRAN members in Vancouver; during these meetings May and Melissa were asked to take several large bins of files back to Ontario.[7] When they mentioned this, Pat recalled an earlier commitment she had made to start this work. And so the collaboration was born: May offering to lend whatever support she could, including contacting colleagues with professional archival experience and funding Melissa's time to assist with this effort; Melissa undertaking to review literature and research other examples of community-based archives; and Pat and Sharon taking responsibility for collecting, producing, and conceptualizing the GRAN material. None of us had any background, knowledge, or experience in archival work; while we certainly saw the value and significance of documenting GRAN's history through minutes, reports, and media clippings, we did not yet view the task ahead as intellectually or politically exciting.

At the start of this journey, we could not have imagined how much our vision would shift. As May and Melissa began to review the literature on feminist, activist, and community-based archiving, underlying complexities and fascinating questions began to emerge. Nor could we imagine that unravelling the stories, the tensions, and the multiple experiences would lead us to a rich and transformative process of collective learning, reflection, and intergenerational exchange. We return to these learnings and shifts throughout the chapter.

TRANSFORMING MEANINGS OF ARCHIVING

As our image of archives as inert records faded, a vision that was far more exciting—if also, at times, daunting—began to emerge. Through learning together, we collectively abandoned the idea that building the GRAN archives was a straightforward task of collecting and organizing records. Instead, our understanding of archival work increasingly grappled with a growing understanding that choosing what to include, for what reasons, and in what ways reflects conscious, deliberate, and selective decision-making.

The *GRAN Archive Policy*, drafted by Pat and Sharon and approved by GRAN's steering committee in August 2015, marks this shift to a reinvigorated vision of archives:

> Our archive constructs the collective memory of GRAN. As such, it is more
> than a simple repository for organizational documents; it also tells the story
> of GRAN and the women who comprise it. It is envisioned as a *living* history,

which implies attention to the ideas, issues, tensions, and experiences that have shaped and continue to shape our movement.

We understand that the ongoing process of establishing, selecting, and updating materials is not a simple reflection of "what happened" but, rather, an assessment of what is most important/relevant/meaningful to the many women, over time, who have and will have responsibility for the collection.

Our growing awareness of the value and complexity of GRAN's activisms also led us to expand our vision of the reasons why GRAN and other social movements create archives. Rather than viewing the archives as a repository for organizational records and a trove to be mined by future researchers, the *GRAN Archive Policy* suggests a broader purpose that envisions a wider use and looks to the future as well as the past:

> The reasons we are establishing GRAN archives are twofold. We believe that members of other organizations/movements as well as academics may find the experiences and struggles of GRAN valuable in understanding the possibilities, obstacles, and collective strength in pursuing change. We also anticipate that the archival process will deepen, and perhaps alter, our ongoing understanding and appreciation of our movement.

We expanded our vision of who might access the archives and decided to increase their accessibility by providing both digital and print archives.

Moreover, this shift meant understanding archiving as a process of generating and preserving the multiple, complex, collective memory of GRAN; this required a new and different recognition of the many different voices GRAN comprises. For example, an early plan to interview key women in order to get GRAN's story "right" shifted to emphasize storytelling, recognizing that there is no single story of GRAN but multiple stories from different standpoints. So the original plan to transcribe a few long interviews turned into the idea of a series of short recorded interviews to feature GRAN members speaking from their different perspectives about their own activist lives and experiences in the movement.[8]

Related to this, we came to understand that GRAN could not leave users of archives with only official records from which to construct their own interpretations of significant events and moments of conflict and tension in GRAN's history. For example, in addition to the relevant documents, Pat and Sharon (in consultation with other GRAN members) decided that the archives would need to include various members' perspectives on GRAN's separation from the SLF, given that this was an important event in GRAN's evolution. Similarly, the archives should comprise both official records and personal reflections documenting the moments in which GRAN first publicly identified as a feminist organization and recording the changing language used to describe GRAN's relationships with grandmother activists in southern Africa (see Chazan 2017). These examples illustrate the ways that reimagining the archives moved GRAN members to actively incorporate materials that would reveal (rather than conceal) the dilemmas and struggles that have shaped GRAN's development. Such decisions have meant working toward including multiple perspectives about the movement's issues and development, to ensure that important perspectives are not silenced.

As we explored together the literature on the archival turn, our collective vision, understanding, and process of archiving were transformed. We carefully questioned what should be remembered, who has authority in the telling and preserving of stories, and how a story is produced and given meaning through archiving. Pat and Sharon put these ideas into practice in drafting the archival policy and in the intentional choice to include moments of tension and a multiplicity of personal narratives in the archives.

TRANSFORMING SUBJECTIVITIES AS AGING ACTIVISTS

Re-visioning the archives broadened the scope of our project and changed GRAN's archival practices, while understanding the archives as a "living history" engaged us in thinking critically about our own subjectivities. Thinking about how to archive stories, movements, and legacies shifted how each of us understood our own ongoing activisms, our roles as people of different ages/generations, and GRAN's development as a movement. We began to experience archives-building as a "particular kind of place where complex subjectivities, and working relations, are created through the act of researching the past" (Lorimer 2003, cited in Ashmore, Craggs, and Neate 2012). While our project (and GRAN's archives) is still very much in development, we have come to recognize that archives-building can change, re-inscribe, and expand the meanings we give to our own positions and identities as aging activists. These shifts emerged in a number of overlapping and contrasting ways, which we present in two reflections to acknowledge how our positions influenced our experiences.

Pat and Sharon's Reflections

Recalling our collective past through archiving has been a mutual and powerful reminder of the many ways we *can* and *do* act together. Actively constructing and reflecting on GRAN's continuing story(ies) and storying brought us (and GRAN members) a different awareness of being part of work that matters. It is not just about writing or recording the stories, but about the ways in which the process of archiving helps to legitimize these stories, and our work, as *something of value*. Renewing awareness of the value of our activist work also brought us toward a more nuanced and layered appreciation of what we do and why we do it, with three implications for our shifting sense of ourselves as activists.

First, the process of archiving both validates and complicates how we understand our positions as "activists" and our ongoing "activisms." Our decision to think of this as an "activist" archives, which was part of our early process, was also more powerful than we anticipated. It compelled us to identify explicitly as "activists"— to wear this identity more openly and more readily.

Second, we have come to understand that archives-building is about asserting GRAN's presence in the historical record by conscientiously crafting how GRAN and the women involved will be remembered. In this way, we came to recognize the process of archiving as a political project—a critical site for resisting the historical invisibility too often accorded those "ordinary" or non-famous people, especially women, who work for social change (Davis 2007). For us, archiving is a way to bring some of the most invisible actors—older women, or aging activists—into the historical record, recognizing that older women continue to work for change well into their later lives. And we are keenly aware that there is more life behind than ahead of us, so this archival work has also been fueled by an urgency to ensure that the stories of our activist lives are not disregarded, misrepresented, or forgotten.

Third, for us and other GRAN members, we recognize that the transformations in our individual and collective meanings of activism can reverberate outward. When we alter the way we consider ourselves as activists, we also begin to open up the possibilities for changing how others perceive us. Just as archives are sites to stake out relevance, to resist invisibility, and to act with agency in telling our stories, they are also sites that can challenge narratives that present older women as passive, disengaged, lacking in power, and diminished (Sandberg 2013; McHugh 2012). These damaging and marginalizing depictions of aging women do not hold up against a living history of GRAN that vividly reflects women's deep engagement in pursuing social justice with energetic determination, solid strategic sense, and sheer hard work. Challenging stereotypes is also deeply personal to us—as grandmothers, we hope that one day our grandchildren will take an interest in the archives. We hope that the archives will remind them that caring about, and working for, human rights and dignity does not end because you grow old, but can form an important part of our older lives.

May and Melissa's Reflections

For us, the process of engaging in activist archiving shifted and blurred our own subjectivities as academics, activists, and archivists. In part, naming this as an "activist archives" project was a reminder that the ways in which we choose to go about research and collaborations in our academic work can be considered "activist." We also thought about our own work for social change and whether and how it might be remembered. For instance, we thought about how our research-as-social-change comes to be documented through publications like this book, as well as within the GRAN archives.

This project also coincided with us coming to understand ourselves as aging subjects, though at different points in the aging process. While we invested ourselves in certain projects to confront ageist narratives of older women because we see the ways in which they elide the incredible activism, resilience, influence, and complexity of the older women in our lives, we also began to reflect on what these limiting narratives do and will mean for both of us as we age. We began to understand that resisting ageism through the archives and other projects was deeply personal as well as bound up in our intergenerational relationships.

Thus, this project has brought us together into an ongoing process of (re)making ourselves (and each other) as activists, as aging, and as archivists, while also complicating the meanings of these subjectivities in our lives. No longer the benign organization of existing files, "archiving" became bound up in legitimizing our work, in enabling us to be "activists" less apologetically, in asserting our relevance in the public record, and in resisting narratives of aging as decline.

TRANSFORMING GENERATIONAL SCRIPTS

Perhaps most centrally, our archival process has emerged as an exciting and uncharted intergenerational journey. We did not foresee that the cooperative efforts of two retired women in their 70s, an academic in her 40s, and a graduate student in her 20s would result in such vibrant intellectual exchange and in such intimate and rich relationships. Our collaboration turned out to be the keystone in our project— shaping its vision, its development, and its momentum. We generated caring and emotive relationships that at various times filled us with enjoyment, excitement, apprehension, urgency, and accomplishment. In contrast to the dispassionate and removed stereotype of archivists, we have been deeply engaged in the intellectual, emotional work of storytelling and meaning-making across three generations (Ashmore, Craggs, and Neate 2012). Our work demonstrates that archives can be sites for intergenerational learning, exchange, and relationship-building and, in turn, how these interchanges can shape archival work. Here again we present our reflections in two parts.

Pat and Sharon Reflect on Their Intergenerational Journey

From our perspective, without the collaboration that spanned three generations there would be no story to tell. Without the tangible and intangible dimensions of our collaboration, the GRAN archives would not emerge as more than boxes of well-organized records. Concrete benefits include Melissa's help in preparing a file plan and devising GRAN's archive policy, and May's provision of key contacts and advice regarding where the GRAN archives might be hosted. But the most important aspects were less tangible and stemmed from May and Melissa delving into the literature on activist archiving and the lively discussions that ensued. Our exchanges opened up the complex, indefinite, and fluid nature of archival processes, contributing to the excitement and the motivation of working on a project with such dynamic and transformative potential. These conversations—infused with shared laughter, concerns, and a sense of discovery—also gave us a language and framework to make sense of the discomfort and uncertainty we felt about the power that is implicit in archives-building. In addition, through May's ongoing research, GRAN members had access to technology workshops that opened up ways of storytelling, as well as a stimulating symposium on activism and aging.[9]

At the same time, our collaboration provided important affirmations for GRAN members, particularly those of us working on the archives. Our conversations with May and Melissa drew us into the special richness of intergenerational learning and sharing that is not bound by age nor by academic/community roles. We also benefited from—and appreciated—the encouragement and support we received from younger people at Concordia, Trent, and York, the Archives Association of British Columbia, and the Canadian Lesbian and Gay Archives. Knowing that younger generations find value in this work, GRAN members stand a little taller and recognize a little more clearly that, as older women activists, we have significant stories to tell about the reasons why and the ways that many Canadian grandmothers work to advance the human rights of grandmothers in southern Africa.

May and Melissa Rethink Generational Scripts

One of the big shifts for us crept up slowly: We became increasingly attuned to just how radical and rare the kinds of relationships are that developed in this project.

Working together, learning together, and enjoying our time together made us keenly aware of the limited opportunities that exist for intergenerational exchange in our society. We became conscious of how much we value Pat and Sharon as colleagues and collaborators, as people who share similar interests, values, and politics. We started seeking opportunities to work together in various ways that extend well beyond the archives (for instance, through the editing of this book!). We also noticed an increasing intimacy to our conversations and communications, in all directions—we interacted as friends, feeling at liberty to express the joys and challenges we were each facing in our lives, and, for us, valuing the support that could be offered by women with so much more life experience. Unlike the inter-generational roles we were each accustomed to, these relationships did not fit neatly along age-prescribed lines of expert-learner, researcher-researched, or storyteller-listener. Nor did they fall into (or completely outside of) familial "scripts" associated with (grand)mother-(grand)daughter relationships.

We came to understand that, through this process, we were in fact challenging certain dominant generational narratives and dynamics. We were not, for instance, involved in any straightforward project of "passing down" knowledge from elder to younger[10] (a dynamic that so often plays out in oral history research with older participants). In addition, we were continuously reminded that our values and politics (which were so much part of our discussions) were more similar to one another than they were different. We came to consider that widely held assumptions of "generational divide" or "generation gap" were far too simplistic to describe how age and aging implicated our relationships. Thus, while the intergenerational dynamics of our collaboration deeply informed how we worked together, the difference in our ages did not determine the contours of our collaboration. This does not mean that age became irrelevant or inconsequential, but rather that age was present in ways that our expectations of intergenerationality could not account for.

REFLECTING BACK, MOVING FORWARD

While archiving is only one way for social movement activists to record, keep, and share the work they do, it has particular significance for aging women who rarely feature as narrators of their activist lives. As our work together developed, so too did our awareness of the spaces that archiving can provide to tell stories, reflect on the meanings of activism, and look towards the future. Our story of the GRAN archives suggests that such spaces can be transformational for each of us as aging activists.

At the start, we anticipated the practical benefits of our archival collaboration but we had little inkling of the extent to which our thinking would change. By the end, we have become acutely aware that archives involve intensely social, political, and emotional processes, they help to shape our understandings of ourselves as activists, and they offer critically important opportunities for intergenerational relationships that alter traditional roles and scripts.

To close this chapter, we build upon these shifts and return to the broader questions we posed earlier in the chapter: How might archiving extend older women's agency and facilitate their "owning" of their activisms? Does archival work have potential to transform dominant narratives of older women and to alter their understandings of their own activisms? What are the possibilities and particularities of intergenerational and community/activist/academic collaboration?

First, our discussion suggests that archiving can inscribe older women's sense of agency, both in taking control of narratives and serving as a powerful reminder of the value of their activist work. Including multiple stories, highlighting the pivotal moments in a movement's history, and inviting members to reflect on times of tension and of celebration open up possibilities for archives, such as GRAN's, to strengthen and nourish the activist work that older women undertake. Archives that capture the expressions of feelings such as pleasure, enjoyment, and sadness through oral interviews, for example, help to foster a sense of community among GRAN members.

Second, by including the voices of individual members and providing multiple perspectives on the struggles and successes that mark GRAN's evolution and development, GRAN's archives invite an appreciation of older women activists as serious and committed, deeply engaged in working for social change. This view shifts the too frequent portrayals of older women's lives as narrow and constricted, and also confronts the "donor-only" appearances of older women in archives. Archives that are engaging and accessible (e.g., short videos with digital access) widen opportunities to underscore the vibrant contributions that older women make to social justice, challenging notions that later life brings disengagement from public life.

Third, our work together suggests the ways in which archiving can create spaces for meaningful, transformational, and enjoyable collaborations that can unsettle typically ascribed generational scripts while helping to bridge community/academic differences in positive ways. Working together in increasingly close relationships and sharing "aha" moments, concerns, and laughter helped to disarm the norms that would otherwise govern relationships among a student in her 20s, an academic in her 40s, and two women in their 70s. No longer viewing ourselves as "researchers" and "volunteers," we became co-learners, helping to situate our knowledge(s) while providing each other with important sources of support and friendship (see Pratt, 2010).

Our intergenerational, academic/activist collaborative project continues as a work in progress.[11] While the archives are not yet a physical reality, our experiences have altered the purpose, thrust, and content of GRAN's archives as well as our relationships and our understandings of ourselves as activists. We are hopeful that our story of the GRAN archives will inspire other activists—young, old, and everyone in between—to take charge of shaping how their movements are remembered, and that it will compel other academics to work with them too. It is surprising and wonderful to explore where an archiving journey might lead.

NOTES

1. May and Melissa (with significant input from Pat and Sharon) have written elsewhere in a more conventional academic manner about the GRAN archives (see Chazan, Baldwin, and Madokoro 2015).

2. Significant discussions of collaborations that surround archiving can be found in Ashmore, Craggs, and Neate 2012; Wexler and Long 2009; and Caswell and Mallick 2014.

3. Influential pieces from this shift include Cook 2001, Cvetkovich 2003, and Osborne 1999.

4. By "subjectivity," we mean the fluid ways that we identify (ourselves) or are identified (by others); our ever-changing, performed sense of self. By using the word "subjectivity," as it is used through much of the feminist archival scholarship, we infer that this fluid way of knowing and performing self is also *subject to* (or comes into being, or is in part made by) broader contextual factors and relations of power.

5. Some, however, have nodded to this; see Wexler and Long 2009 and Wallace et al. 2014.

6. By heteronormativity we are referring to the ways in which heterosexuality, with its rigid, binary conceptions of gender, is taken as common sense and normalized through our institutions. Connected to this, family structures rooted in reproductive heterosexual relationships are assumed to be the "default" or most natural form of family arrangement. This conception of the heteronormative family reinscribes rigid gender roles, makes reproduction appear to be the basic purpose of "family," and thus obscures other forms of kinship and intimacy. For further discussion, see Eng 2010; and Farrier 2015.

7. This was not possible until much later.

8. This aligned with a digital storytelling workshop put on by Aging Activisms (in collaboration with Ageing + Communication + Technologies) in Montreal in the spring of 2016. Four GRAN members recorded media capsules of their own histories with activism and how these are implicated in their ongoing organizing with GRAN (see www.agingactivisms.org/montreal-media-capsules).

9. See www.agingactivisms.org/montreal-media-capsules and www.agingactivisms.org/aging-activisms-2015.

10. Also known as "heteronormative narratives of knowledge transmission" (Farrier 2015) or "generativity," in cultural gerontology.

11. We would like to thank Suzanne Dubeau, assistant head archivist, and Anna St. Onge, archivist, Digital Projects & Outreach, Clara Thomas Archives and Special Collections, York University, for their help in reaching an agreement in principle to house GRAN's archives.

REFERENCES

Ashmore, Paul, Ruth Craggs, and Hannah Neate. 2012. "Working-with: Talking and Sorting in Personal Archives." *Journal of Historical Geography* 38: 81–89.

Bly, Lyz, and Kelly Wooten. Eds. 2012. *Make Your Own History: Documenting Feminist and Queer Activism in the 21st Century.* Sacramento, CA: Litwin Books.

Caswell, Michelle. 2014. "Seeing Yourself in History: Community Archives and the Fight against Symbolic Annihilation." *The Public Historian* 36(4): 26–37.

Caswell, Michelle, and Marika Cifor. 2016. "From Human Rights to Feminist Ethics: Radical Empathy in Archives." *Archivaria* 81: 23–43.

Caswell, Michelle, and Samip Mallick. 2014. "Collecting the Easily Missed Stories: Digital Participatory Microhistory and the South Asian American Digital Archive." *Archives and Manuscripts* 42(1): 73–86.

Charpentier, Michelle, Anne Quéniart, and Julie Jacques. 2008. "Activism among Older Women in Quebec, Canada: Changing the World after Age 65." *Journal of Women & Aging* 20: 343–359.

Chazan, May. 2015. *The Grandmothers' Movement: Solidarity and Survival in the Time of AIDS.* Montreal, QC: McGill-Queen's University Press.

Chazan, May. 2017. "Contingent Meanings, Shifting Practices: Grandmother to Grandmother Solidarity as Transnational Feminist Praxis." *Gender, Place, Culture.* DOI:10.1080/0966369X.2017.1377159.

Chazan, May, Melissa Baldwin, and Laura Madokoro. 2015. "Aging, Activism, and the Archive: Feminist Perspectives for the 21st Century." *Archivaria* 40: 59–87.

Cook, Terry. 2001. "Archival Science and Postmodernism: New Formulations for Old Concepts." *Archival Science* 1: 3–24.

Cvetkovich, Ann. 2003. *An Archive of Feelings: Trauma, Sexuality, and Lesbian Public Cultures.* Durham, NC: Duke University Press.

Danbolt, Mathias. 2010. "We're Here! We're Queer?: Activist Archives and Archival Activism." *Lambda Nordica* 3–4: 90–118.

Davis, Angela. 2007. How Does Change Happen? [video]. www.youtube.com/watch?v =Pc6RHtEbiOA

Dunbar, Anthony W. 2006. "Introducing Critical Race Theory to Archival Discourse: Getting the Conversation Started." *Archival Science* 6: 109–129.

Edwards, Peggy, and Kathleen Wallace-Deering, with Linda Watson. 2011. *A Story Evolving: Advocacy in the Canadian Grandmothers to Grandmothers Movement.* Toronto, ON: The National Advocacy Committee of the Grandmothers to Grandmothers Campaign. www.grannyvoices.com/docs/story-evolving.pdf

Eichhorn, Kate. 2013. *The Archival Turn in Feminism: Outrage in Order.* Philadelphia: Temple University Press.

Eng, David L. 2010. *The Feeling of Kinship: Queer Liberalism and the Racialization of Intimacy.* Durham, NC: Duke University Press.

Farrier, Stephen. 2015. "Playing with Time: Gay Intergenerational Performance Work and the Productive Possibilities of Queer Temporalities." *Journal of Homosexuality* 62: 1,398–1,418.

Flinn, Andrew, and Ben Alexander. 2015. "'Humanizing an Inevitable Political Craft': Introduction to the Special Issue on *Archiving Activism and Activist Archiving.*" *Archival Science* 15(4): 329–335.

Grandmothers Advocacy Network (GRAN). 2014. *Strategic Plan 2014–2018.* www.grandmothersadvocacy.org/wp-content/uploads/2014/01/GRAN-STRATEGIC-PLAN-2014-18.pdf

Hogeland, Lisa Maria. 2001. "Against Generational Thinking, or, Some Things That 'Third Wave' Feminism Isn't." *Women's Studies in Communication* 24: 107–121.

Juhasz, Alexandra. 2006. "Video Remains: Nostalgia, Technology, and Queer Archive Activism." *GLQ: A Journal of Lesbian and Gay Studies* 12(2): 319–328.

Lorimer, Hayden. 2003. "The Geographical Field Course As Active Archive." *Cultural Geographies* 10: 278–308.

McHugh, Maureen. 2012. "Aging, Agency, and Activism: Older Women as Social Change Agents." *Women & Therapy* 35(3): 279–295.

Osborne, Thomas. 1999. "The Ordinariness of the Archive." *History of the Human Sciences* 12(2): 51–64.

Pratt, Geraldine. 2010. "Collaboration as a Feminist Strategy." *Gender, Place and Culture* 17(1): 43–48.

Richards, Naomi. 2012. "The Fight to Die: Older People and Death Activism." *International Journal of Ageing and Later Life* 7(1): 7–32.

Román, David. 2006. "Remembering AIDS: A Reconsideration of the Film *Longtime Companion.*" *GLQ: A Journal of Gay and Lesbian Studies* 12(2): 281–301.

Sandberg, Linn. 2013. "Affirmative Old Age—The Ageing Body and Feminist Theories on Difference." *International Journal of Ageing and Later Life* 8: 11–40.

Wallace, David A., Patricia Pasick, Zoe Berman, and Ella Weber. 2014. "Stories for Hope—Rwanda: A Psychological-Archival Collaboration to Promote Healing and Cultural Continuity through Intergenerational Dialogue." *Archival Science* 14: 275–306.

Wexler, Geoff, and Linda Long. 2009. "Lifetimes and Legacies: Mortality, Immortality, and the Needs of Aging and Dying Donors." *The American Archivist* 72(2): 478–495.

REFLECTION 8

Following Nan to the Kiji Sibi

Jenn Cole

Jenn Cole (mixed ancestry Algonquin Kiji Sibi Watershed) is a scholar and performance artist. She is passionate about teaching performance and creative expression as research and scholarship practices. She writes about the activist elements of intimacy created by imperfect storytelling and feminist performance adaptations, while her performance practice explores storytelling, trans-generational autobiography, and the sharing of food together as an expression of vulnerability and relational exchange that is pivotal as we try to cultivate a sense of home.

In this piece, Jenn creatively stretches conceptions of the archives and brings us back to the broader theme of this section, "being remembered." Jenn shares her process of Biskaabiiyang, returning home by returning to herself. She traces what it meant, in public performance installation, to collaborate with audience members to map family stories across generations of First Nations grandmothers and settler, logging, fur-trading grandfathers (murky details!), and a Nan who always made tea, at whose table you could ask any question without fear of failure. In reflecting on her embodied performance of remembering her grandmother, Jenn resonates the importance of intergenerational relationships (and preserving, remembering, and circulating the memories of these) as a resistance to colonial interruptions to identity, land, and belonging. Her performance could be understood as a form of "activism" broadly defined, while the map she creates through it an archives of sorts, to be continually produced by future generations.

I am just beginning. I am just beginning something from a long time ago.

I used to be very quiet about it. I was afraid to admit I did not know the way home. I was afraid of going the wrong way.

My Nan microwaved Red Rose tea in glass mugs and we drank it at her table in Belleville, Ontario. Over tea, you could say anything to Nan. You never had to worry about it coming out all wrong. It came out the way it came out. She was a wise lady.

I learned the term *Biskaabiiyang* from Leanne Simpson, who describes the process as returning home to oneself by reflecting on how one has been personally marked by colonialism, focusing on the possibility of return. I have questions about who I am and where Algonquin identity and settler identity live at odds within me. My family history is one of fur traders, log drivers, First Peoples, sharing and stealing land, suppressing and passing on traditions. My relatives come from the Ottawa River Watershed, which is a hot spot for colonial history and contemporary identity politics that make my head spin. Beginning to learn about the Indian Act. Trials. Broken Treaties. Families moved off the land so the government could build the nuclear reactor that sustains the town closest to my home. Learning old family stories. Learning about family members! Oh, hello! Reflecting with big gratitude on all the plants and smells and sensations I got to know by living on Algonquin land. Sandy soil. Sweet fern. Blueberries. Granite. The line of the river against the mountains. English words for older things. Convoluted processes proceeding.

In November, 2016, I sat on a blanket in the Marriott Hotel in Minneapolis at a theatre conference and invited audience members to help me to map my way home by sharing their grandparent stories with me. They read cards from tea bags I stitched on my Nan's sewing machine that either gave instructions for me to animate my fold out paper map with conté river lines and ink flora genealogies or that invited dialogue about grannies and grandpas. Some of these cards read: Tell me about your grandmother and marriage; tell me about your grandfather's hands; share a family recipe or remedy; and do you know any stories about when your grandmother was a little girl?

One person's grandmother was called the Puerto Rican Elizabeth Taylor. She was quite a scandal, having been married five times. A mother made watery soup her son missed only once he left home. A young woman went to India to visit the palace of her grandmother's youth and found an unimpressive bungalow. Another did not want to make her late grandmother's cookies in case they did not turn out. Instead, her family made a functioning gingerbread Ferris wheel. A relative, five years old, was the only one to glimpse an interracial family marriage through a peephole in a curtain. A woman drew her grannie's bedroom so I could see where they slept together at sleepovers.

The process of story sharing was joyful, warm, and full of surprises. As we talked, I archived my own family's stories and mark-making in the map book. My grandpa's tentative drawings of trees from forestry school, my Nan's dad's drawing of how to cross-track a moose in winter so you can sketch him, or the words from the Nibi Song that Doreen Day wrote with her grandson, a love song I have been learning to sing to the waters of the Kiji Sibi. I began to say, "I do not know the way home. I am just learning the way. I believe our grandparents packed down some trails through the grasses and the snow. I think they may have left us some pieces of maps. They might be hard to read. Let's look at them together and begin to figure them out."

When I think of where I come from, it is a particular spot at the edge of the Ottawa River. I like to take the long way to get there. My grandparents are from nearby, little towns I always thought were their own places, not tiny parts of the large territory called Kiji Sibi. Bissett Creek, where Grandpa step-danced on tables while his dad fiddled, where my mom grew up with deer slung frozen over the backyard maple bough in winter. You sawed off what you wanted for dinner. Mattawa—in a community they used to call "Squaw Valley"—where my Nan's dad hung out in hunt camps all year long, sketching bear cubs and creek ice.

Land and grandparents. I am lucky to have grown up on the land my grandparents loved and understood. They knew how to lay trap lines and nibble backyard leaves and keep a fire going. I am so grateful to know some of this too.

Why is it important to remember? Because the stakes of loss are both personally and politically grave. My Nan loved to watch people powwow. She did not know how to dance. I don't either. She should have been out there dancing, though. That was the shape of her heart. If I do not follow this road of reconnection with my Algonquin-ness, there is no one to share it with my son. Knowing very little, I am in the position of having to find my place in relation to my Anishinaabeg identity or to end knowledge of it in our family altogether. The good news is that this makes remembering from the heart politically powerful. I feel personally and politically invested in seeking the resurgence of my own Indigenous heart.

My Nan said that when my grandpa's dad died, they went through his things and his (his mother's?) medicine book fell apart. Pages written in the Anishinaabeg language blew away and floated down the creek. No one knew how to read or speak the language anymore, so they didn't think the book had any value.

When my mom started working at what was then called the Indian Friendship Centre in North Bay, my grandpa, embarrassed, said, "What would you want to work in a place like that for?"

One piece of diaspora is the shame left over from racism, my grandpa thinking that being Native didn't do anyone any good. His dad never taught him the

Algonquin language. They were three generations of fur traders and log drivers. Cannot speak the language. Never lived on the reserve. No paperwork. (Actually, I have a card that says I am a member of the Métis Nation of Ontario. Unfortunately, it does not come with knowledge or community or answers in any immediate way.)

I learn from tracing family stories, stories that brush against histories of settlement and displacement, of abuse of and deep care for this land and these waters, against the stories of others, that we are already together. In this world. I need others in order to do the work of return partly because this is an extension of the way we are already. As well, I come from generations of unremembered and unshared details. And a few good stories, too! Grief and fear of going the wrong way can turn easily to paralysis. Sharing stories with others makes gathering family history feel good. Makes an impossible tangle of doubt and unbelonging into chatting and sharing tea. And, as Jill Carter told me, I had better keep that map so that my grandkids can keep it going.

I am taking the long way home. I am just beginning. I have plenty of tea.

CLOSING

Activist Theirstories and the Future of Aging Activisms

May Chazan, Melissa Baldwin, and Pat Evans

And yet the sun is rising.
And yet the planet spins.
And yet, the children—Anishinaabe, Syrian, Jew—trudge up the hill toward school.
And yet the duck sits idly on the Otonabee, drifting slowly tailward.
And yet the oak leaves rustle in the iridescent breeze.
And yet the lips part, the ribs stretch, the heart beats.
As long as your veins are home to blood coursing, there is more to the story.
There is more to this story.
Keep on.
(Ziy von B, from Reflection 5, "And Yet," 2016)

RETURN

As the three of us consider our "closing" remarks, facing down the moment when we are meant to knit this book neatly together, we return to these beautiful, hopeful, and ever-open 81 words offered by Ziy von B. Like others in this volume, including Jenn Cole (Reflection 8), *we return*. We return to the many insights offered throughout. We return to why and how we embarked on this journey. We return to ourselves—noting who we each were when we set out and who we are becoming together. We return to the words and works of contributors: to the poems, the essays, the conversations, the photos, and the reflections shared with us. We acknowledge each author, each connection, and our gratitude.

We pause here—page 233—to re-read this poem out loud, as it lies tucked quietly in Reflection 5. "And yet, the sun is rising ... the children—Anishinaabe, Syrian, Jew—trudge up the hill toward school ... There is more to this story. Keep on." We picture Ziy's children on that hill, not trudging but soaring, in that moment before it registers that this may not have been the intended image. We imagine Monique Mojica (Reflection 3) on the bus with her little one, teaching him about borders and refugees as others listen in. We think of waaseyaa'sin christine sy (introduction to Part II and Poems 1 and 4), who, at the moment of her writing, needed to receive Monique's story. In her email to us, she called Monique's piece an "elixir"; she wrote about that bus ride in her introductory essay. We flash to Ingrid (from the opening of Chapter 1), driving that bus, day after day, to put her children through school: keeping on, surviving. We imagine Jenn's child, still so very small. He will be working on that map, too, one day. And Keara Lightning (Poem 2), we hold the tenderness of her poem. She does not feel the womb-y waters; she burns bright and eternal with or without little ones in her future, and her Kokhum knows this. Connection.

But did our readers appreciate Ziy's poem? Did they read it aloud? Or was it missed? Was it made less prominent by its positioning, its length, its access to space, its font? This small, quiet, less obvious one—like so many "activists"—was its message fully received? We consider for a moment the difficult decisions we are making as the editors of this volume—the uneasy power we hold. We have selected, placed, and guided each entry; we have often acted with uncertainty, although always with care. What will this volume precipitate, intentionally and not? How will it be received? (How) will it be carried forward?

It is from this particular moment of return, then—from this place of gratitude, connection, and self-consciousness—that we offer our "closing." We offer it in the spirit of the story to which Ziy alludes—a story forever open to interpretation and always unfinished. We also offer it with appreciation for the distilling brilliance of poetry. Indeed, in 81 words, Ziy's poem knits together three of the most profound learnings gifted to us in our editing process. These learnings—personal and scholarly, conceptual and applied—offer an entry point to extend, deepen, connect, and complicate studies and practices of activist aging. From these learnings we begin to articulate future directions for ourselves, for Aging Activisms (our research collective), and for this field more generally.

THREE LEARNINGS

(1) We Are Connected Relationally and Cosmically

Perhaps what emerges most strongly for us is what we call a *politics of connection*. The intellectual, political, creative, and emotional task of conceptualizing aging and activisms must begin from an awareness of *connection*, rather than from certain categorical divisions often used in aging and social movement studies. We appreciate in some instances the salience of considering "later life" versus "middle age," "settler" versus "Indigenous," "environmental movement" versus "economic development," "decline" versus "success," "young" versus "old," "artistic creation" versus "activism," and so on. And yet, when we read and listen closely to activists and scholars, it is the murkiness of these categories and the importance of connection that surfaces.

Contributors to this volume ask us to consider—conceptually, but also personally, politically, spiritually—how activist aging shapes and is shaped by particular lands, places, moments, and relationships. We are asked to explore connections to each other across time; to all of our relations, both humans and non; to those who have come before us and to generations yet unborn. As Ziy's words evoke the rising of the sun, the spinning of the Earth, the rustling of the breeze, the floating duck, the trudging children, and the river—indeed, the Otonabee River—these are not outside of the story of what it means to act, resist, come together, age, or develop. These are the story.

(2) To "Keep On" Is to Enact Activist Aging

The introduction to this volume sets out a broad and pluralized conceptualization of "activisms," in hopes that contributors' words might further animate such a definition. Yet, we did not direct contributors to do so; we did not make this an explicit goal of the volume to those writing the poetry, chapters, or reflections. It is all the more pertinent, then, that so many explicitly sought to widen what counts as activisms and who counts as an activist.

From early on in the volume, we were struck by discussions of activisms as resistance, as survival, or, in the words of christine at the opening of Part II, as "persisting life." We have learned that to "keep on," as Ziy asks us to, is itself an activist practice for many. And, as "keeping on" invokes time, continuity, and intergenerationality, it speaks so tenderly to what we mean by activist aging.

At the same time, we tread carefully. Keeping on is different for different people. It comes with uneven challenges, with generational trauma, with disabled body-minds, with deliberate erasures from lands, records, and narratives, with racialized histories, with systemic poverty, and with unearned privileges, too. We sit with this tension.

(3) There Is Always More to the Story

Finally, through our editing process, we were confronted several times with the limitations of "the story" this volume could tell—with the limitations of our structure, our assumptions, and our knowledges. As noted in the book's introduction, we initially conceptualized this book as a series of research chapters written by academics and reflections written by activists. Quickly, however, some of the chapters were proposed as collaborations between the people we had initially grouped as academics and those we had considered activists—our structure was too simplistic. Clearly, the academics in this volume are also activists and the activists have equally important analyses and knowledges to share.

We were then called upon by two invited contributors to consider orality, conversation, or storytelling as their preferred approach to knowledge sharing. Setting aside the constraints of chapter/reflection formats, we worked, in our imperfect and still limited way, to embrace these brilliant and vital contributions (Chapter 3 and Reflection 3) on their own terms.

We later struggled with the realization that some of the most radical, unsettling, and decolonial offerings on activisms, aging, and intergenerationality that we knew of already existed as poems or creative prose. Some of these were written by scholars and activists connected to our research collective. So, we sought permission to incorporate some of these pieces to mark each part of the book, deeply aware of how these extend, deepen, and challenge both what precedes them and what follows, in ways that would not be possible through any form of essay or editorial note.

Engaging with the tensions of representing "bodies" only through text, we invited the set of bold, brave, and baring photographs that grace the middle of the book. These compelling artworks bring our own bodies into reading in ways not possible in the other pieces. And yet we hold the absence of their voices as a tension, and we hope that these beautiful humans are *seen* and not only looked at.

"There is more to this story," Ziy reminds us. Indeed, we are always limited by our words, by our concepts, by our knowledge systems, by our categories, by our structures, and by our societal assumptions. A better, more critical, and more ethical study of activist aging needs to always ask: *What else? What form does it take? How can we get at it?* It is ultimately this line of questioning that we have opened and wish to leave open with this book.

THE FUTURE OF AGING ACTIVISMS

We return now to the conceptual framework and scholarly contributions of this book; to what we hope we have opened up and to what has yet to be done. In doing so, we raise what we deem to be the burning questions for future scholarship in this field.

Part I introduced the volume's core concepts and offered context. Two decades ago, older women's activisms began to garner scholarly attention; analyses of age or aging began to appear in feminist social movement studies (e.g., MacDonald and Rich 1983). But what and who, we ask, has remained less prominent? Where shall we turn to deepen and extend this work? The contributions to Part I begin to portray the *plurality* of older people's activisms. Chapter 1 speaks to the politicized nature of (grand)motherhood by drawing on life histories with white settler activists; it insists on a broad conceptualization of activisms, including everyday acts of resistance and survival as politicized actions, particularly in the context of women living in situations of domestic abuse (Pain 2014). Chapter 2 features the tactics deployed by older women involved in RECAA, who work in creative ways to end elder abuse. Many RECAA members are recent immigrants and racialized in the Canadian context, and their perspectives, tactics, and ways of organizing offer important insights into thinking about older people's activisms.

These chapters and their accompanying reflections provide a glimpse into how overlapping systems of power and privilege fuel different activisms. The section's themes of resistance, survival, and resilience ripple through the volume, as do the authors' refusals to relegate activism to attendance at formal protests. Collectively, they say, to paraphrase the legendary Miss Major Griffin-Gracy—a long-time trans activist in her 80s from the United States—from the 2016 film *MAJOR!*: "My work did not end 40 years ago; I am still here and look at what I am doing today!" These contributions offer counter-narratives to the well-known assumptions of aging as decline; they also refuse the neoliberal, ableist, and ageist jibber-jabber that reverberates through discourses of successful and active aging. From the outset of the volume, older activists are contemporary social changers—no question. Their worth does not depend on physically attending protests; they are creative, determined, knowledgeable, resourceful, savvy, and tough. Their power also lies in the small acts that bring them together, their collectivity, their ongoing emotional labour.

But what and who, we ask, has remained less prominent? Where shall we turn to deepen and extend this work? There is always more, indeed. Part I is carefully cradled between two poetic offerings, *Grandmother* and *Firekeeper*, both written by Indigenous activists and scholars, both providing stark reminders of the Eurocentricity of this field and of who else is still here—persisting. Contributors to Part II open a space for a more explicitly decolonial analysis, and it is from here that we begin to understand activist aging as *a politics of connection*. Elder Shirley Williams Pheasant (Chapter 3) reminds us that, for her, walking for the water is motivated by relationship; water is animate, it is her relation. Monique (Reflection 3) offers the continuum, evoking a version of intergenerational persistence that extends beyond the living, several generations forward and several back. Keara (Poem 2), from her younger perspective, tells us that this continuum is strong and the fire remains lit. But there is also soreness. The legacy of trauma cannot be overlooked. Care and continuance co-exist, while no person, no culture, no ceremony, no activism can remain static in time. Understanding activist aging as a politics of connection also speaks to the possibilities (and discomforts) of settlers working in meaningful relationship with Indigenous activists, as discussed in Chapter 4 and Reflection 4.

Studies of aging and activism rarely engage with critical race perspectives or decolonial frameworks, and this volume only barely begins this urgent work. Part II sits with the tensions we, the editors, embody each day as uninvited settlers on Anishinaabe territory. Why, we asked ourselves in conceiving of this section, have studies of aging and activism yet to fully grapple with settler colonialism, decoloniality, and Indigenous knowledges? What do First Peoples—Elders, olders, knowledge-holders, and youngers, from different places and communities across Turtle Island—have to say about aging and activism? Is the often-assumed linearity within which we embed time, the lifecourse, and aging a colonial construct, and what would it mean for this to be unsettled? What about the language and terms we use—do these alienate some, fail to resonate with others? How could a decolonial analysis challenge our understandings of aging as decline, of gender as binary, of activism as formal protest? We offer these lingering questions with an understanding that this is the work to be done; indeed, it is our work to do. This is part of what it will mean for us to unsettle ourselves, our minds, our writings, our research, and our activisms (Regan 2010).

Part III further opens up activist aging, through a focus on embodiment and performance, giving us pause to consider the consistent push in anti-oppressive activist work, and indeed at times in this volume, *to make visible*. In her introduction, Sally Chivers reflects on becoming visible under the "normate gaze," pointing out that being visible does not necessarily mean being *valued*, and "inclusion" is not necessarily *meaningful*. The contributors to this section understand this: They seek to hold that gaze long enough to challenge what lies under it; they refuse its devaluation. In doing so, they crip, queer, and un/sex studies of activist aging.

Part III contributes to efforts among some scholars to have aging and disability studies speak to and with one another (e.g., Putnam 2007; Aubrecht and Krawchenko 2016; Stone 2003). What can studies of critical disability offer to thinking about aging activisms? What does it mean to intercept not only ageist but also ableist discourses in this field? For us, this has meant that we do not engage with earlier research that suggests that activism or "civic engagement" in later life is valuable as part of a package of active aging—that it will prevent the onset of aging-related disability and help people remain youthful (and able-bodied and minded) (Lips and Hastings 2012; Hutchinson and Wexler 2007). It has also meant that part of why we advance an expanded version of activisms well beyond outward protest is to allow for a cripping of what counts as activist tactics. We value the knowledges and contributions of people with disabilities of different ages, understanding that activisms might be different from different embodiments.

However, while this focus on embodiment opens so many important lines of inquiry, here too there is more to be considered. In particular, we sit uneasily with the continued erasure of aging queer, two-spirit, and trans bodies; of aging queer, two-spirit, and trans activisms (Brown 2009; Ophelian and Florez 2016). The future of aging activisms, we believe, requires more LGBTQIA2S+ and especially transgender voices, and more nuanced and sophisticated analyses of gender and gender expression, particularly as these intersect with race, colonization, and age. We must meaningfully learn from these experiences and knowledges as we go forward. There is much work to do.

Finally, Part IV considers the theme of being remembered: the importance of remembering activisms and of transmitting knowledges. It asks how activists of different ages become agents of archives and, more generally, take up various forms of memory work. Recognizing that this work informs who and what is remembered, who and what is erased, and how, the contributors to this section remind us that record-keeping and archiving are also forms of activism. Their contributions collectively bring archival studies together with aging research—again in a rare but much-needed scholarly alliance. At the same time, as noted in the book's introduction, they refuse a unidirectional or simplistic version of knowledge transmission and instead frame intergenerational memory work as more complex and multi-directional, with younger, middler, and older nurturing each other as co-creators of their movements' stories. Here we ask, as Laura Madokoro does in her introduction: Why are aging, activism, and the archives rarely considered in tandem? What does memory work look like for different activists, across different movements? Why does it matter? What is at stake?

We have structured this book into these four parts largely to help readers grapple with the complexity of information and ideas. However, certain themes interweave the volume and are intimately interconnected to one another: plurality, persistence, survivance, decoloniality, race, power, gender, bodies, visibilities, memory, continuity, knowledges, and others. In attending to these themes, this volume makes some significant contributions toward extending the "what, who, and how" of existing scholarship on activist aging. It brings together the varied perspectives and insights of people who identify as able-bodied, disabled, Indigenous, settler, white, racialized, older, middler, younger, straight, LGBTQIA2S+, cis, and/or non-binary. It unsettles one-dimensional views of activism, insisting instead on a conception of activisms (pluralized) that includes protest, rally, advocacy, arts-based work, ceremony, land-based practices, survival, record-keeping, performance, and many other ways of acting for change. And it calls into question the epistemological boundaries of research in this field.

To studies of social movements, this book brings the much-needed analytic of age, aging, and intergenerationality. At the same time, it effectively intervenes in dominant aging narratives—victimizing narratives of aging as decline, neoliberal discourses of "active aging," and assumptions about "aging" as relegated to "old age." These important interventions, together with the critical approach throughout (i.e., the aspirational and unfinished project of bringing intersectional feminist, decolonial, critical race, queer, and crip analyses into scholarship on activist aging), expand, deepen, and offer new directions to the new and growing field of age/ing studies.

Overall, this book has opened a conversation about what power and privilege mean for understanding activist aging. In looking to the future, both of our work as an activist-research collective and to the future of studies in this area, we call for more critical race perspectives and analyses; for decolonial and Indigenous perspectives; and for centring different ways of knowing. We support more work on aging trans activisms; the cripping and queering of aging studies; and an expansion of aging and intergenerationality beyond the tropes of later life and passing-down. Finally, we insist that these themes connect and overlap, but we would like to understand how; what they mean in different places, on different lands, in different territories; and what relations they invoke.

ACTIVIST THEIRSTORIES

We draw the volume to a close with a series of activist theirstories. In conceptualizing this as the book's closing, we initially framed what follows as a series of "herstories," to oppose the hegemonic use of male-dominant language. However, over the course of this project, we have increasingly understood the imperative of advancing more gender-expansive, non-binary approaches, and thus we offer here the term "theirstories." In advancing *their*stories as a framework for what follows, we *return* one more time, to the words of Angela Davis in the opening of this book: to the idea that those who work the hardest in the least glamourous jobs in pursuit of social change are often omitted in the histories of their movements. *Theirstories* signals our thinking around, and our hopes for, the future of aging activisms. We wish to make explicit that gender does *not* become binary as we age; we challenge the heteronormativity of aging studies (Marshall 2017; Sandberg 2008), the coloniality of gender (Lugones 2008; Simpson 2016), and the ageism in queer studies (Siverskog 2015).

We turn, then, to the strong and vibrant voices of six activist storytellers—Anne Caines, Abigail Myerscough, Gillian Sandeman, Elizabeth Vezina, Rose Marie Whalley, and Jesse Whattam—as they reflect on the shifting meanings and practices of their activisms during their lives. In their own words, they tell their stories as activists of different ages, as people whose activisms took shape on Turtle Island and whose activist roots lie elsewhere, and as activists whose experiences of structural disadvantages and systemic privileges differ, sometimes sharply. Their stories reveal the complex and multiple expressions that their activisms embrace, ranging from quiet approaches to overt actions, often, but not always, shifting over time in ways that attune with aging and the changing circumstances of their lives.

These storytellers are connected to one another, to us, and to the place from which we write. They are among the many who have gathered with us in Michi Saagiig Anishinaabeg territory, in the community of Nogojiwanong (Peterborough, Ontario). They are among those in our research collective who came forward to offer their contributions, answering our call for personal reflections pivoting around four questions, which recall the critical lifecourse perspective first identified in the book's introduction: What drew you into activism? Have your activisms changed at different times in your life? Over time, what has sustained your social change work? What form(s) do(es) your resistance work currently take?[1] Guided by these questions, these activists tell their stories and we present them together, one following the other, with no intervening text.[2] This allows a powerful portrayal to emerge of the remarkable diversity as well as the common themes that motivate and characterize their activist experiences and practices.

The stories told by these six extraordinary "ordinary" activists illustrate in vivid ways many of the core themes of this volume: the significance of everyday, less-visible activisms; the influence of (direct and indirect) experiences of oppressions on people's resistance work; and the changes to their activisms that often occur as they age and as their circumstances alter. But emerging so clearly from these six narratives are also aspects of these storytellers' activisms that have so far received little attention. These less-considered themes make possible even more textured understandings of the nexus of aging and activisms. There is indeed always more to the story.

First, storytellers of different ages describe the *importance of learning* in helping to propel, strengthen, and sustain their activisms. Learning opportunities can arise via informal channels, such as other activists, as well as more conventional forms of education; many speak of these as critical to increasing their awareness of structural oppressions and as helping them to understand their feelings of injustice. Second, these activists recall *significant individuals* who have instilled and nurtured their activisms. These are sometimes well-known and much-admired activists and sometimes figures from their own lives, such as parents, grandmothers, and teachers. But in a tweak to the often-assumed generational scripts, which assign older people the role of knowledge transmitters and mentors, these significant figures also include children identified as "developmentally delayed," and the young people who serve as inspirations to certain older activists. Lastly, these activists highlight the importance of *self-care*, renewal through nature, and taking periods of reducing, withdrawing from, or changing the pace of their activist work. Their stories reveal the incredibly valuable contributions they make in their work for social justice, to which they give little emphasis or even attention. While these themes are echoed in other places in this book, they become especially evident and powerfully resonant as their stories, one by one, unfold.

Activists of different ages, backgrounds, and abilities have a prominent voice in this book in keeping with a critical framework that questions, widens, and repositions what are viewed as legitimate sources of knowledge. We cannot think of a better way to close than with the voices of these extremely thoughtful and committed activists. We invite readers to attend to what has yet to be fully revealed to them as they revel in just how creatively these folks are keeping on.

Anne Caines, 73[3]

I came to Montreal as an immigrant in 1979. I am a citizen now and my children were born here; I have my first grandchild who is now 3. Working for social change has been a very important part of who I am since my early childhood. I was born in Singapore at the end of World War II and these early years were very formative ones. My father was Japanese and my mother Portuguese and Irish. My father had been interned as a prisoner of war in India by the British for the greater part of the war. My mother remained in Singapore and experienced the Japanese occupation.

The immediate postwar situation was unsettling. I witnessed race riots that involved Chinese, Malays, and Europeans; we also heard of uncles killed or beaten and left for dead. Our family was Eurasian, a mixture of Asian and European: Some of us look Asian, as I do, and others looked Italian, Portuguese, or white.

Even at a young age, I never took anything at face value—reacting to how people perceived a racially mixed identity really made me quite rebellious. Certainly, we felt racism as children but we didn't know what to call it. I just knew that I did not like being in the middle of a race riot or considered an oddity. I am giving you this background because in many ways it has influenced my life profoundly and is significant to understanding why I have always been drawn to work for social change, specifically, have always worked towards inclusivity of peoples of diverse identities and backgrounds.

I thought I would become a teacher. However, my first teaching experience in London, England, convinced me of the importance of looking outside, into community and society. The school was a school for "sub normal" children (I still can't get over calling children by such an ableist label as "sub normal" in the late 60s, even though this label no longer exists). These were children who had failed in the so-called "normal" school system to read or write or were there because they had adjustment problems. I had the reception class: 15 children, ages 6–13. They became my first children, my family. They were amazing individuals who had already experienced discrimination and rejection from society. Somehow I could not see how to prepare these children to integrate back into a system that they knew had failed them and would most likely fail them again.

I was very fortunate to find a course in community development/action and the opportunity to examine the consequences of labelling and the mindset and attitude that these children would grow up to be taken care of as educationally "sub normal" adults. Those two years of reflection and writing about my first family changed my lifecourse. I became a community educator/activist.

The context of my activism has changed, but not my feelings towards social justice. Social justice for me has always been equated with fighting for human rights. In a very real sense I have always considered myself to be an immigrant of the world. This is not a unique experience for immigrants. When I was a child we travelled between, Singapore, Hong Kong, Japan, and eventually emigrated to San Francisco when I was 11 years old. My parents spoke English in the home and so we thought, "Oh, this is where we belong! We are going to be Americans and we are going to love it!" We realized we weren't Americans.

My activism as a community worker has been varied. In the States I worked helping women, who were jailed for prostitution and petty crimes, to obtain bail while awaiting a court appearance. In England I worked in youth clubs; in Canada I worked with groups on environmental issues. In Quebec my children brought me into their school system—I was on the school committee of my son's very multicultural, immigrant school. I am also very grateful to the South Asian Women's Community Centre for giving me the opportunity to work on women's and immigrants' rights within Quebec. I am a founding member of RECAA (see Chapter 2), an organization that works across age, gender, and cultural lines to raise awareness of elder mistreatment.

I follow a personal rule: When you are going to work for social change, put yourself in a place where you will learn something about what the world is about and how to change it in a way that is going to improve the quality of life for every-one. That's what I was looking for as a child: respect for who I was.

My third grade teacher, Mother Lennon, still inspires and sustains me in my activism. My children say, "You changed your life when you were eight?" They laugh but it's the truth. In Singapore I was always being punished for actions that I did not consider naughty. Mother Lennon, I thought, would be like all the rest, but when I acted out, instead of a scolding, she responded with laughter and love. In hindsight, I realize I was learning that, in social action, justice and love go together.

I have always believed that activism must also take you out into the streets, to be counted for what you believe in and what you are fighting for! Today I march for policies and actions that affect climate change and actions that marginalize and deny legal and human rights to immigrants. We must change laws that inhibit family reunification and see that migrant workers have the same rights as all work-ers. We need to be part of the solution to the refugee crisis. We have to end racial profiling and be generous to the millions of displaced refugees worldwide.

Abi Myerscough, 25

I have always joked that I will "get arrested for something"; it was just a matter of finding that one thing that would push my activism over the edge. I have always known I was a feminist. Before I knew the theory behind it or could name it, I always questioned why, as a girl, I was expected to do certain things but never the same things as my male classmates.

Looking back across my (so far) short lifespan, I do not remember either of my parents being particularly politically or socially active. But my grandmother and great-grandmother were. Both of them worked sewing upholstery for Jeep and Chrysler vehicles for most of their lives. My grandma was just months shy of a full pension when the factory closed, leaving her and many of her colleagues to fight a lengthy legal battle.

My grandma also rallied for Indigenous rights, aiding the people of Ipperwash when they moved into the army barracks to reclaim their stolen land. She ran clothing and food drives, rallying alongside and participating, at their request, in ceremony. She had married a Native man and remained an ally and admirer of the Ojibway peoples and culture all her life. I remember the walls of her cottage were lined with Native artwork, intermingled with political cartoons taped to the fridge or on the front door. She always taught me, as my mother did, to be proud of my Indigenous heritage. She was a true activist; both she and my Nana were all smiles as they told their stories to me as a child, and from this I somehow took up their fervour. I know she is proud of me. Have you ever heard the saying that whenever you find a dime it means that someone who has passed is thinking of you? Well, the day after I applied to the master's program in Canadian Studies at Trent University to study aging, I found a dime on my walk to class. I knew I made the right decision. That is why I am an activist and how I became who I am today.

No matter how hard I sometimes struggle through school or my activism, I always try to make my family proud and honour my grandmother's memory. My professor in a research course said, "You can't make change unless you do something about it." This always stuck with me, because as long as I want to be a student and write about lofty ideals that I "hope" get put into motion, I need to spend just as much time to actively work towards it. So, as I stand today, my work is sustained by the notion of moving beyond the theory and education, and becoming active in order to realize my childhood dream of becoming a lifelong student.

Throughout my undergraduate degree in Women's Studies and Canadian Studies at Trent University, I spent a lot of time looking at gender roles in the sport of hockey, trying to understand why girls are limited by the way masculinity shapes this sport. That plan to study gender roles in hockey changed one day in my fourth year of university, in a gender studies course, when we were asked to read an article about long-term care homes in Ontario. I writhed in anger as I read about the lack of support and resources available for seniors and staff. Growing up, my sister and I accompanied my mom to the various long-term care facilities where she worked and we witnessed injustices within these institutions. It enraged me to see the problems that residents faced along with the hardships and stresses the employees experienced.

My problem has always been that I love knowledge and learning so much that I have trouble finding focus, so in the end it's not so much what I'm going to do, but what I'm *not* going to be able to do. For now, I am just dipping my toes into this academic world, but when I finish my program I hope to move into a more activist-oriented role, and actually put my theory into practice. Nothing was more inspiring than seeing the aging women at the 2015 Aging Activism Symposium talk about their lifelong activism. It reminded me of my grandmother and how, had she still been alive, she would have undoubtedly been a Raging Granny or a member of GRAN, just kicking ass and taking names, trying to make the world a better place for those they will leave behind. That is my life goal. I want to keep being active for as long as I possibly can, and inspire others to join in the fight.

Gillian Sandeman, 80

I grew up in an era of huge social change in England when, just after the war, the government put into place the underpinnings of the social safety net. I saw the problems of poverty, racism, and inequality as a student volunteer at a settlement house in the slums and teaching English to African immigrant men. So, initially my activism was close to the traditional charity model: There's a problem; I can help.

I grew up in a family that valued education and careers for girls but it wasn't until I experienced discrimination based on my gender and marital status that I understood the need to be an outspoken feminist and to embrace opportunities in fields where women were not always welcome. I was prevented from registering for a PhD course at the University of St. Andrews because I was pregnant. And at Trent, I and other "faculty wives" were denied proper recognition and advancement as academics because we were the female halves of faculty couples.

My understanding of the need for political activism began in Newfoundland in the early 60s. There I saw deep poverty and deprivation in the outports, a malfunctioning denominational education system, and a constant emigration of the young seeking opportunities on the mainland. I began my affiliation with the NDP after we came to Peterborough in 1965.

Becoming increasingly frustrated with my life at Trent, I thought a lot about the kind of work I really wanted to do. And in 1973 I became a probation officer, much to the surprise of the young men on probation and the all-male jail staff, because there had never been a woman probation officer in Peterborough. I found the work rewarding and began to understand and critique the criminal justice system—which is not a system at all but a mélange of badly relating parts.

As the Peterborough's NDP member of the Ontario Provincial Parliament (1975–1977), I served as the opposition critic for Corrections. I worked hard at questioning the minister and raising issues, such as the number of deaths in prison and the use of solitary confinement for juveniles. It is disheartening to see that these issues haven't gone away: There are too many Ashley Smiths.[4]

When I was defeated [in the 1977 provincial election], I wanted to continue working in the area and was hired as the executive director of the Toronto Elizabeth Fry Society, an agency very involved with advocacy for women in the criminal justice system. The Elizabeth Fry Societies across Canada were particularly concerned with trying to get the old Prison for Women closed, and finding ways of getting the women closer to their homes and into good rehabilitation programs. I was a member of one of the many task forces asked over the years to make recommendations to the government: Our conclusions were so sensible, and radical, that our report, like all the others, was ignored.

A big part of my activism has been looking at who the decision makers are and how one can encourage them to make the right decisions. One way is to work directly with them, engage with them, and gain their trust—not to be bought out by them, but to be respected by ministers, government, the opposition, and civil servants. More recently, I've been proud to be involved with that kind of advocacy as a founding member of GRAN.

The like-minded, skilled, wonderful people that you meet and the important issues that bring you together are what sustain me. Now I am consciously withdrawing. I see that there is much to be done, but I see lots of younger, wonderful activists, including my grandchildren. I am in awe. This is great and the work will carry on, and that is sustaining as well.

I continue to be somewhat involved with GRAN. But much of my activism is quiet and local. Until recently, I was on the board of a local credit union because cooperative movements have always really interested me. I sit on the board of an organization that provides and advocates for services that allow people to live at home. I am now very busy with Jamaican Self-Help, a small volunteer-run international development organization based in Peterborough.

Some of the things I've done have been "firsts": I was the first woman Fellow at Peter Robinson College at Trent University, Peterborough's first woman probation officer, and its first woman to sit in the provincial legislature—one of seven women and 119 men.

When I look back, I was not formally prepared for most of those things that I have done. I certainly wasn't prepared to be a politician. With a PhD in English, I certainly wasn't prepared to be a probation officer or to take on the Elizabeth Fry Society. I wasn't prepared to chair large and unruly party conventions. My activism has been based on a willingness to speak up about things that are important in any and all settings, however unfamiliar.

Elizabeth Vezina, 70

Many factors combined to get me involved in social change. They included my age and retirement, my return to university, and the birth of grandchildren.

Retirement from work left a huge void in my life, but it also afforded me the opportunity to reinvent myself. With the children on their own (finally) and my no longer working 60 hours and more a week, quite suddenly I had massive amounts of time, which initially I did not know how to employ. There was also an intellectual gap in my life as I had been solving fairly complex problems for many years (designing and implementing computer systems) and I had enjoyed the challenge. Time was no longer something that expanded forever into the future but was to be limited to, at best, a couple of decades. Having lived an extremely privileged life, it was definitely time to give something back to future generations. However, I was at a loss as to what form that could take. I had never been involved in any volunteer work or activism of any sort.

In an effort to solve some of the above dilemmas, I returned to university to complete a BA in cultural anthropology. Although I had been aware of some of the problems our world was experiencing, many of the courses I took gave me a much better understanding of some of these issues, especially the degradation of our environment and the many forms of social injustice.

While I was attending university, one of my grandchildren was born. I distinctly remember holding her tiny body all wrapped up in pink and thinking what a world she had been born into and how little I had done in my life to make it any better. I still tear up at the thought.

The last factor that tied all these influences together was a volunteer project in one of my anthropology courses. I turned down many of the options that I found initially, as they involved making meals or taking care of children, and quite frankly I had done enough of that in my life. An article in one of the university's newspapers drew me to the Montreal Raging Grannies. It has been a perfect fit. Membership in this activist group is intellectually challenging, personally rewarding, and—as I do most of their technical work—effective, as they draw much media attention and in the process a great deal of fun.

I have come late in life to activism. Since I was a teenager, I have always pushed the boundaries of what it meant to be a woman, but those were personal actions and never involved other people in an organized way. As a manager in business, I always tried to promote, hire, and encourage women, but again this was only on an individual basis.

Sustaining me are a realization of the wonders of our universe, an understanding of how little we truly know about that universe, the growth of a huge global movement for change, and the incredible women heroes that are contributing to that movement.

I am privileged to live in the Laurentians, north of Montreal, on a quiet lake surrounded by forests and hills. Every day I walk the dog in this environment and every day the woods enchant me with their serenity and their constant change. It invokes a feeling of oneness with nature and I get to witness its resilience and abundance. This counterbalances my terror in knowing that many of the planet's ecosystems have reached—and in many cases surpassed—tipping points that foretell their demise.

Women have always been an integral, important component of what makes our communities work, but for centuries that work has, for the most part, been unacknowledged. Now we have strong well-known women leaders who steer our work, motivate our actions and act as role models for women everywhere—Maude Barlow, Vandana Shiva, Elizabeth Warren, and Naomi Klein, to name a few. It is a joy to work with the Raging Grannies, a group of older, creative, energetic, funny women who share most of my aspirations and hopes. Being involved in an activist group also alleviates some of the guilt of my complicity in the sad state of affairs the world is currently experiencing.

Today, I am a proud member of the Montreal Raging Grannies. I help in the organization and documentation of our "gigs" (protests). We protest many issues and work to bring them to the public's attention. Our mandate is a very broad one as we work to bring peace and social justice to the world as well as protect the environment.

Rose Marie Whalley, 72

I was born in the north of England in 1943. My mother, a young German-Jewish refugee, met my father when she enlisted in the British Army as a cook. My father had spent most of his 45 years in the army, first fighting for king and country during World War I and later, as he put it, guarding the shores of the British Empire.

By the time I was four, my father worked as a postman. In spite of his service to his country, he did not earn enough to adequately provide for his family. My mother frantically tried to trace her family lost in Europe whilst, at the same time, looking after three small children: Her grief and frustration knew no limit. We lived in dingy circumstances at the back of an empty shop in a working-class neighbourhood. In spite of my parents' best efforts, there was not enough food, heat, clothes ... although no one had much, we had even less. In addition, there was no support from neighbours: Mother looked different, had a strange accent and was ostracized—Germany was the enemy and they did not understand anti-Semitism. From the beginning, I knew that what happened in the world affected you as an individual, it was real. In the 50s, through the crackling airwaves of the old wireless came the sounds of the civil rights movement from the lunch counters in the Deep South. Inspired, I too rebelled ...

My first social justice causes were nuclear disarmament and ending apartheid in South Africa. I was 18 or 19. There were huge demonstrations in London, as well as marches. Nothing was or is more important than the nuclear threat. The marches were meaningful and energizing. As a young teacher in London, I was part of a boycott of South African fruit. We'd stand outside the grocery stores chanting "Cape fruit, fresh from the gun," a play on the commercial slogan "Fresh from the sun." I was a foot soldier, never a leader. I enjoyed the street, leafleting, and making signs. Doing something concrete was appealing.

The war in Vietnam was beginning to loom large. I joined protests. In 1967, now married, I moved to the United States where my husband studied. I found a job—administering a leftist printing press operation—and it was there, in the hustle and bustle of preparing packages of articles to be sent to college campuses, that talk turned to feminism. I was instantly hooked.

At the same time, I was involved in helping young men escape the draft and head for Canada. One day, something went wrong and, apropos of nothing, I had to leave the United States. In June 1971, I rolled into Montreal on a Greyhound bus with a toddler and a few cardboard boxes to begin my life in Canada. I found my niche in the fight for daycare and abortion rights. I was with young mothers, and we were passionate to throw off the mantle of patriarchy and create a better world. I worked in a daycare centre funded by a grant. That, together with our feminist/anti-capitalist analysis of society, allowed for creative community experiments and spinoffs: housing co-ops, food-co-ops, clothing and toy exchanges. Women demanded appropriate health care, birthing centres, abortion rights—home births and midwives were illegal in Quebec! We marched and marched.

What has sustained me over the years is that my goal is still waiting to be realized. I believe the inherent injustices of capitalism cause human and environmental misery; racism and patriarchy are expressions of capitalism. I am part of a global community seeking to end injustice. I joined the Canadian Voice of Women for Peace and met inspiring peace activists of my mother's generation, women like Kay Macpherson, Muriel Duckworth, Ursula Franklin, and Marion Dewar who worked against militarism and never gave up. The voices of my foremothers echo in the darkness: It's one step forward and one step back, but keep going. I have never felt that there is nothing we can do to change the world. It's just the stars in the sky that we cannot change.

Increasingly in the 1980s, I was becoming frustrated and tired. I had a full-time job and a teenager, and I thought of myself as a hands-on activist, not a theoretician. I had little patience for endless long meetings based on consensus decision-making. Over the years I'd attended events to protest the wars in Central America, the treatment of Aboriginal people in Canada, the Israeli occupation of Palestine, police brutality, and labour issues. I saw them all as part of the fight against capitalism.

In 1986, around Christmastime, we were leafleting downtown urging people to boycott South African goods. This particular Saturday, the cold wind was penetrating, the snow and ice firmly underfoot. I got the beginnings of frostbite on my knuckles and realised I'd have to find another context for my activism. I discovered the warmth and coziness of the radio studio. Working in radio meant that I could also work with all kinds of groups on all kinds of issues. The mic became a piece of chalk. For 25 years, radio has been my main form of activism. For the last 13 years I have worked with a small group of older feminists to push the feminist agenda using the airwaves. We have a one-hour show, "Old(er) Women (A)Live (OWL)," that runs once a month on our local community radio station, CKUT in Montreal. We are slowly venturing into podcasts. Imagine people miles away hearing something that resonates and getting up and, shoulders to the wheel, trying their best to move the world towards peace and justice.

Jesse Whattam, 25

I was drawn into social change work at an early age. My youngest sister has Down syndrome, so I often witnessed difference as the basis of how people treated her. My other sister and I saw my parents advocating for her in the school system and we grew up supporting her against bullying, confronting our classmates who used derogatory language or abusive actions. Seeing our small school community's mentality and ideology shift, even slightly around dis/ability and language, may have been the first instance of change I was a part of. Despite the small scale, it stuck with me.

Even though neither of my parents would consider themselves activists, my parents had a big influence on my drive to work for social change. I witnessed my mother being a caregiver in so many ways, for our family and community, and she showed me the importance of caring for others and the diversity of ways it can happen. My dad was my coach and is a teacher. He taught me what it means to be a leader, how it doesn't mean telling people what to do, but has a lot to do with vision, listening, and supporting others. I grew up with a strong sense of community within my neighbourhood, and this taught me about the way that communities work together. We were responsible for our collective well-being. I see that as necessary not only on a local level, but also national and global.

One of my first jobs was at McDonald's, and that really motivated me to be a part of tearing down capitalism … I just remember thinking: *Is this really how we want to work and live? With these incredibly dehumanizing hierarchies? Is this really how we want to nourish our bodies or produce our food?*

I had an early, albeit limited, understanding of how all our liberation is tied together. As my understanding has changed, deepened, and widened, my activisms have transformed. When I was 11, my school had a program called SAGE Quest (Scholastic Arts and Global Education), and it was there that my global awareness was really fostered. My activism was very volunteer-based in a charity model, but we were taught that charity was inadequate, and to connect local issues to the larger economic, social, and political systems.

In a high school social justice program I really began to understand the term "activism." We learned about organizing: A group of us ran a campaign to educate and raise awareness about local poverty. We volunteered with local organizations and met radical movers and shakers in Hamilton. At that point, my activism was a mix of grassroots organizing and volunteering and learning from those around me.

I started university at Trent in International Development Studies. Inside and outside of the classroom, I learned more about the complexities of systems of oppression, such as colonialism, and my immense amount of privilege and complicity in perpetuating those systems. I had the opportunity to take Indigenous Studies courses that completely transformed my understanding of the reality of oppression, leading me to realize that, no matter what type of social change work I do, it is on stolen land—and responsibility and accountability comes with that understanding.

Soon after moving to Peterborough, I joined a student/community social and environmental justice organization, Ontario Public Interest Research Group, and for three years worked as its food security coordinator. I learned so much about student change work, the challenges involved, the opportunities, the hope, and the heartbreak. I watched and was a part of the food bank becoming a community, growing from the ground up, people working together to create a more inclusive space.

Doing student change work in a way that is personally sustainable has definitely been a learning process. I have started to learn what self-care means for me, what will fill me up and how to recognize what depletes my energy. I am learning balance and how this will help me be more effective in the activism and student change work I wish to do. I have an amazing support network, which has kept me surrounded by love and encouragement. Time in nature has kept me grounded and never fails to give me perspective and peace of mind, even if just for a moment. I have been sustained by being surrounded by like-minded people who keep me inspired. I find a constant process of learning more and listening to new perspectives sustains me.

Since leaving my position at the food bank and graduating from my undergrad, I have recognized the intense burnout I am experiencing. Currently, my activism is quieter. I am in a process of deep reflection and allowing myself to absorb all I have learned. I still go to events and support movements, but am not doing frontline organizing.

For three years, I have been on the board of directors of the Peterborough Student Housing Co-op, which seeks to ensure students have affordable, safe, and supportive housing. For the past year, I have been working at Trent as a research assistant to May Chazan, whose research focuses on why and how older women across North America are doing social change. It has been inspiring to learn from all of the women, because everyone brings a different perspective, and it's been incredibly enlightening to hear the diversity of ways they have dedicated parts of their lives to creating social change. It has also been interesting working in academia, even for such a brief time, because I have seen the possibility of radical projects and politics.

One thing I have learned is that the form of my activism is in a constant state of change, influenced by the changing socio-political context and the happenings in my personal life, but it's always exciting—that's for sure!

NOTES

1. We have also facilitated several workshops through our research collective to create a series of activist digital stories around these same questions. See: agingactivisms.org/our-stories.

2. Activists shared their thoughts through either a recorded interview or through their own written responses, and we acknowledge the work of Jesse Whattam in compiling, collecting, and editing these pieces. All transcripts were edited for clarity and to conform to length requirements, and each storyteller was offered an opportunity to approve these changes. Ages cited are at the time they told their stories.

3. Anne, Elizabeth, Rose Marie, and Jesse all have full "theirstories" that can be listened to at www.agingactivisms.org/montreal-media-capsules. They were interviewed as part of the digital storytelling workshop put on by Aging Activisms in collaboration with Ageing + Communication + Technologies at Concordia University in April 2016.

4. Ashley Smith was confined to a segregated cell in a correctional institution when she died in 2007 at age 19 from self-inflicted choking. Guards had been told not to enter her cell as long as she was breathing. In 2013, an Ontario coroner's inquest determined that her death was homicide.

REFERENCES

Aubrecht, Katie, and Tamara Krawchenko. 2016. "Disability and Aging: International Perspectives." *Review of Disability Studies* 12(2/3): 3–11.

Brown, Maria T. 2009. "LGBT Aging and Rhetorical Silence." *Sexuality Research and Social Policy* 6(4): 65–78.

Hutchinson, Susan. L., and Wexler, B. 2007. "Is 'Raging' Good for Health?: Older Women's Participation in the Raging Grannies." *Health Care for Women International*, 28, 88–118.

Lips, Hilary M., and Sarah L. Hastings. 2012. "Competing Discourses for Older Women: Agency/Leadership vs. Disengagement/Retirement." *Women & Therapy* 35: 145–164.

Lugones, Maria. 2008. "The Coloniality of Gender." *Worlds & Knowledges Otherwise* Spring 2008: 1–17.

MacDonald, Barbara, and Cynthia Rich. 1983. *Look Me in the Eye: Old Women, Aging and Ageism.* Tallahassee, FL: Spinster's Ink.

Marshall, Barbara. 2017. "Happily Ever After? 'Successful Ageing' and the Heterosexual Imaginary." *European Journal of Cultural Studies.* DOI:10.1177/1367549417708434.

Ophelian, Annalise (producer/director) and StormMiguel Florez (co-producer/editor). 2016. *Major!* [documentary film]. What Do We Want Films with Floating Ophelia Productions. www.missmajorfilm.com

Pain, Rachel. 2014. "Seismologies of Emotion: Fear and Activism during Domestic Violence." *Social & Cultural Geography* 15(2): 127–150.

Putnam, Michelle. 2007. *Aging and Disability: Crossing Network Lines.* New York: Springer Publishing Company.

Regan, Paulette. 2010. *Unsettling the Settler Within.* Vancouver, BC: UBC Press.

Sandberg, Linn. 2008. "The Old, the Ugly and the Queer: Thinking Old Age in Relation to Queer Theory." *Graduate Journal of Social Science* 5(2): 117–137.

Simpson, Leanne. 2016. Untitled Keynote Address. *National Women's Studies Association 37th Annual Conference.* Montreal, QC: November, 2016.

Siverskog, Anna. 2015. "Ageing Bodies that Matter: Age, Gender and Embodiment in Older Transgender People's Life Stories." *Nordic Journal of Feminist and Gender Research* 23(1): 4–19.

Stone, Sharon Dale. 2003. "Disability, Dependence and Old Age: Problematic Constructions." *Canadian Journal on Aging* 22(1): 59–67.

Contributor Biographies

EDITORIAL TEAM

May Chazan is a parent, professor, and activist. With her own ancestral roots in Eastern Europe, she is grateful to live, teach, write, and nurture life in Mississauga Anishinaabe territory. She is a Canada Research Chair in Gender and Feminist Studies and a faculty member in Gender and Women's Studies at Trent University, Peterborough, Canada. She is also on the executive committee of the Trent Centre for Aging and Society. May is inspired by how social justice movements form, operate, and generate change, and by how, across enormous differences in power, privilege, and world view, alliances are forged and maintained. In 2015, May published *The Grandmothers' Movement: Solidarity and Survival in the Time of AIDS* (McGill-Queen's University Press). Prior to that, she co-edited the volume *Home and Native Land: Unsettling Multiculturalism in Canada* (Between the Lines Press, 2011). Since 2013, she has been leading the Aging Activisms research collective—researching, thinking, gathering, and stirring the pot with and alongside many of the contributors to this volume.

Melissa Baldwin, co-chair of Aging Activisms, just completed an MA in Canadian and Indigenous Studies at Trent University, looking at the Peterborough Poetry Slam as resistant space-making. Along with Maddy Macnab, Melissa co-hosted a radio show, *Aging Radically*, on Trent Community Radio to create spaces for inter-generational conversations about activism across people's lives. Melissa has worked as a research assistant to May since 2013, co-authoring several journal articles and conference papers with her over this time. As a genderqueer settler person and an uninvited guest, Melissa is grateful to be living, learning, loving, growing, and rabble-rousing in Michi Saagiig Anishinaabe territory.

Pat Evans is a former co-chair of the Grandmothers Advocacy Network (GRAN), a cross-Canada movement of older women who work to strengthen the human rights of grandmothers, vulnerable children, and youth in southern Africa. Previously, Pat was a faculty member in the Schools of Social Work at York and Carleton universities, where her research and teaching focused on gender and social policies, especially related to women's paid and unpaid work. Working with GRAN, May, and Melissa allows her to blend the challenges and tensions in activist work with opportunities to reflect on its meanings for older women and its potential for social change.

CONTRIBUTING AUTHORS

Gabriela Aceves Sepúlveda is assistant professor in the School of Interactive Arts and Technology at Simon Fraser University. As both an interdisciplinary media artist and cultural historian, her research focuses on Latin American feminist media and contemporary art and design history and practice. Working at the intersections of video and performance, she uses video and multimedia installations to explore the social, political, and cultural structures that shape our sense of self. She is currently working on a monograph on the histories of feminist media in 1970s Mexico. Her articles have been published in *Platform: Journal of Media and Communication* and *Artelogie: Recherches sur les arts, le patrimoine et la littérature de l'Amérique latine.*

Mary Anne Ansley is a Peterborough/Nogojiwanong resident and Ojibwa living with spina bifida from birth. After graduating with her sales and merchandising diploma from Sir Sandford Fleming College, Mary Anne worked for many years in the retail sector. She held a number of positions including cosmetician, committee events member, head co-coordinator for stock-taking, stock counter for three suppliers in Toronto, and she was in the management trainee program for Eaton's Canada. She has been living on CPP and ODSP since 2009. She has been actively involved in committee volunteer work for women living with disabilities through Women Building Inclusion, the Peterborough Domestic Abuse Network, Survivors Advisory Committee, and the YWCA Peterborough-Haliburton Crossroads. She takes on public and guest speaking engagements, leadership positions on planning committees, committee membership, and participates in seminars, workshops, and community events. To date she has created two digital stories and a profile video that was screened in Toronto in November, 2015, for "Reclaiming Your Voice," and has been involved with creating booklets for the community on surviving domestic abuse. In 2015, Mary Anne was recognized with the Volunteer Service Award from the YWCA Peterborough-Haliburton, and received the Certificate of Excellence from the Peterborough Domestic Abuse Network.

Ziy von B is a queer Jewish parent, community organizer, writer, and performance poet whose art works to blur boundaries, forge connections, and address injustice. Born in Toronto with grandparents and great-grandparents hailing from Poland and Lithuania, Ziy is grateful to call Nogojiwanong (Peterborough) home.

Anne Caines is of Irish, Portuguese, and Japanese descent. She was born in Singapore and grew up in Japan and San Francisco. She received a diploma in community development at the University of Manchester, UK, and has continued to be involved in community activism ever since. Since immigrating to Montreal, Canada in 1979, she has been a member of the South Asia Women's Community Centre. She is a founding member and current coordinator of Resources Ethnoculturelles Contre l'Abus envers les Aîné(e)s / Respecting Elders: Communities Against Abuse (RECAA).

Nadine Changfoot is an associate professor of Political Studies at Trent University and also a senior research affiliate with Re•Vision: The Centre for Art and Social Justice at the University of Guelph. Her research is feminist and collaborative, addressing and producing art at the intersection of politics, arts activism, and community-campus engagement that include methods and ethics of research creation for digital storytelling and complex cross-sectoral partnerships that include the state, non-profit sector, aggrieved communities and individuals, and academy. Nadine partners with disability, First Nations, older-adult identified women, and queer and trans individuals to screen their digital stories to audiences in health care, educational, and advocacy settings, and to create knowledge at the edges of the academy for social change. She is a research lead on Bodies in Translation: Activist Art, Technology, and Access to Life; and Community First: Impacts of Community-Campus Engagement.

Sally Chivers is a professor of English at Trent University. She is the author of *From Old Woman to Older Women: Contemporary Culture and Women's Narratives* (Ohio State University Press, 2003) and *The Silvering Screen: Old Age and Disability in Cinema* (University of Toronto Press, 2011), and co-editor of *The Problem Body: Projecting Disability on Film* (Ohio State University Press, 2010). She is a member of the international interdisciplinary research team "Reimagining Long-Term Residential Care: An International Study of Promising Practices," which conducts rapid ethnographies within care homes in six countries to determine how long-term care could be improved. Her individual research focuses on care narratives in the context of austerity, with a focus on advice and advocacy.

Jenn Cole (mixed ancestry Algonquin Kiji Sibi Watershed) is a scholar and performance artist. She is passionate about teaching performance and creative expression as research and scholarship practices. She writes about the activist elements of intimacy created by imperfect storytelling and feminist performance adaptations, while her performance practice explores storytelling, trans-generational autobiography, and the sharing of food together as an expression of vulnerability and relational exchange, which is pivotal as we try to cultivate a sense of home.

Andrea Dodsworth was born in Peterborough/Nogojiwanong and raised in Maynooth, Ontario. As a child, she came to Peterborough/Nogojiwanong every week for therapy at Five Counties Children's Centre and moved to the city in 1993 because it was a nice fit for her, being a small city, not too far from home and with a significantly high number of the population comprising people with disabilities. Andrea has been an active member of the community since 1993 and is a graduate of the Recreational Leadership Program at Sir Sandford Fleming College. She has been employed as a radio dispatcher for the Ontario Ministry of Transportation, a camp administrative assistant, and a camp counselor with Merrywood Easter Seals Camp, and as an assistant to the Municipality of Maynooth Municipal Deputy-Clerk, yet she underlines that she has been deemed unemployable by ODSP. She has been recognized as an athlete and a disability advocate, and has been awarded the City of Peterborough Senior Female Athlete of the Year for Wheelchair Track and Field (1996), the lifetime achievement Holnbeck Award (2014) (awarded each year by the City of Peterborough to an individual or individuals who have volunteered their time to improving the lives of people who have disabilities), the Province of Ontario 10th Anniversary AODA Champion Award (2015), and the Peterborough Downtown Business Improvement Association Friends of Downtown Award (2016). Andrea serves as a volunteer on the following City of Peterborough Committees: Accessibility Advisory Committee, Accessible Transit Advisory Sub-committee, and the Built Environment Sub-committee. She is vice-chair of the Council for Persons with Disabilities and a member of the Kawartha Participation Projects Foundation Board of Directors. She also does accessibility consultations with the Peterborough Downtown Business Improvement Association and works with downtown businesses to make their spaces accessible. Andrea volunteers in her community because it is her way of saying "thanks" to those who have helped her over the years to become the person she is today.

Peggy Edwards is a writer and retired health promotion consultant based in Ottawa, Canada. She has worked with Health Canada, the Canadian Public Health Association, and the World Health Organization, and is the co-author of three bestselling books on healthy aging and grandparenting. She is an activist and leader in the Grandmothers Advocacy Network (GRAN) and the Grandmothers to Grandmothers Campaign, which supports African grandmothers who are raising their grandchildren in the context of the HIV/AIDS crisis.

Marlene Goldman is a professor in the Department of English at the University of Toronto. She is the author of *Paths of Desire* (University of Toronto, 1997), *Rewriting Apocalypse* (McGill-Queen's, 2005), and *(Dis)Possession* (McGill-Queen's, 2011). She recently completed a book entitled *Forgotten: Age-Related Dementia and Alzheimer's in Canadian Literature.* Her work currently entails leaving the ivory tower and becoming a catalyst for changing the public's gothic approach to dementia. More precisely, with the aid of an Insight Grant from SSHRC, she is currently using film as a means of transforming the public's perception of people with dementia.

Jean Koning has dedicated her life to standing in solidarity with the First Peoples of Turtle Island. Since the 1960s when she worked for Children's Aid on Manitoulin Island, she has been spreading awareness of the vast inequality experienced by First Peoples in Canada, and learning what it means to stand in solidarity with Indigenous peoples. Koning has served with Project North and the Aboriginal Rights Coalition (now a branch of KAIROS) and has worked closely with Aboriginal Anglican Church people throughout southwestern Ontario, as well as with First Peoples. She is currently a member of the Kawartha Truth and Reconciliation Support Group, a group of First Peoples and settlers who learn together as they explore the brutal truths about colonial history, and who work to promote justice, healing, and reconciliation in all possible ways. She is a force in the Peterborough activist community and more widely.

Constance Lafontaine is the associate director of Ageing + Communication + Technologies (ACT) and works with the director to manage the project from Concordia University. As part of her work with ACT, Constance develops and leads participatory-action research and research-creation projects with Montreal-based partners. She also explores the intersections of animality and human and non-human aging, including probing multi-species temporalities. Constance is also completing a PhD in Communication Studies at Concordia University, where she focuses on the intersections between discourses of global warming and contemporary animal spectacles, focusing on polar bear displays in Canada. She has completed undergraduate degrees in Communication and Political Science and a Master of Arts in Communication at the University of Ottawa.

Niambi Leigh, born in Jamaica and living in Nogojiwanong/Peterborough, is a poet whose work explores the intersections of race, emotions, and mental illness. One of the organizers of Black Lives Matter Peterborough/Nogojiwanong, Niambi's poetry is lyrical, deeply felt, and always rooted in storytelling. Their work reminds you that the act of breathing is an expression of strength.

Keara Lightning is a member of Samson Cree Nation, who has had the privilege of growing up as an uninvited guest on Anishinaabe and Haudenosaunee territories. As an activist, she has worked on fossil fuel divestment campaigns and in climate-justice organizations, as well as Indigenous student and community groups. She hopes to continue writing and learning Cree language.

Maddy Macnab recently completed her MA in Canadian Studies and Indigenous Studies at Trent University, Nogojiwanong (Peterborough, Canada). She is a researcher with the Aging Activisms activist-research collective, and she co-hosted the intergenerational community radio show *Aging Radically* from 2015 to 2017. Her work as an emerging researcher and community organizer focuses on feminist oral history, the politics of migration, and settler solidarities.

Laura Madokoro is an assistant professor in History and Classical Studies at McGill University. Her research explores various facets of the history of refugees and humanitarianism. She is especially interested in questions relating to settler colonialism, human rights, and race. Her current SSHRC-funded research explores the history of sanctuary in Canada from Confederation to the present, with a view to building towards a larger translocal history of sanctuary among white settler societies. Madokoro is the author of *Elusive Refuge: Chinese Migrants in the Cold War* (Harvard University Press, 2016), which considers the history of migration and resettlement of Chinese refugees to the white settler societies of the United States, Canada, Australia, New Zealand, and South Africa.

Monique Mojica (Guna and Rappahannock Nations and a member of the Chocolate Woman Collective) is passionately dedicated to a theatrical practice as an act of healing, of reclaiming historical/cultural memory, and of resistance. Spun directly from the family-web of New York's Spider Woman Theater, her theatrical practice embraces not only her artistic lineage, by mining stories embedded in the body, but also the connection to stories coming through land and place.

Maureen Murphy has had a camera in her hand since the age of 10. Her photographs have appeared in local and community newspapers, magazines, on the cover of government reports, in advertisements, as well as on multiple websites. She has a strong belief in making a contribution, and one of the ways she does this is by photographing people.

Abigail Myerscough is pursuing graduate studies at Trent University on the Ontario elder care system, specifically interrogating women's experiences. She has become politicized not only around issues of aging and gender inequality, but also about her own positioning as a young woman from a "mixed" Indigenous-settler background. She brings this growing politicization to her research.

Carole Roy is an associate professor in the Department of Adult Education at St. Francis Xavier University in Nova Scotia. She was involved in the peace movement in Victoria, BC, in the 1980s, where she met the women who later became the Victoria Raging Grannies, starting the iconic movement of creative older women activists who speak out with flair and pizazz on issues of concern. She has published *The Raging Grannies: Wild Hats, Cheeky Songs, and Witty Actions for a Better World* (Black Rose Books, 2004), as well as articles on the Raging Grannies and other wise women activists. She has also worked with Magnus Isacsson on the documentaries *Les Super Mémés* (French) and *Granny Power* (with Jocelyne Clarke). She is grateful to the Raging Grannies and other boldly daring women for a vision of vibrant and dynamic aging.

Gillian Sandeman was born in England. She was married in 1957 and moved to Canada shortly after. Juggling her roles as mother, grandmother, and great-grandmother, her work life has included teaching at two universities, being a probation and parole officer, serving as the Member of Provincial Parliament for Peterborough, and directing the Elizabeth Fry Society of Toronto, among other positions. She is a fierce advocate for incarcerated women and served on the founding board of the Grandmothers Advocacy Network.

Kim Sawchuk, a feminist media studies scholar with a commitment to critical thinking and research creation, has research interests that span the fields of art, gender, and culture, examining the intersection of technology with people's lives and how that changes as one ages. Her long career of research and writing have addressed the embodied experiences of technology and their discourses, mobile media, and the politics of geo-location and the transition to wireless infrastructures, with particular attention to age, aging, and their cultural impact. Sawchuk is a professor in the Department of Communication Studies, the associate dean of research and graduate studies for the Faculty of Arts and Science at Concordia University, and the principal researcher of Ageing + Communication + Technologies (ACT).

Sadeqa Siddiqui was the coordinator of the South Asian Women's Community Centre, a services support and advocacy organization in Montreal, for 30 years. She retired in 2012. She is now an active member and president of Ressources Ethnoculturelles Contre l'Abus Envers les Aîné(e)s/Respecting Elders: Communities Against Abuse (RECAA), where she works towards the respect of elders in the cultural communities of Montreal.

Ruth Steinberg is an Ottawa-based photographer specializing in portraiture and fine art photography. She holds a BFA from the University of Manitoba and graduated from the two year Portfolio Program at the School of the Photographic Arts Ottawa (SPAO). She was the Artist-in-Residence, Short-term Projects at Enriched Bread Artists in Ottawa during the fall of 2014. There, she initiated the series *What the Body Remembers*, a thoughtful and provocative series of nudes of women aged 55 and older.

Sharon Swanson is a retired educator currently residing in Kelowna, BC. Sharon did her undergraduate degree at UBC and her graduate work later in life at Ottawa University. For over 50 years, she taught at all levels, from grade one to teachers' college, spending the final 20 years as a training consultant for senior managers in the federal public service. During the last decade Sharon has been a strong supporter of the Grandmothers for Africa campaign and a devoted activist for the Grandmothers Advocacy Network (GRAN). She has held leadership roles in both organizations, currently deeply committed to the GRAN Archives project and developing new archiving knowledge and skills. Although an activist since the days of the Vietnam War and living in both the United States and Australia, she remains actively engaged with both local and global issues. Sharon wants her children and grandchildren to see firsthand that their voices and actions can make a difference in the world.

waaseyaa'sin christine sy is Anishinaabe of mixed ancestry from Lac Seul First Nation and Sault Ste. Marie, Ontario. She presently lives and works in the territories of the W̱SÁNEĆ and Lekwungen people where she lectures in Gender Studies at the University of Victoria. She is a mother; actively engaged in supporting Anishinaabeg endurance through language, ceremony, land-based practices, and critical thought; and is presently taken up with the muse that is "being out of territory"—a first in her life. sy has won awards for poetry, short story (fiction), and academic writing. She is the blog-author of *Anishinaabewiziwin*. Through a queer Indigenous materialist feminist theory, her PhD research examines historical and Anishinaabe knowledges about womyn's relationship with the sugar bush and interprets this for a contemporary and future practice of land (re)matriation.

Elizabeth Vezina reflects that, unlike many of the Raging Grannies, she is new to social activism. Work had been the centre of her life for 30 years, so retirement has meant a reshaping of her life. She felt not only that it was time for a change, but also that she needed to give back to the society that had provided her with so much. A return to university for a degree in anthropology, the birth of her grandchildren, and the growing realization that our planet is on a path of destruction helped shape the direction of her transformation. Being part of the Montreal Raging Grannies has given meaning to her life, keeping her very busy, providing a community of like-minded women, challenging her intellect, and often tickling her funny bone.

Rose Marie Whalley grew up in a working-class neighbourhood in the north of England. She is a retired teacher, a mother, and a grandmother. As a young woman, she was involved in working to ban nuclear weapons, ending apartheid in South Africa, working to end the war in Vietnam, and engaging in consciousness-raising groups on feminist issues. Living in Montreal for over 40 years, she has continued working on the feminist agenda against militarism, against poverty and job insecurity, for human rights and reproductive rights, and for accessible child care. In 2003, she helped to found a small radio collective, "Older Women Live," to raise awareness of the negative effects of ageism and to inspire the next generations to continue the struggle for a just world.

Jesse Whattam, Trent University, has deep involvements with a number of community-based social-justice organizations in Peterborough. For three years, she worked at the Ontario Public Interest Research Group as the coordinator of a local food bank. As a young person who is continually inspired by the passionate activist community in Peterborough, Jesse is a relentless community organizer, especially around poverty and food security.

Elder Shirley Ida Williams Pheasant is a member of the Bird Clan of the Ojibway and Odawa First Nations of Canada. At age 10, she attended St. Joseph's Residential School in Spanish River, Ontario. Elder Shirley started teaching in the Native Studies Department at Trent University in 1986, in order to develop and promote Native language courses. Now an Elder, she remains a professor emeritus in Indigenous Studies at Trent. She has published one book, *Aandeg*, meaning *The Crow* (Lakefield, Ontario: Waapoone Pub. & Promotion, c1990), as well as numerous articles and teaching materials on the Ojibway language and culture. Elder Shirley led the Revitalization of the Nishnaabemowin Language Research Project and the Lexicon Dictionary, a collection of Ojibway and Odawa words organized and presented by themes. In 2017, Elder Shirley received an honorary Doctor of Laws from the University of Ontario Institute of Technology in recognition of her remarkable Anishinaabemowin language teaching and pedagogy and her extraordinary community leadership. She is currently a water walker and a member of The Sacred Water Circle, a volunteer run, non-profit initiative that brings together Indigenous and non-Indigenous people to work for the benefit of water.

Index